HERMITS

HERMITS

The Insights of Solitude

—————◆—————

PETER FRANCE

St. Martin's Press ⚏ New York

Library of Congress Cataloging-in-Publication Data

France, Peter.
    Hermits : the insights of solitude / Peter France.
        p.   cm.
    ISBN 0-312-15546-8
    1. Hermits.   I. Title.
BX2845.F73   1997
305.5'68—dc21   97-10024
                                                      CIP

First published in Great Britain by
Chatto & Windus Limited

First U.S. Edition: July 1997

10 9 8 7 6 5 4 3 2

To Felicia

Acknowledgements

I am very grateful for the helpful comments of friends on the island of Patmos, including Carraigh B. Thompson, Barbara Bonfigli and Jacqueline Delia. The book *Hermits and Hermitages of Patmos* (in Greek) by Sister Anthousa of the Monastery of Evangelismos was an early inspiration, and my ideas were clarified and considerably enriched by conversations with my spiritual father, Bishop Kallistos of Diokleia.

Peter Scorer of the Department of Russian, Exeter University, helped with advice and research material on the hermits of Russia, and Robert Lax not only set me right about his friend Thomas Merton, but convinced me that the riches of the solitary life are still available, most particularly to the hermit who loves people.

Euan Cameron, friend and editor, has been with the book since the conception of the original idea. It has been greatly helped by his critical vigilance; the errors of fact or lapses in taste that remain are all my own work.

I acknowledge with gratitude the following permissions for quotation: St Vladimir's Seminary Press for *Russian Letters of Direction*; New Directions Publishing Corp. for *Seeds of Contemplation*; Farrar, Straus & Giroux for *Disputed Questions*; and the Merton Legacy Trust for *Contemplation in a World of Action*.

Contents

PROLOGUE

Dawn in China

The human impulse to take off and live alone is an ancient one and societies down the ages have varied in their responses to it. From the earliest times there have been people who felt at their best in company and others who felt happiest on their own.

The two attitudes were at the heart of the earliest philosophies of the good life which took shape in China in the sixth century BC, Confucianism and Taoism. They shared a common aim: to teach people how to be fulfilled. Both accepted that a sense of self-confidence and serenity were essential but they differed on the way to achieve this. The system of Confucius was through discharging social obligations; that of Lao-Tse was through avoiding them.

Traditional Chinese society had developed a clearly defined system of social relations: between father and son, sovereign and subject, husband and wife, brother and brother and, finally, friend and friend. Reciprocal obligations recognised by everyone and teachable to children had been established for each relationship.[1] The basic human virtue, according to Confucius, is *jen*, which can be understood as humanity as expressed in doing the right thing by your fellow human being. This is inborn but flowers first in the environment of the family and is then extended to wider social relations. The virtuous individual is respectful in private life and loyal in dealing with others. He develops self-confidence through the respect he wins from his friends and his status in society. Confucius held that knowledge is 'to know man'[2] and that wisdom is 'to attend to the welfare of the people'.[3]

Lao-Tse had little use for society and was completely indifferent to the social status of the individual. Social organisation was anathema to him and social participation of any kind an impediment to the freedom and so to the proper development of the individual. He was an older contemporary of Confucius and had been an official at court but, tradition has it, he became disillusioned with court life and fled through the western passes. The guardian of the route persuaded him, before leaving, to compose the *Tao te Ching*,[4] which became a manifesto for the solitary life.

The essence of its teaching is that it is by withdrawing rather than by asserting ourselves, through retreat rather than pursuit, by inaction rather than action that we acquire wisdom. We have to unlearn the superficial cleverness that we have developed to get on in society, to cease to compete with others, and to learn to live alone.

Solitude is healthy, according to the Taoist, because it removes us from the mutilating pressures of society and exposes us to the healing influence of nature. We are part of the natural world and should allow our personalities to be shaped by natural forces. The short-lived storms of wind and rain suggest the futility of violent action; vegetable growth matures, culminates and subsides in response to a natural impulse. The person who seeks truth should imitate this.

The highest goodness is like water. Water is the symbol of humility. It always seeks the lowest place, it 'dwells in regions which people detest' and yet it is good and necessary to all living things: 'it benefits all things and does not compete with them'. Further, water best illustrates the principle of *wu wei*, or effective inactivity, because it is soft and yielding but can wear away rock: 'There is nothing softer or sweeter than water and yet there is nothing better for attacking strong and hard things.'[5]

The *Tao te Ching* articulates, in a poetic form, a floating group of ethical principles which had long been in existence in China before the age of Lao-Tse and which were to inspire hermits in other lands for two and a half thousand years. They reject ambition, aggression, acquisitiveness and material prosperity. In place of these learned responses to organised society they teach humility, poverty, independence and self-knowledge:

> He who rises himself on tiptoe cannot stand;
> he who straddles cannot walk.
>
> *
>
> He who knows he has enough – is rich
>
> *

Hermits

He who overcomes others has force;
he who overcomes himself is strong.

*

In habitation, stay close to the land;
in meditation, go deep in the heart.

*

To speak little is natural.
High winds do not last all morning;
heavy rains do not last all day.

*

There is no greater sin than desire,
No greater calamity than envy,
No greater adversity than pining for
    something for oneself.
Therefore he that knows enough is
    enough will always have enough.

Introduction

The island of Patmos, where I spend most of my time, has been, for over a thousand years, a place for hermits. Their tiny white houses were hidden away deep in remote valleys or on the peaks of mountains. They were monks from the Monastery of St John who felt called to the solitary life and were given permission by the abbot to live alone during the week and return to the monastery at weekends to take part in the liturgy and to receive the sacrament.

One of them is responsible for this book, although he died sixty years ago. The ruins of his hermitage, little more than a shallow cave among a group of rocks on a mountain slope, catch the last rays of the setting sun across the valley from my house. Every evening I look across and think of the man who spent years of solitude in that place.

But it was something more than this daily reminder of a man who chose to live alone that started me on the research into the hermit life; it was the occasion of his quitting the cave. When I asked my neighbours about him they told me that he was already an old man when he settled there. Women from the nearby farms used to visit him on Fridays and take a little bread and fruit or cheese. They also used to take to him their problems, and his reputation for dealing with them spread; the Friday visitors swelled into a stream of suppliants so numerous and insistent that he eventually fled to a barren island to recover the solitude he had lost.

Many hermits have suffered the same intrusion and many have had to run away from the invasions of the curious. But what caught my attention in the story of my local hermit was that his disruptive popularity had been the consequence of his giving sound advice. And that advice had little to do with the spiritual path he was following. The problems these women carried to him with his Friday provisions had to do with their relations with husbands and children, their sick animals, their quarrels with neighbours, the choice of husbands for their daughters. They brought their sexual tensions and the anxieties of married and family life to a monk committed to lifelong chastity and solitude. They asked advice on the many problems of living together in society from somebody who had chosen to live outside it.

This seemed worth investigation. Is it possible that solitude confers insights not available to society? Could it be that the human condition, even the ways we relate to each other, is better understood by those who have opted out of relationships?

The question is a particularly urgent one today when the success and stability of our lives are judged by the quality of our relationships. They have been elevated to the *sine qua non* of the fulfilled life. We are obsessed by them. Books, magazine articles, radio and television programmes regularly appear on the making or repairing of relationships. When they treat of solitude it is only to provide a setting for examining 'the problem of loneliness'.

Current psychological dogma sees us as sociable animals who need the close companionship of others from the cradle to the grave. Our psychological health is demonstrated by a capacity to form relationships. Without them we are warped: our criminals today, from shoplifter to serial killer, are understood as people whose attempts at close attachments have been unsuccessful. No other explanation is necessary or is sought.

The psychologists are backed by other behavioural scientists currently in favour who seek to explain all human behaviour in terms of its animal origins. These point out that we must be genetically programmed to need each other to survive: in the animal world, the function of the herd is to maintain the security of its members. Predators are confused by a multiplicity of potential prey and tend to hang around picking off the ones on the outskirts. So, in evolutionary terms, the animals that belong and can form relationships are more likely to survive to pass on their genes. The loners lose out. And this is why it is thought by some biologists to be natural, and therefore virtuous, to form attachments, as it is unnatural and depraved to live alone.

The pressures on all sides to bond make those who, for whatever reason, find themselves alone uneasy and even guilt-ridden in their situation. Even worse, they reduce the possibility of success for the relationships which they constantly promote. If, as we are told, our lives can be fulfilled only by our intimate attachments to others, then those attachments are from the beginning under a weight of responsibility that cripples their growth. Even more importantly, this current insistence on relationships not only spoils our chances of relating – it gets in the way of our discovering the value, perhaps the necessity, of solitude.

My research threw up many parallels with the hermits on Patmos and it soon became clear that one of the ironies of the human situation is that those who have chosen to live outside society have always been eagerly sought out for advice on how to live within it. Hermits have built up great reputations not only, as might be expected, for heroic asceticism or spirituality but for insight into the ways of the world. They have often found it diffi-cult to preserve their seclusion from the crowds who came to disturb it in search of counsel. They have something to say to us today even in an age so uniquely averse to solitude. Hermits can make clear the fruits of the solitary life as well as re-ordering the priorities for those of us who live among people.

A book which seeks to gather together and present the insights of hermits has to exclude those who had nothing to say. Many thousands of recluses have lived their solitary lives and gone to their graves in silence. Further, if a man or woman spent a lifetime in complete solitude, any wisdom they might have acquired could not have survived them. So the hermits who can contribute to our lives today either had visitors who preserved their sayings or else they gave up their solitude at some stage.

The first glimmerings of the value of solitude seem to emerge in ancient China, when, in contrast to the social ethic of Confucius, the poetry of the *Tao te Ching* hints at the pleasures to be found in rejecting society and following the example of nature. At about the same time, or a little later, the Greeks were emerging from a Homeric culture in which an individual's personal dignity depended on the honour or respect he could win in society. Through the teach-ing of Socrates, a warmly sociable character who needed to be alone from time to time, they learned to be choosy about those whose good opinions they sought. The followers of Socrates carried his social discrimination further and many rejected completely the society which had demonstrated its depravity by putting him to death. The Cynics, who claimed allegiance to Socratic principles, were the first outsiders, despising the comforts and even the decencies of civilisation to assert the supremacy of the individual.

Their attitudes were encouraged by the conquests of Alexander the Great, in whose empire the individual was significant as a citizen of the known world, not as a unit of a city-state. The Cynics thrived and were teaching their high-minded rejection of material possessions throughout the worst excesses of the Roman Empire. In this they found common cause with the early Christians, many of whom adopted a style of living close to that of the Cynics.

The Desert Fathers demonstrated their rejection of contemporary society by choosing to live outside it in areas which had been considered unfit for human habitation. They became hermits to escape the distractions of life in the village or city and found that with solitude came peace, a clearer perception of the way to spiritual health and, perhaps more surprisingly, an awareness of the self-deceptions of those who lived in society. It is in the revelation of these distortions of the human personality that they have most to teach us. The tales told by them, and about them, are a rich treasury of psychological insight expressed with humility, compassion and humour.

The tradition of the Desert Fathers was maintained by the hermits of Mount Athos and from there it passed to the solitaries who found their 'desert' in the vast forests of Northern Russia. Most of these lived lives of quiet unremarked asceticism in the remoteness of their caves or wooden huts but some, still following the example of the Desert Fathers, became spiritual guides or *startsy*. These then attracted followers and often founded communities which became monasteries. Others protected their solitude by living in separate huts close to but not usually in sight of each other. These were called sketes, and the most famous of them, at Optina, was renowned all over Russia during the nineteenth century for the quality of the *startsy* who lived there and the penetration of their insights. Thousands made the pilgrimage to Optina, peasants, soldiers, statesmen, intellectuals and writers such as Gogol, Dostoevsky and Tolstoy.

As the Russian skete of Optina was approaching the peak of its fame as an exemplar of fifteen centuries of Christian tradition, an idiosyncratic graduate of Harvard College was setting up, on the other side of the world, a personal experiment in the solitary life. Henry Thoreau set out to experience and examine, from first principles, the economic, psychological, dietary, sartorial and spiritual consequences of living alone. He built himself a hut by a lake and kept a journal. He was only twenty-eight years old when he started the experiment, but he reported a wide range of insights – from a suspicion of new clothes to the transcendental influences of the natural world.

Thoreau was an enthusiast for the spirituality of the East. He practised meditation, called himself an occasional yogi and adopted as his motto '*Ex Oriente Lux*'. The solitary life which he attempted is, within Indian culture, not something to experiment with nor the consequence of a spiritual conversion but the normal and natural conclusion of every lifespan. All human beings ideally mature, according to Hindu philosophy, into hermits. That philosophy was revived by Thoreau's contemporary Ramakrishna, who went into solitude to gain enlightenment and then returned with a body of teachings that, carried to Europe and America, sparked off a revival of interest in Eastern religion that continues today. The essence of the teaching, that all faiths are in their inner essence the same, makes it enriching to all.

Sometimes the true value of the solitary life has been brought home most clearly to those who have sought but failed finally to achieve it. Charles de Foucauld, in his youth a dissolute aristocrat, aspired for most of his adult life to become a hermit in the remotest part of the Sahara desert. He found that separation from his own culture made him more available to the Tuareg, who honoured him as a saint and martyr after his assassination. He called himself a hermit, dressed as a hermit and lived alone for many years in the desert, but he was never completely alone. Out of his search for solitude emerged the inspiration for hundreds of followers who dedicate themselves to the service of others.

Another frustrated hermit was Thomas Merton, the most powerfully persuasive apologist for the solitary life of all time. Intensely sociable and a compulsive communicator, he lived for most of his adult life as a Trappist monk under a vow of silence. During that time he struggled with the conflict between his wish to live as a hermit and his need for companionship, his urge towards the contemplative life and his desire to pass on the insights he found in contemplation. His vow of obedience to a superior who opposed his wishes kept him for twenty-two years from moving into his hermitage. During that time he assembled a powerful array of historical witness in support of the solitary life and, when he finally achieved a measure of solitude, he was able to articulate its benefits with both passion and precision.

Merton's closest friend is now a friend of mine and lives on Patmos. Robert Lax is a hermit in society, perhaps pointing the way ahead for today's contemplative. He is a poet who lives alone and yet loves people. Every day he walks in the streets and talks to many friends he has made in thirty years on the island and to any strangers he thinks may need help. He is concerned, compassionate and sensitive. He is a close and loyal friend and will say that friendships are an important part of his life, but every evening he returns to an empty house and centres himself within its silence as he has for over forty years. Out of that silence and solitude emerge the insights of his poems and the revelations of his conversation on living alone in the world today.

The selection of viewpoints and personalities from ancient China to present-day Patmos is inevitably a personal one. This is not an exhaustive compendium of hermits of the world in chronological order. It is influenced, no doubt, by my interests as a convert to Eastern Orthodox Christianity, though I must explain that I have none of the certainties and little of the missionary zeal that often accompany late conversions. I feel rather that I have been allowed in on compassionate grounds and am standing, still blinking and mystified, just inside the gates hoping to be slightly more open to the truths to which the Church bears witness. (Fortunately for me, the Orthodox Church is mystery-friendly.) The omission of the Western medieval hermits is not due to lack of interest on my part, but is simply because there have been many books devoted to them and also, perhaps, because the continuing tradition of the Desert Fathers is less well known in the West.

Finally, the book is a record of some of the most penetrating insights, described in the words of hermits over two thousand years, into the need we all have for a time of solitude in our lives.

CHAPTER ONE

The Emergence of the Individual

The Greeks, who first taught the Western world what could be achieved by living together, were also the first people in that world to work out a philosophical justification for living alone. Greek society in the age of Pericles reached unsurpassed levels of achievement in philosophy and the arts, and even gave birth to science; but that same age, which was called 'golden' because of the glories created by the city-state, was also the first to discover the significance of the individual. Although the Greeks never developed a hermit culture, they were the first to work out a philosophy of solitariness – one which stressed the value of the individual outside a social context. So, as they are the founders of our civilisation, they are also the inspiration of those who have chosen to live outside it.

The world of classical Greece which gave birth to European civilisation was not a place in which to be solitary. Man, said one of the most influential of all Greeks, Aristotle, is a political animal. By this phrase, echoed by political philosophers down the centuries, he did not mean that we are all born to take an active interest in party politics but that it is in our nature to live in a *polis*, or community. Human beings, Aristotle taught, achieve their full potential by working for the common good, and their drive to do so is not implanted by society through an education in Civics but is an innate instinct.

An ancient Greek myth explains this.[1] When the gods were first creating the animal kingdom, they gave to the brothers Prometheus and Epimetheus the power to choose the characteristics of each member as it was created. Epimetheus, who had more zeal than intelligence, persuaded Prometheus to let him do it by himself and he began distributing the gifts of the gods with enthusiasm. To some animals he gave horns and claws so that they could hunt for their food; to others he gave fleetness of foot to run away. To the different creatures as they came into being he handed out great strength, keen senses, thick skins and furs to ward off the cold. The last animal to be created was Man. By this time, Epithemius had nothing left to give. So Man was put on earth a bare, forked, unprotected thing until Prometheus, taking pity on humans, stole fire from heaven and gave them technology.

But technology demands communal effort, and humans could not use it to survive unless they could learn to cooperate and live in communities. So Zeus sent Hermes with two gifts from his own personal store: a sense of shame and a sense of justice. Hermes asked if he should distribute these gifts only to some individuals and not to others – like the practical skills of carpentry and house-building. But Zeus said no: a community cannot survive only through its experts. If it contains laymen in the arts of communal living as there are laymen in the practical skills it will fail. So all men were given a sense of shame and justice. 'And,' Zeus added, 'implant this custom in them from me: that if there should be one without a sense of justice or shame from doing wrong he should be put to death as a pest of the community.'[2] So the *arete* of Man, the purpose for which he was created, his true virtue, is to live in communities. Man is, by nature, a political animal.

The Greek society described by Homer was one in which people were motivated almost entirely by public opinion. It is an example of what anthropologists have called a 'shame culture' rather than a 'guilt culture' – that is, one in which the main spur to activity is public esteem rather than the pricking of a private conscience. The highest good at which an individual could aim was the achievement of *timi* or public honour. (So fundamentally important was *timi* in this sense that it came to mean also the basic price or value of an object.) Achilles asks, 'Why should I fight if the good fighter receives no more *timi* than the bad'[3]. When Hector takes his baby son in his arms in a famous scene of the *Iliad* he prays that the boy '. . . may become, as I have been, pre-eminent among the Trojans, as strong and brave as I . . . And let people say, as he returns from the fighting: "This man is better than his father." May he carry home the bloody spoils of the enemy he has killed and bring joy to his mother's heart.'[4] The prayer strikes a harsh note with us today because the highest good the father can wish for his son is the noto-riety that comes from fighting and plunder. But it is enough to gladden his mother because she knows that success as a warrior is the sure way to that public celebrity which was the spur to all human activities. The human being was significant only so far as he or she was acknowledged and praised by society.

Greek religion in the earliest times was a communal activity. The gods that were worshipped were those of the community, and the acts of worship were expressions of communal solidarity. But there was an early movement which departed from the usual worship of the Olympian gods in the direction of a more personal religion. Those who practised the cult of Orpheus banded themselves into ascetic brotherhoods and tried to purify their souls through diet and dress. The Orphic cults were based on the myth that Orpheus had introduced to Greece from Egypt the worship of Dionysus. Soon after his birth, Dionysius was entrusted to the Titans, who, under Hera's orders, tore the child to shreds and boiled his flesh in a cauldron before eating it. The Titans were then blasted by the fire of Zeus, who created, from their ashes, a new race of men. These were composed of the eaters and the eaten, so that they each had within them the divinity that was a piece of the god. The *soma*, or body, was the *sema* or tomb of the divine. The Orphics taught that by abstinences and purifications the divine might be preserved pure within the body and protected from the soiling of the carnal appetites. Their practices were ascetic and mystical. The preachers of the Orphic doctrines were the first pre-Christian missionaries in the Mediterranean world. They were specially powerful at Crete and do not seem to have penetrated the religion of mainland Greece to a great extent until their most famous convert, Pythagoras. Pythagoreans, exponents of an intellectualised Orphism, practised continence and abstinence and – some of them – silence. These religious observances of asceticism, of withdrawal from society, of stressing the individual's duty to work out his salvation with diligence, were all part of the transition which gave birth to the individual as set apart from society and so provided the first religiously based ideological justification for solitude.

Yet Greek society continued for the most part to maintain the social ethic of Homer, which survived into the age of Plato:

> If you were to look at the ambitiousness of men, you would be surprised how irrational it is, unless you understand that the love of fame and the desire to win a glory that shall never die have the strongest effect upon people. For this they are ready to face any danger – even more than for their own children: to spend their substance, to endure any physical hardship, to give their lives for it

. . . the nobler a man is, the more is undying fame and immortal *arete* the spring of his every action.[5]

Anything which exposed an individual to the contempt or ridicule of others or which caused loss of face was intolerable. It was a matter of personal honour for a wronged person to seek revenge, and a prosecutor in an Athenian court would openly admit this as a reason for bringing a complaint.[6]

In time of war, the Greeks sought and won honour by hand-to-hand combat on the battlefield. In peacetime, they bought it. The Attic farmer was as concerned as the Homeric hero to be publicly recognised. In the golden age – the fifth century – this recognition was attested by the possession of citizens rights, the loss of which was called *atimia*. As in every society, the wealthy were given public respect. Greeks enjoyed accumulating money and felt no pangs of conscience in pursuing it. Money was necessary to the good life and to keep friends. The poet Pindar wrote that a man who loses his money loses his friends, and quoted the words of Aristodamus of Argos which became proverbial:

'Money, money makyth Man,' he said
When he lost his possessions and friends together.

Theognis, an elegiac poet of the late sixth century BC, who had lost all his lands in a political revolution, said that poverty is worse than old age or shivering ague and that a man should avoid it even by flinging himself from a precipice or drowning himself in the sea. As poverty was degrading, wealth was elevating and allowed a citizen to buy and surround himself with beautiful objects to the delight of his family and the admiration of the society in which he lived.

Socrates

So when we come to Socrates – an unprepossessing figure who walked barefoot; whose meat and drink were of the poorest; who wore the same cloak, summer and winter; who claimed that the most valuable possession he had was his leisure and that to be content with little is to approach the divine – a sea change has begun. It would be a misrepresentation, of course, to claim Socrates, that most sociable of men, as a hermit. His whole life was spent in public – the market-place, the streets, the gymnasia. He had no liking for the country and rarely went there. 'Fields and trees', Plato makes him say, 'will not teach me anything; the life of the streets will.' He loved the market-place because there he had opportunities to talk with and therefore learn from his fellow Athenians.

But the market-place also, paradoxically, reinforced his asceticism by allowing him to experience the pleasures of abstinence. He once happily remarked, surrounded by the great variety of goods for sale: 'How many things there are that I do not want!' In his indifference to possessions and public opinion Socrates had the cast of mind of the solitary; but it was combined with an intense sociability that kept him in the city. He did not need to live in the desert to prove his independence. He was well able to assert and maintain it through his conversations. He was sociable but not committed to company. He could stand absorbed in his own thoughts from one dawn to the next if a thought struck him and he felt the need to unravel its potentialities. Dinner might cool and friends be kept waiting while Socrates pondered alone.

In another important respect Socrates cleared the philosophical ground for the solitaries: he argued for replacing the approval of society as the spur to human activity by the individual conscience. The aim of the wise man was no longer the plaudits of the masses but *autarkeia*, or self-sufficiency.

A contemporary of Socrates, Hippias of Elis, had also preached a doctrine of self-sufficiency but, in his case, it was a demonstration of his own virtuosity rather than of abstemiousness. He taught that the greatness of the *polis* was based on its economic independence and that every individual could achieve the same greatness and become a *polis* in himself by learning the arts of self-sufficiency. According to Plato, he once presented himself at the Olympic festival, where his fellow Sophists enjoyed parading themselves, wearing clothes and ornaments all of which he had made with his own hands, including an engraved ring and an ornate Persian belt.[7] Socrates taught a different self-sufficiency: for him the wise man was not the one whose abilities had been expanded to fill his needs, but one whose needs had contracted to balance his abilities.

Such a person seemed to others deprived. Antipho, the Sophist, once approached Socrates and, in the presence of a crowd whose attention he was trying to capture, said:

I thought, Socrates, that those who studied philosophy were to become happier than other men; but you seem to have reaped from philosophy fruits of an opposite kind; at least you live in such a way as no slave would continue with his master: you eat food and drink drink of the worst kind; you wear a dress that is not only bad but the same in summer and winter, and you continue shoeless and coatless. Money, which cheers men when they receive it, and enables those who possess it to live more generously and pleasantly, you do not take . . . you must consider yourself to be but a teacher of wretchedness.[8]

Socrates answers that, since he doesn't take money for his conversations, he is at liberty to talk to the people he likes. As for his diet: 'he who eats with most pleasure is he who least requires sauce'. The purpose of changing dress in winter and summer is surely to enable people to go out in the different weather conditions, but Socrates points out that he has never had to stay at home because he was too hot or too cold, or because his feet hurt. He then rounds off his apologia for the ascetic life with words that inspired later generations: 'I think that to want nothing is to resemble the gods and that to want as little as possible is to make the nearest approach to the gods; that the Divine nature is perfection and that to be nearest to the Divine nature is to be nearest to perfection.'[9]

As to public opinion, Socrates seemed indifferent to it during his life and, during his final hours, gave a reasoned explanation of the need to avoid dependency on it. In the year 399 BC he was locked away under sentence of death in the state prison in Athens. The execution had been stayed because of the annual ceremony in which the Athenians commemorated the delivery of their city by Theseus from the tribute exacted by the Cretan Minotaur. Ships sailed from the Athens to the sacred island of Delos, and while they were absent from the city no one could be put to death there. As Socrates and his executioner waited for the return of the fleet, his old friend Crito came to visit him with a plan for escape. Socrates was unwilling to run away and pointed out that a philosopher should uphold the law. One of the arguments Crito used to persuade him to fall in with the plan was that, if he refused, Crito would be blamed:

CRITO: Most people will never believe that it was you who refused to leave this place although we did our best to persuade you.

SOCRATES: But, my dear Crito, why should we pay so much

attention to what 'most people' think? The reasonable people, who have more claim to our consideration, will believe the facts as they are.

CRITO: You can see for yourself, Socrates, that we have to think of popular opinion as well. Your situation right now is enough to show that the capacity of people for causing trouble is no small thing, in fact it has no limits if you once get a bad name with them.

SOCRATES: I just wish that ordinary people had a boundless capacity to do harm, because they might then have a limitless capacity to do good, which would be a marvellous thing. Actually they have neither. They cannot make a man wise or stupid; they just act at random.

Socrates goes on to say that serious thinkers have always held that only some of the opinions in popular circulation should be respected, others not. And, as was his way, he illustrates this by concrete examples:

SOCRATES: When a man is in training and taking it seriously, does he take notice of all praise and blame indiscriminately or does he only pay attention when it comes from his doctor or trainer?

CRITO: Only when it comes from the qualified person.

SOCRATES: Then he should fear the criticism and welcome the praise of the one qualified person, but not when it comes from the general public?

CRITO: Obviously.

SOCRATES: So he should regulate his work and his exercises as well as his diet in accordance with the judgement of his instructor, who has expert knowledge, rather than by the opinions of the general public.

CRITO: Yes, that is so.

And Socrates goes on to point out that the athlete who tries to train according to a regimen dictated by popular opinion is likely to damage himself. The conclusion is that popular opinion is an unsafe guide to human conduct and is more likely to lead to harm than good.[10] This is a view which overturned the long-established priorities of the Greeks; it was a view which led them to put to death the wisest of their number.

7

The Cynics

After the death of Socrates, some of his followers picked up his indifference to popular opinion and carried it further, into an open scorn for society. They became the outsiders: rejecting material possessions, wandering the countryide with staff and begging bowl and claiming that the *polis,* far from being the natural environment for humanity, was the great distorter of human values.

Socrates had no more devoted pupil than Antisthenes, who walked from Piraeus to Athens every day, a round trip of over ten miles, to hear his master. Xenophon reports Socrates as saying that Antisthenes never left him, and Plato says that Antisthenes was with Socrates at his death. Antisthenes was not a full-blooded Athenian. His mother was from Thrace, possibly even a slave, and so he had no strong attachment to the city-state of Athens. He followed Socrates in teaching the importance of individuality and self-sufficiency. And, whereas Socrates thought of possessions as irrelevant to the pursuit of the good life, Antisthenes went one further and erected a scorn for wealth into an ethical principle. Since the appetites can distort a person's perception of the truth, and since wealth feeds the appetites, the wise man will avoid wealth and seek to control rather to indulge his desires.

> As I see it, wealth is not a material possession that one can keep in one's house as if it were an object, but a disposition of the Soul. Otherwise it would be impossible to explain why anyone who already possesses material goods should expose himself to peril and fatigue for no other reason than to acquire more wealth . . . For my part, though I confess I have no money at home, I don't want any because I only eat as much as will satisfy my hunger and drink to quench my thirst. I dress in such a way as to be as warm when out of doors as Callias in all his finery.[11]

In fact, Antisthenes was quite comfortably off and the torn cloak he wore to make public his scorn for material possessions was an affectation. When he turned the cloak one day so that the tears were more obvious, Socrates remarked to him: 'I can see your vanity peeping through the holes in your cloak.' As Socrates echoes the spirit of Chuang-Tsu, so there is in his most devoted pupil a pre-echo, perhaps, of Tolstoy, whose servants spread silk sheets on the peasants' beds so that their master could sleep in comfort when experimenting with humility. Antisthenes cannot be enrolled as a precursor of the genuine hermits since he was given to parading an assumed poverty to make an impression on his fellow citizens; but in his philosophy of rejecting possessions and regarding civilisation as a corrupting influence on the natural goodness of mankind he was a bridge between Socrates and the Cynics.

Antisthenes was also important in the early history of Cynicism because he promoted the causes of the two principle patron saints of the Cynics: the hero, Herakles, and the king, Cyrus. Both demonstrated virtues which the Cynics adopted and passed on to hermits of later ages. Antisthenes wrote books about both.

Herakles was a generally admired hero figure because of his performance of the twelve labours, or *ponoi*, imposed on him by the gods. He piled up *timi* through demonstrations of courage and strength in overcoming obstacles, and his real virtue lies in the stoicism with which he accepts that which he cannot change. This is the Herakles of Homer, of Hesiod and of Pindar. But there is a subtle change in later stories of Herakles which reflect an attitude to toil, pain and labour which was accepted and later taught by the Cynics: that ease is to be avoided and that true virtue consists in the willing acceptance of avoidable discomfort.

The *Horai* of Prodicus, a precursor of Socrates from the mid fifth century BC, tell the story of how the young Herakles, before deciding on how he should shape his life, goes into the wilderness and meets two beautiful women. One is elegant and modest in her appearance and demeanour. She is Arete. The other wears a semi-transparent dress and is heavily painted and sensual. Her name is Kakia, or Evil. The second approaches him and tells him that he can choose a life of pleasure and indulgence, living off other people and never experiencing toil or *ponos*. But Arete says that the gods never give any real good to humanity without *ponos*. The earth only produces crops after cultivation; cattle cannot be raised without toil; to excel in the martial arts the body must be healthy, and it can only become so through exercise. The people who follow her way have moderate enjoyments, not luxuries for which they have not worked. The young men are encouraged by praise from the old, and the old are honoured by the young. They celebrate the great achievements of the past and tackle with vigour the problems of the present. They are friends to the gods, loved by their friends and honoured in their native land.

There is never any doubt as to which of the two ways Herakles will choose. His choice is still in the context of the culture which is driven by public approval; but the significant change from earlier stories of Herakles is that here he deliberately choses the *ponoi*.

They are not imposed from the outside and he does not undertake them to benefit others but to complete his own path to virtue. This preference for the career of hardship when an easy life is on offer is the mainstay of the Cynic philosophy.

The second Cynic patron erected the preference for hard living over civilised ease into a national principle of education. The Persian king, Cyrus is celebrated in the *Cyropaedia* of Xenophon (b. Athens *c.* 430 BC). This book in eight volumes is more a historical novel than true history, but it is significant in that the system of education which it promotes is one which accepts that the harsh conditions of a natural life – that is, one lived close to nature – are more conducive to morality and happiness than the sheltered existence of civilised people. This is a revolutionary idea in the golden age of the city-state and one which gives a philosophical basis to those who later chose to leave the city for a solitary life. Cyrus is represented as an ideal king and a morally superior being, not because of his specific achievements, but because he was preeminent in that virtue which all men should possess: the *arete* that comes from living a natural and ascetic life. His system was an individual-ethical one in which the human being is of primary and the state of secondary importance.[12]

In their deliberate decision to adopt the ascetic rather than the easy life, the Cynics considered that they were opting for the natural way of living over civilisation. They prepared the philosophical way for later hermits by their preference for *physis*, or nature, over *nomos*, or culture. The idea of *physis* for the Greeks was that of property or characteristics. So that they would say it is in the 'nature' of wild animals to bite, or of dry wood to burn. As for people, their nature was part of their inheritance from their parents and they were most comfortable when acting in accordance with it. But civilisation often forced them to act according to the laws or custom of others. This could produce economic and political stability but it was at the cost of moral integrity. It is a conflict echoed by the hermits down to our own time.

The laws imposed by culture had been undermined by Herodotus, who demonstrated that they were relative rather than universally valid:

Darius, after he got the kingdom of [Persia], called into his presence certain Greeks who were at hand, and asked what he should pay them to eat the bodies of their fathers when they died. To which they answered that there was no sum that would tempt them to do such a thing. He then sent for certain Indians of the race called Callatians, men who eat their fathers, and asked them, as the Greeks stood by, and knew by the help of an interpreter all that was said, what he should give them to burn their fathers when they died. The Indians exclaimed in horror and asked him not to use such language. Such are the rules of custom, and Pindar was right in my judgement when he said: 'Custom is the King over all.'[13]

The Cynics were individualists, proclaiming the supremacy of the individual over social rules, and they quoted the story from Herodotus in support of their view that *physis*, or nature, was constant and stable whereas *nomos*, or custom, was varied and changing. Nature was the core of the individual when the artificialities of society had been stripped away. So the Cynics tried to live on an irreducible minimum because this was *kata physin* – according to nature.

Diogenes

The best-known pupil of Antisthenes, who most flagrantly demonstrated in his own life the rejection of civilisation, living outside society and living alone, was Diogenes of Sinope. He became far more famous in his own lifetime than his master and there are some difficulties of chronology in the relationship. Diogenes Laertius records that Antisthenes at first repulsed him with a stick, but Diogenes placed his head directly under it and said: 'Strike, for you will not find any stick hard enough to drive me away so long as you go on speaking.' Whether or not they actually met is uncertain, but the link in their philosophy is undeniable.

Diogenes was from Sinope, on the coast of the Black Sea, which had been founded as a Greek colony in the seventh century BC by the Ionians of Miletus. It was the terminus of a great caravan route from the River Euphrates to the Black Sea. His father, Hikesias, was a magistrate there and seems to have had some responsibility for the currency – possibly as a money-changer – because he was exiled, together with his son for debasing it. Diogenes reacted to the order of banishment by saying: 'The Sinopeans have condemned me to banishment; I condemn them to stay at home!'

This, at least, is one of the stories recorded by Diogenes Laertius. Diogenes made much use of the phrase '*paracharatein to nomisma*', (altering the currency), and told the story that he had been directed to do so by the oracle at Delphi. The Greek word '*nomisma*', or currency, is connected with *'nomos'*, meaning law or accepted standard of behaviour. So when Diogenes was told to alter the currency, he came to accept this as a divine command to change the ways people behaved. Sceptical critics have put this story down to a later invention and pointed out that the claim to have received a command from the Delphic oracle is simply an attempt to claim a link with Socrates, but the metaphor is an apt one.

Diogenes had one other teacher of philosophy as well as Antisthenes: an Athenian mouse. He was, so the story went, musing on life one day when he noticed a mouse running about in a carefree fashion. It wasn't afraid of the dark; it wasn't looking for a secure spot to lie down in or the comfort of a bed, or indeed any of the comforts that humans spend so much energy in seeking to acquire. And in the example of that mouse he found a remedy for his poverty and a basis for his philosophy.

According to Diogenes Laertius, he was the first to 'double his cloak out of necessity' and sleep in it; he carried a wallet in which he kept his food and all worldly possessions. He was once made so feeble by illness that he needed a staff to support him and took to the habit so that even when restored to health he carried a staff with him on his journeys. The cloak, the wallet and the staff became the badges of the Cynics.[14]

Diogenes carried to extremes a number of Socratic ideas: frugality became with him asceticism; the famous Socratic irony which pretended ignorance as a mode of argument became *parisia*, an outspoken frankness which licensed all speech; *sophrosiny*, the moderation of sensual desires, became *apatheia*, an insensibility that could amount to callousness. And the indifference which Socrates professed to popular opinion became, with Diogenes, *anaideia*, a total shamelessness demonstrated by his practice of masturbating in public. Plato is said to have referred to Diogenes as 'Socrates gone mad'.

An instance of his madness was the occasion when he went to a meal at Plato's house and trampled over all the embroidered cushions with his muddy feet. 'Thus I trample on the pride of Plato', he cried. 'With the pride of Diogenes', replied Plato.

He was particularly upset by lavish interior decorations. At one rich man's house, finding himself surrounded by carpets and cushions, he spat on the owner's face, and then wiped it with his cloak and apologised, saying it was the only dirty place in the room he could find to spit. Diogenes enjoyed a joke and once, when watching an incompetent bowman at an archery contest, walked over and sat down right next to the target, explaining that it was the only place where he felt safe.

He was fond of demonstrating that the independence conferred by his isolation from society made him even more powerful than its greatest: 'Aristotle has to dine when Philip thinks fit; Diogenes can dine at any time he chooses'. The most famous instance of this was when the young Alexander the Great visited Diogenes one day and asked if he, the most powerful ruler the world had ever known, could do anything for the destitute philosopher. 'Yes,' Diogenes replied: 'get out of my sunlight'.

Diogenes was the outsider – the stranger – the spectator at what Pythagoras had called the festival or fair of life. He pronounced it a world of fools with totally distorted values. 'Things of value are bartered for things that are worthless and vice-versa. A statue fetches 3,000 drachmae while a quart of barley flour is sold for a couple of copper coins.' Even the coins were false and did not represent a true system of values. They had to be defaced and put out of circulation. Diogenes had a mission to attack all convention, custom and tradition. But unlike Socrates, or even Antisthenes, his attack was not through argument, but by example. When one of his students asked to borrow a book, he replied: 'You are a silly fellow. If you wanted figs you wouldn't be satisfied with painted ones. But you take no notice of the practice of virtue and study only those who write about it.'

He had a great reputation for ridicule and repartee. He often said that it was strange that men should compete with each other in punching and kicking but never in the pursuit of virtue. He noted that young men would sacrifice to the gods to procure good health while at the same time eating and drinking so much as to destroy what health they had. Instead of anointing his head with oil, he anointed his feet, explaining that the perfumes from his head were lost in the air but those from his feet mounted to his nose.

When asked what was the right age for marriage, Diogenes replied: 'For a young man, not yet; for an old man, not at all.' He mocked those who were upset by bad dreams, saying they didn't care what they did when they were awake and then made a great fuss about what they fancied they had done when they were asleep. He constantly repeated that the gods had given men an easy life but that it had been spoiled by their seeking after honey, cheese cakes and unguents.

He was once at a banquet where the guests threw bones at him as if he were a dog. On his way out he cocked his leg against them. When asked why people give money to beggars but not to philosophers, he replied that it is because they think they might well end up one day as beggars but will never become philosophers.

He said that education gave sobriety to the young, comfort to the old, riches to the poor and was an ornament to the rich.

When he was taken prisoner by pirates and put up for sale as a slave, he was asked what work he could do. His reply was 'Govern men'. And he told the auctioneer to put him up for sale as a master. Seeing Xeniades, a richly dressed man in the crowd, he said: 'Sell me to that man. He needs a master.' And Xeniades bought him and took him to Corinth as tutor to his sons. Diogenes taught them to improve their memories by learning poetry, to cut their hair short and not to wear ornaments or shoes. He was popular in the household and, as he grew older and death approached, the sons asked him how he would like to be buried. He replied 'face downwards', and when asked why, explained that the Macedonians were rising in power so rapidly that the world would shortly be turned upside down and he would then be the right way up.

Diogenes was one of the earliest and most colourful of technophobes: he said that Prometheus had been justly punished for bringing to man the arts and skills that led to the establishment of cities and the artificiality of modern life. 'In this', notes Bertrand Russell in his *History of Western Philosophy*, 'he resembled the Taoists and Rousseau and Tolstoy but he was more consistent than they were.'[15]

An epitaph to Diogenes credited him with 'pointing out to mortals the surest path to a contented life, to glory and lasting happiness'.[16]

There are echoes of the Hindu mystics in the teaching of Diogenes, and these may well have come from direct contact. The port of Sinope, where he was born and raised, was a prosperous distributing centre for merchandise from India. Pliny says that the Euxine Sea (Black Sea) served as a route for commerce between India and Greece.[17] It is likely that the Indian merchants accompanied their goods as far as Sinope. There they would need a money-changer and that is quite possibly what Diogenes' father did for a living. So Diogenes may well have had had opportunities in his boyhood to learn about the ways of the Indian people.

The ancient Greeks knew something about Indian culture.

Aeschylus mentions the people of India in *The Suppliants*;
Herodotus describes India at some length,[18] and there was a tradition that Pythagoras had visited India and, as Apuleus reports,
'obtained from the Brahmins the greater part of his philosophy'.[19]
Diogenes Laertius says of Democritus, a contemporary of Socrates:
'Some say that he associated with the Gymnosophists of India'.[20]

The most famous Greek to associate with the Indian gymnosophists was Alexander the Great, who, on hearing of their fame
as philosophers, sent his steersman, Onesicratus, to meet them. It
was a good choice. Onesicratus had been a pupil of Diogenes
before taking to the sea, and his visit to the Indian holy men convinced him that, as his master had always insisted, Cynicism was
not a school of philosophy but a way of life.

The oldest and wisest of the gymnosophists was called
Mandanis and he 'commended Alexander for his love of wisdom,
even though he ruled so vast an Empire; he was the only philosopher in arms he had ever seen'. [21] He then explained to
Onesicratus that his teaching was aimed at removing both pleasure
and pain from the soul through training the body in ascetic practices. He asked whether such practices were taught in Greece, and
when he [Onesicratus] answered that Pythagoras taught such doctrines and also bade people abstain from meat as did also Socrates
and Diogenes, Mandanis replied that he thought the Greeks
sound-minded in general but that they were wrong in one respect,
in that they preferred custom to nature; for otherwise, Mandanis
said, 'they would not be ashamed to go naked like himself and live
on frugal fare'.[22]

We shall be returning to Hindu theories of renunciation more
fully in Chapter VIII. There is no reason to suppose that they were
directly or mainly responsible for the Cynic teachings which had a
greater influence on early European civilisation: the impulse to
withdraw from society seems to be a universal human one. But the
Greeks were aware that a far older civilisation than their own had
accepted as its wisest representatives those who lived outside
organised communities.

Crates

The most famous pupil of Diogenes became so celebrated in his
own time that he was mentioned in the comedies of Menander and
Philemon. A collection of his sayings was put together by the

philosopher Zeno, and Plutarch wrote his biography. This last distinction could well have had more to do with the eccentricities of
his life than with the significance of his teaching.

According to tradition, Crates was a wealthy man who
renounced his possessions. One story is that he sold his farms to
shepherds and then, following Cynic practices of renunciation,
threw the money into the sea. A more interesting tale, recorded by
Diogenes Laertius, is that, he sold all his lands and deposited the
money with a banker, having drawn up an agreement with a
moral: if his sons should turn out to be ordinary, ignorant people
they should inherit it, since they would need the money; if they
should blossom into philosophers, they would not, and the money
should go to the poor.

Crates lived a life of renunciation and poverty on the outskirts
of society. He was never a hermit – indeed, his nickname was 'the
door-opener', because he was welcome in every house – but he
was, like the hermit, an outsider: his authority was simply that of
the uninvolved, and he used it to settle family disputes, of which he
became a famous arbiter.

He taught a simple, practical asceticism: 'Prefer not the oyster to
the lentil, to avoid confusion.'[23] His message was that luxury and
extravagance cause revolution and tyranny in the cities. They must
be replaced by simplicity. A third-century-BC historian of the
Cynics, Teles, describes the life of a student of Crates:

> Metrocles says that when he studied under Theophrastus and
> Xenocrates, though he had a liberal allowance from home, he was
> actually afraid of starvation and was constantly in a state of want
> and penury. But when he transferred to Crates he could have
> maintained a second person besides himself without any
> allowance. For formerly it was essential to have sandals . . . a
> cloak, a retinue of servants, a well-furnished household, to
> contribute to the common table fine wheated bread, dainties
> above the common level, sweet wine, and to furnish the
> entertainments which came his way . . . But when he changed over
> to become a follower of Crates there was none of that. Living on
> a much simpler scale he was satisfied with a rough coat and barley
> bread and common herbs and felt neither regret for his former
> mode of life nor dissatisfaction with that of the present . . . If he
> wished to anoint himself he would go into the baths and use oil-
> lees; sometimes to he would go to the furnaces of the smithies,
> roast a sprat, mix a little oil and sit down and make his breakfast.
> In summer he would sleep in the temples, in winter in the baths. [24]

It was through his student Metrocles that Crates formed a relationship which caused amazement and merriment in antiquity. Metrocles sent word to his family to say how happy he was to be a student of Crates and how much he admired his master. His sister, Hipparchia, came to visit them out of curiosity. She fell violently in love with Crates and threw over her younger and more eligible suitors, threatening to commit suicide unless she could marry him. Now Crates was not built to excite passion. In fact he was so unprepossessing in appearance that he was always laughed at when he stripped for his physical exercises. He took off all his clothes and said he was showing Hipparchia all his possessions – all she would be getting if she became his wife. This final argument failed and they were married. Hipparchia went everywhere with Crates, wore the Cynic clothes and became a famous philosopher in her own right.

Little survives of the genuine written work of Crates, but the spirit of his message survives in 36 epistles, written over his name by well-known Cynics or supporters of Cynicism in the Augustan age (42 BC to AD 17). They are evidence not so much of what he actually taught but of what a later age thought of value in his philosophy:

3. Crates to his students:
Take care of your soul, but take care of the body only to the degree that necessity requires, and of externals not even that much. For happiness is not sensual pleasure on account of which we need externals, but virtue is complete without any externals.

8. To the youths:
Accustom yourselves to wash with cold water, to drink only water, to eat nothing that has not been earned by toil, to wear a cloak and to make it a habit to sleep on the ground. The baths will never be closed to you, the vineyards and flocks fail, the fish shops and shops which sell couches go broke, as they will to those who have learned to wash with hot water, to drink wine, to eat without having toiled, to wear purple clothing and to rest on a couch.

11. Crates to his students:
Practise being in need of only a few things (for this is the closest thing to god, while the opposite is the furthest), and it will be possible for you, because you are midway between gods and irrational beasts, to become like the superior race and not the inferior.

15. Crates to his students:
Law is a good thing, but it is not superior to philosophy. For the

former compels a man not to do wrong, but the latter teaches him not to do wrong. To the degree that doing something under compulsion is worse than doing it willingly, to that degree is law worse than philosophy. For this treason, do philosophy and do not take part in government. For it is better to know the means whereby men can be taught to do right than the means whereby they are compelled not to do wrong.[25]

The popularity of Crates as an arbiter in domestic disputes is revealing about Greek society of his day. The state ceremonies and the mystery cults could satisfy a demand for religion but were of no value in everyday affairs. The two great schools of philosophy – the Academy and the Peripatetics – were scholarly and scientific in spirit, so the ordinary citizen could expect about as much help from them with everyday problems as he or she could today from NASA. Friends were there to help, and it is interesting that most ancient discussions of friendship insist that the function of a friend is to give advice. But friends knew little more than you did yourself. So a man like Crates, detached from ordinary living, could give impartial counsel related to a known standard of values. He was more important to the average Athenian of his day than Theophrastus and the learned Academicians. And he was laying the foundations in Western Europe of a way of life and a social role for the solitary, long established in the East.

The Cynics and Christianity

The conquests of Alexander the Great were to advance the cause of the Cynics. He thought in terms of empire, not of the city-state. The greatest of Greek philosophers before his time had been men of the city: Plato and Aristotle held that the fulfilment of human potential could only take place within the city, but as the city-states began to lose their influence and be merged in a greater cosmopolitan whole these ideas began to be replaced by that of the individual as citizen of the world, with an importance and value transcending that of the city.

In the first century AD there were Cynics wandering the streets of Rome and preaching against the civic order. They were expelled from the city in 71 to 75 for teaching opinions 'contrary to the age' and in AD 94 Domitian expelled all philosophers from the city, some of whom fled to the Western Celts. In Eastern Europe a community of outlook grew up between the Cynics and the early

Christians in their hostility to the Græco-Roman civilisation, and the Church Fathers saw much in the ideals of the Cynics with which they felt a close sympathy.

There were even Christian Cynics and Cynic Christians, the most famous of the latter being Peregrinus, born in the closing years of the first century. He became the leader of a Christian community in Palestine and was imprisoned by the Romans. Hailed as a new Socrates, he was released by the Governor of Syria, to prevent his being turned into a martyr. He went home and surrendered all his dead father's property to the State, being as a result proclaimed a 'true disciple of Diogenes and Crates'.[26] He went to Alexandria and studied under the famous cynic Agathoboulos but was expelled from the Christian Church for profaning its rites. He spent some years teaching Cynic philosophy at Athens before immolating himself on a funeral pyre at the Olympic games of 165.

A more notable contribution to the early history of the Church was made by was Maximus the Cynic, who adopted the Cynic garb and the Christian faith at an early age. He grew up in the mid fourth century, when the Arian disputes split the Church. He opposed the Arians, supported the Creed which was accepted by an ecumenical council and became known as the Nicean Creed, and was appointed to the See of Constantinople. He was welcomed there by Gregory Nazianzen and was publicly addressed as:

> the best and most perfect of philosophers . . . one who follows our Faith in an alien garb, nay perhaps not in an alien garb if the wearing of bright and shining robes is the mark of angels as it is so depicted. This man is a Cynic not through shamelessness but through freedom of speech, not through gluttony but through the simplicity of his daily life . . . a dog who greets virtue not with barking, but with hearkening; who fawns on what is friendly because it is good, who snarls at what is alien because it is bad.[27]

St Gregory of Nazienzen (329–389) had a warm sympathy for Cynicism and welcomed its ideals of poverty and simplicity, as did his close friend St Basil the Great (330–379), who declared that Diogenes had been the heathen exemplar of the poor monk. Both spent periods of their lives as hermits and adopted for a time a style of living which came close to that of the Cynics. The ascetic orders of Christianity to which we shall now turn were directly connected with the Cynics and form a bridge between the ancient and modern worlds.

CHAPTER TWO

The Desert Fathers

The desert is the uninhabitable place. It is the region of desolation and solitude that surrounds and threatens the fertile plain. Along the Nile valley, the desert is a silent presence always visible to the dwellers in towns and villages as they live in comfort on the rich dark soil. Its bare hills are the 'waste howling wilderness'[1] of the Old Testament, the haunts of demons; and yet men and women have always been drawn from the comfort and security of their homes in the valley to the barren caves above in search of solitude.

St Antony of Egypt was the most famous of the Desert Fathers, and his life inspired thousands to leave their homes and follow him. He was the son of rich Christian parents who died in his youth, leaving him well provided for a life of ease. But one day in church he heard the words of Jesus to the rich young man that he should sell all he had and give to the poor. Antony felt the words were spoken to him and he obeyed them. He went to learn from a local hermit how to live in solitude and then moved away to live in the tombs on the outskirts of villages, then further into the desert, and finally to a deserted fort at Pispir, on the east bank of the Nile about fifty miles south of Memphis. He lived alone without seeing a human face for over twenty years, being brought supplies of bread and water every six months. Sometimes the friends who brought these supplies would hear terrifying shrieks and groans from behind the locked doors. Eventually they could stand this no longer and they broke down the doors expecting to release a wasted and emaciated maniac. Antony emerged healthy, sane, balanced and full of advice on how to lead the ascetic life. He went to Alexandria to support the Christians who were being persecuted there and spent the rest of his life alternating between retreats into solitude and emerging to help and advise others.[2]

Within Antony's lifetime thousands of men and women flocked

to the desert in search of religion. There were reported to be five thousand monks on Mount Nitria, to the west of the mouths of the Nile. The monastery of Tabennisi, near Dendara, had seven thousand men and women living in different styles – communal and solitary – under its supervision. Less than forty years after Antony's death a traveller through Egypt and Palestine reported that the population of desert dwellers almost equalled that of the towns. These men and women were not, of course, all drawn to the desert by the fame of Antony. Many lived their lives there without hearing his name. They came for a variety of reasons – some no doubt were criminals escaping justice or citizens evading tax – but the majority were on a spiritual quest of some kind which they felt they could not pursue in the society of their day.

The Christian Church was then as ambivalent about asceticism as it is today. From its roots in Judaism, it inherited the tradition that the desert was a place of spiritual power where God had revealed himself to Moses and to Elijah. John the Baptist had lived there with the clothes and severe diet of a prophet before announcing his great message to the world. Christ had fasted for forty days and forty nights in the desert, frequently retired there to pray, and instructed his disciples to follow his example in prayer and fasting. So the severe austerities of the prophets were part of the tradition with which Christ had associated himself. But on the other hand he was known as a man who openly ate with publicans and sinners. He contrasted his own way of life with the asceticism of John the Baptist, recognising that, by doing so he had acquired a reputation as a glutton and wine-bibber.[3] And his first miracle had been to keep the wine flowing at the wedding feast and to improve its quality. So Christ could not be held up by the ascetics as an example of unremitting self-denial.

The Church had a further problem with asceticism. At the end of the first century it had to face its first great crisis in the struggle with Gnosticism. This was a bundle of mystic beliefs which predated Christianity but which were fused with it in various sects. The keynote of Gnosticism is the duality of spirit and matter. The world and the flesh are evil, standing in opposition to God. So the ultimate aim of life, according to the Gnostics, is liberation from matter and this is achievable through a complex series of arcane practices and passwords known only to the initiated. But because, in the Gnostic belief, the spirit is in bondage to the flesh in this life, severe asceticism is in order. Wine and meat are forbidden, and marriage is looked on as merely licensed fornication. The early Church on the other hand taught that the whole creation of God is good. She became suspicious of ascetic practices, since they often were the outward signs of Gnostic beliefs.

There were also divisions among Christians over the question of poverty. Christ's message was undeniably focused on the poor, and many Christians of the apostolic age had sold their worldly goods and lived in communities awaiting the second coming. But, as the generations passed after his crucifixion, they found it increasingly hard to live in daily expectation of his arrival on clouds of glory and Christians came to accept that they had to settle down to a possibly long period of coexistence with the world. So there had to be accommodations to its ways. During the second and third centuries the early Churches came to acknowledge legitimate wealth, power, even luxury as not necessarily being contrary to their faith. Some individual Christians were not prepared to make such accommodations. They seperated themselves from society and became solitaries.

They were the outsiders. They provoked the hostility and resentment of their contemporaries and the satirical malice of historians. They inspired some of the finest invective of Edward Gibbon:

> . . . the Ascetics, who obeyed and abused the rigid precepts of the Gospel, were inspired by the savage enthusiasm which represents man as a criminal and God as a tyrant. They seriously renounced the business and the pleasures of the age; abjured the use of wine, of flesh and of marriage; chastised their body, mortified their affections, and embraced a life of misery, as the price of eternal happiness.[4]

When, almost sixty years ago, Helen Waddell introduced the writings of the Desert Fathers to the twentieth century, she referred to the 'slow-dropping malice of Gibbon' in his account of their effect on civilisation and went on to quote 'the more humane distress of Lecky':

> There is perhaps no phase in the moral history of mankind of a deeper or more painful interest than this ascetic epidemic. A hideous, distorted and emaciated maniac, without knowledge, without patriotism, without natural affection, spending his life in a long routine of useless and atrocious self-torture and quailing before the ghastly phantoms of his delirious brain, had become the ideal of the nations which had known the writings of Plato and Cicero and the lives of Socrates and Cato.[5]

William Edward Hartpole Lecky (1838–1903) was an Irish historian and philosopher who wrote a *History of Rationalism*, published in 1865. A lover of civilised values and champion of eighteenth-century rationalism, Lecky was offended by the rejection of the social and philosophical priorities of the Age of Reason. He was, as we shall see, an inaccurate and unintentially comic observer of the Desert Fathers.[6]

As for Gibbon, whose distinction as a writer of ancient history is unassailable, it may be fairly observed that he was temperamentally antipathetic to asceticism: he detested enthusiasm in any context; he was fond of good food, wine and fine clothes. Towards those who rejected the tangible pleasures of the flesh in favour of the insubstantial searchings of the spirit, he was simply uncomprehending. But the case he makes, that the Desert Fathers tortured themselves in this life in order to win a comfortable billet in the next, has been widely accepted as a true analysis of Christian asceticism and deserves an answer.

There were, of course, the extremists. We shall come across stories of them trying to outdo each other in discomfort and deprivation. But there are as many stories cautioning against heroic austerities as there are celebrating them. And the historian Palladius, 'a faithful Boswell to the more austere saints and a whole-hearted admirer of virtues not his own',[7] who records them was more a teller of tales than a careful scholar. It is significant that Simon Stylites, so often the exemplar of historians who dismiss the Desert Fathers as half-crazed fanatics, was expelled from his monastery for excessive austerities, found distasteful by his contemporaries among the monks, and only acquired a reputation in the modern age through the contempt of Gibbon.

There is no doubt that the hermits chose a life of solitude and hardship because they believed it would help their spiritual progress. The ultimate aim of that progress was the salvation of their souls, and a frequent question from the monk to the elder was 'What must I do to be saved?' It is in this question that we most frequently misunderstand them. We are all heirs to Gibbon in our tendency to think that this question means 'What shall I do now to be saved after death?' But the *soteria*, the 'salvation', the monks are seeking is not a secure place in an eternity of heavenly bliss which begins when they die. It is, first of all, a state which begins in the present life and continues uninterrupted by death. When a man meets God it is at the point where eternity intersects with time, and, for these Christians, the awakening of the divine in man places him on the plane of eternity.

Secondly, this activation, through the grace of God, of man's divine spark steers him towards perfection – in the Greek sense of completion or the achievement of his natural end. This is the 'salvation' which the hermits seek. It signifies, here and now, integrity, health, freedom from fault and illness. So to be 'saved' is not just to escape hell – it is to escape, in this life, everything that leads to hell: sin, the devil and the 'world' in the biblical sense. Salvation is at the same time eternal happiness and a state of peace and well-being in the present world through the health of the soul.

This is why the hermits' apophthegmata – the stories of the Desert Fathers' deeds and sayings – can speak so movingly to us today down the centuries and across such a wide cultural gap. They deal with essentially human virtues and follies. Paradoxically, these men and women who fled from human society developed, in their solitude, a uniquely subtle awareness of human psychology. They lay bare the self-deceptions we all practise. They teach us why it is important to be self-aware and how we can come to know ourselves. The sins they struggle against are the thoughts and deeds that undermine human integrity, and the methods they use in the fight are ones which can lead us all to spiritual and psychological health.

Although their spiritual experiences were frequently intense, the Fathers were reticent about them. The stories we read are more to do with how they should treat each other. Helen Waddell writes: 'Of the depth of their spiritual experience they had little to say: but their every action showed a standard of values that turns the world upside down. It was their humility, their gentleness, their heart-breaking courtesy that was the seal of their sanctity to their contemporaries, far beyond abstinence, or miracle, or sign.'[8]

Their lives, though for the most part conducted in isolation, were remarkably similar in domestic conditions. The hermitage would be a hut of stone with a roof made from branches. It had a door which could be closed and locked, for we often read of visitors knocking there. Inside was a reed stool on which to sit when working, a reed mat on which to sleep, and a sheepskin. This last item seems to have been the only one which a hermit would carry away if changing locations. In fact some of the stories mention that a hermit took up his sheepskin and left the cell to indicate that the move was a permanent one. There was a lamp or candlestick, a jar of oil for the lamp and one of wine for visitors. There would also be another jar of brackish water for the hermit to drink and in which to steep the palm leaves to soften them for working. The preserved food would be dried peas and lentils, and these, after soaking, could be cooked and seasoned with herbs from an outside garden.

In these conditions men and women lived in solitude for many years, sometimes in groups whose caves were separate but within easy walking distance of each other, meeting for a liturgy on Sundays but otherwise seeing only the occasional visitor or young monk in search of the Way. Some built up a reputation for their austerities; others inspired followers through their wisdom. The latter were called 'abbas', a world close to the Hebrew 'rabbi' or teacher. Antony was the most famous, largely because of the widely popular *Life*, written in Greek and acclaimed as the work of St Athanasius. There were others whose words we shall meet below. Arsenius, born in Rome of a noble family, who held high office at the imperial court in Constantinople before fleeing the world in AD 394 was said to have worn the most splendid clothes in the court and the vilest in the desert. Moses, in contrast, was a black slave who became a monk and retired to the desert near Petra in 475. Of John Colobus little is known except that he was a dwarf; and Poemen's identity is obscured by the fact that, as almost three hundred stories survive with his name attached, that name must refer to at least two different Fathers. The conditions of the desert were so harsh and dangerous that women could hardly survive there, but Theodora lived in solitude as a monk for many years and was only discovered to be a woman after her death, when her body was being prepared for burial.

Most of the Desert Fathers are known only from the apophthegmata about them which have survived. These stories of how they dealt with each other and the problems they faced have come down to us with all the unvarnished directness of camp-fire tales. They are not carefully edited illustrations of some overarching theory about the human condition. They often seem inconsistent and contradictory, because, as the Fathers always insisted, the advice they gave was always to a particular individual facing a unique situation. It was never intended to have a universal application. And yet the human condition brings us all into situations that echo each other and we can draw profit from a wisdom that throws light on our own.

No writing about the Desert Fathers is as compelling as the apophthegmata themselves. These were written down towards the end of the fourth century and they form, for all their fragmentary and episodic qualities, the most ancient and valuable record of early Christian monasticism. By the fifth century, they had already begun to be collected in two different ways: by author and by topic. Since we know little of the authors, it seemed preferable to select and present them here in groups which deal with the subjects of greatest importance to the Fathers and to ourselves. I have translated them as directly and simply as I could,[9] trying to preserve their effect, which has been described as 'like the flash of a signalling lamp – brief, arresting and intense'. [10]

It is an effect which can, it seems, have revolutionary and far-reaching effects on those exposed to the Desert Fathers. Palladius, whose account is the most important source document for their history,[11] prefaces it with a prayer the present reader may like to bear in mind:

> May this account, then, be a sacred reminder for the good of your soul and a constant medicine against forgetfulness. May it dispel the drowsiness that arises from senseless desire, indecision, and pettyness in necessary affairs. May it free your character of hesitation and meanness of spirit. May it rid you of excitability, disorders, worldly conceit, and irrational fear. May it improve your never-failing desire and your pious intention, and may it be a guide both to you and to those who are with you, not only your subordinates but your rulers as well.

Solitude

For the Desert Fathers, solitude was not merely an escape from distractions; it was a teaching presence. To remain silent and alone is to be open to influences that are crowded out of an occupied life. These influences, some felt, were enough to bring about spiritual health. We may well have a duty to our fellow human beings, and good works are praiseworthy; but self-knowledge can only come through solitude.

> There is a story of three ascetics who became monks. One gave himself the task of reconciling enemies according to the words 'Blessed are the Peacemakers'; another committed himself to visiting the sick; and the third went off to the desert. The first wore himself out trying to keep men from fighting each other and,

disillusioned, went to visit the one who cared for the sick. He found that he too had become discouraged by the unending task and was ready to give it up. So they went to the desert to see how the third was getting on. They told him their problems and asked if he had made any progress. He was silent for a moment and then poured some water into a vase and said: 'Just look at this water'. They did, and it was murky. A little later he said to them: 'See now how the water is cleared'. And they could see their faces in it like a mirror. And he said to them: 'This is like the man who lives among other men and because of their turbulence cannot see his own sins, yet when he lives alone, especially in the desert, he can see his failings.'

*

A brother came to Scete to ask for a word from Abbas Moses. He said: 'Go and stay in your cell; your cell will teach you everything.'

*

A brother asked Abbas Hierax: 'How shall I be saved?' The Abbas said: 'Stay seated in your cell. If you are hungry, eat. If you are thirsty, drink. Do not speak ill of anyone and you will be saved.'

*

An abbas said one day to Abbas Ammonas: 'I am troubled because I can't make up my mind between three ideas: to wander in the deserts, to set out for a foreign land where nobody knows me, or to shut myself up in a cell without seeing anybody and only eating on alternate days.' The Abbas replied: 'None of the three is right for you. Just sit in your cell and eat a little every day and keep continually in your heart the words of the publican[12] and you will be saved.'

*

Abbas Moses said: 'The man who flees man is like a ripe grape, the one who lives among men is like a green grape'.

But to flee from society in order to escape its problems is not the solution. Solitude is not for the simply unsociable:

Abbas Lucius once said to Abbas Longin: 'If you haven't first conducted yourself well among men, you won't conduct yourself well in solitude'.

*

An abbas said: "It is better to live among the crowd and keep a solitary life in your spirit than to live alone with your heart in the crowd'.

Sometimes, in spite of all his efforts, the fame of a solitary would make him attractive to the rich and famous. Then extreme steps had to be taken:

A nobleman came one day to see Abbas Simon. Hearing of his approach, the hermit girded himself and went out to prune a palm tree. As the party arrived, they shouted: 'Old man, where is the anchorite?' He answered: 'There's no anchorite here'. So they went away.

*

Another time, another nobleman came to see him. The servants came before and said to the abbas: 'Abbas, get ready, the nobleman, who has heard of you, comes for your blessing.' And he said: 'Yes, I'll get ready'. He put on his patched garment and, taking bread and cheese in his hands, sat at the entrance enthusiastically eating. When the nobleman arrived with his train, he scorned him, saying: 'Is this the anchorite we've heard of?' And they turned and went back home.

*

The local Governor heard one day about Abbas Moses and came to Scete to see him. Somebody told the Abbas so he fled into the marsh. Now the Governor and his party came across him there and asked him: 'Tell us, old man, where is the cell of Abbas Moses?' And he said: 'What do you want with him? He's a madman'. So the Governor left. Later he went to the brothers and told them what had happened and they asked him what this man was like. When he replied that he was scruffy, large and black, they told him who it was: the Abbas Moses.

*

The blessed Archbishop Theophilus came to see Abbas Arsenius once with a nobleman and asked the Abbas for a word of profit. After remaining silent for a time, the Abbas asked him: 'And if I give you one, will you keep it?' They promised to keep it. Then the Abbas said to them: 'Wherever you here that Arsenius is – stay away'.

*

One of the Fathers came to visit Abbas Arsenius and as soon as he knocked at the door the Abbas opened, thinking it was one of the servants. When he saw it was somebody else, he threw himself on his face on the ground. The visitor said: 'Get up, Abbas, so that I may greet you', but the Abbas lay on the ground and replied: 'I shan't get up till you have gone away'. After having entreated him for a long time the visitor left and he got up.

Part of the authority of the hermit issues from his situation as a separate and uninvolved individual outside the boundaries of society. He is aware of, but not swayed by, the pressures that shape the lives of others. He is the outsider – the stranger. So he can arbitrate in situations where disputing parties are looking for impartiality. This was not, of course, an authority the hermits sought; it became an embarrasment to them and many had to uproot themselves to escape the demands for them to act as judge in the lives of others. But the need to live as a stranger was often stressed:

> Abbas Poemen said: 'If a monk masters his belly and his tongue and lives the life of a stranger, you can be confident – he will not die'.

*

> Somebody said to Abbas Pistos: 'Father, what does it mean, to live as a stranger?' And he said: 'Be silent and say that you have no right to speak about anything. That is to live as a stranger'.

*

> A brother asked Abbas Poemen: 'How should I be in the place where I live?' The Abbas said :'Have the mentality of a stranger in the place where you live so you don't too readily express your opinions and you will be at peace'.

*

> One day Abbas Longin asked for the view of Abbas Lucius on his thoughts, saying: 'I want to live as a stranger'. The old man said to him: 'If you don't master your tongue you'll never be a stranger no matter where you go. Simply master your tongue and you are a stranger.'

The main characteristic of the stranger, it seems, was the refusal to comment. The Fathers felt that words had great power for good or evil and should be used with care:

> Abbas Macarius used to say that a bad word will make even a good person bad but a good word will make even a bad person good.

*

> A brother told Abbas Sisoes: 'I want to control my heart but I can't.' The Abbas replied: 'How can we control our hearts when we keep open the door of our mouths?'

*

> Abbas Diadochus said: 'Just as if you leave open the door of the

public baths the steam escapes and their virtue is lost, so the virtue of the person who talks a lot escapes the open doors of the voice. This is why silence is a good thing; it is nothing less than the mother of wise thoughts.'

Silence could communicate. One of the stories of Antony is that he was visited by three brothers over a period of years. Two of them constantly asked him for his advice and for the words that could save their souls. The third remained silent until, one day, Antony asked him if he had not anything to ask. He replied: 'It is enough for me that I am with you, Father'. This communication simply through a presence rather than speech is at the heart of the Orthodox tradition.

Theophile the Archbishop went one day to Scete and the brothers asked Abbas Pambo: 'Say a word to the Father so that he can be edified'. The old man said to them: 'If he is not edified by my silence, he will not be edified by my words'.

*

Abbas Isaias said: 'Love to be silent rather than to speak. For silence heaps up treasure, while speaking always scatters'.

Asceticism

This is the most misunderstood aspect of the lives of the Desert Fathers, contrasting as it does with the classical ideal of a sane mind in a healthy body. Self-inflicted pain seems to us the sure sign of a sick mind, and, carried to extremes, can lead to the twisted and emaciated forms in which it became the tradition for artists to portray the hermits. There were indeed many such, and they drove themselves to extremities in an unhealthy spirit of competition which led them to outdo each other in austerities.

But too often the perversions and exaggerations of asceticism are taken as the norm for which that much abused word more properly stands. The Russian mystic Vladimir Soloviev wrote: 'If the suppression of the flesh is taken not as a means for good or evil but as an end in itself, we get a pecular kind of false asceticism which identifies flesh with the physical body and considers every bodily torment a virtue. Although this false asceticism of self-laceration has no evil purpose to begin with, in its further development it easily becomes an evil: it either proves to be a slow suicide or becomes a peculiar kind of sensuality.'[13]

The Desert Fathers were not exempt from this behaviour but, as we shall see, they recognised and condemned it. The story below of Abbas Macarius shaming the austere monks of Tabennisi is a famous example. But there remains the puzzling fact that there are sayings from the Fathers which claim that good health is not so much a condition of spiritual development as a threat to it. This can only be understood in the light of their insistence that we all need to recognise our state of dependence. The human being who exults in good health and possesses a hearty appetite and a good digestion is liable to slide into the error of feeling himself or herself to be self-sufficient. This shuts the door to spiritual progress. A sharp reminder of our vulnerability to the pangs of hunger, the ache of sleeplessness, the nagging urge for sex, brings us back to a condition from which we can start to advance.

Abbas Daniel said: 'To the same degree that the body flourishes, the soul vegetates; as the body vegetates, so the soul flourishes'.

*

One day the brothers came together at Abbas Joseph's hermitage. He was particularly ebullient and full of fervour and he said: 'Today I am King because I rule over my passions'.

*

A brother came to Abbas Macarius one day and asked how he could be saved and the Abbas told him to go to the burial ground and insult the dead. So he did so, hurling insults and stones at the graves. When he got back, Macarius asked him if they had responded and the brother said they had said nothing so Macarius told him to go and praise the dead. He went to the burial ground and sang the praises of the men buried there. When he reported back, Macarius asked how the dead had taken his congratulations and the brother replied that they had said nothing. So the Abbas said: 'You know all those insults you hurled at them and they said nothing and all the praises you heaped on them and they said nothing; you also, if you want to be saved – be a dead man, taking no notice either of the injustice of men or of their praises. Behave like the dead and you will be saved.'

*

The great Abbas Macarius was unsurpassed in his austerities. Palladius tells the story of his setting out one day to visit the monastery of Tabennisi because he had heard of the strict life led by the monks there. He put on the old clothes of a labourer and asked to see the Abbot, Pachomius. 'I beg you to receive me into your hermitage', he said, 'that I may become a monk.' But Pachomius replied that he was obviously an old man unused to the ascetic life and that the severe austerities of the brethren would be beyond him. For seven days Macarius pleaded to be allowed to try and was finally admitted on condition that he would be expelled should he not be able to put up with the hard life.

There were then fourteen hundred brethren in the monastery and Macarius studied their different kinds of asceticism. One ate only every evening, another every other day and yet another every five days. One would remain standing all night and sit down only by day. Just before Lent began, Macarius collected a heap of moistened palm leaves and stood in a corner plaiting them day and night for the forty days until Easter. He ate no bread and drank no water and remained standing for this time, neither speaking nor sleeping, only munching a few cabbage leaves on Sundays to give the appearance of eating.

The brethren were very put out that this strange old man could do without more things for longer than they were able and they sent a deputation to the Abbot to demand that this 'bodiless man' whose practices put them to shame should be expelled from the monastery – either he must go or they would.

But God revealed to Abbot Pachomius the identity of his guest and he took Macarius into his oratory and greeted him: 'I am grateful to you for having given this lesson to my children so they might not become haughty about their own ascetic practices.' Then he asked Macarius to return to his own hermitage.

*

Abbas Poemen said: 'Just as smoke chases away bees and then all the sweetness of their labours is spoiled, so corporal well-being chases the fear of God from the soul and so all its good activities are lost'.

*

He said again: 'If the monk detests two things, he can become freed from worldly ties'. And the brother asked: 'What are they?' He replied: 'Corporal well-being and vain glory'.

*

Another abbas called on one of the Fathers who had just cooked a few lentils. He said: 'Let's just say a little office'. And he went through the whole psalter. Then the other recited all of the two great prophets. And, as morning came, they forgot to eat and the abbas went away.

Sex

It is surprising, given the priority, power and urgency with which we have invested the sexual appetite, that its problems were not a major preoccupation with the Desert Fathers. They had to go without it and we are constantly being told that repression is a bad thing and that sex, like steam, builds up a head if it can't find an outlet. Perhaps one explanation is that their sexual appetites were suppressed rather than repressed. That is, the Fathers confessed their carnal thoughts to each other rather than pretending they didn't have any.

There are relatively few apophthegmata which deal with sexual problems. This cannot have been due to embarrassment or censorship, because the few stories that treat of sexual desire do so without a hint of reticence:

> A monk struggled at Scete because the enemy put into his mind the thoughts of a very beautiful woman he lusted after. Another brother arrived in Scete from Egypt and told him that she had died. He took his tunic and, at night, went and opened her tomb, dried the pus from her corpse with his tunic and returned to his cell. He kept the smell close to him and said to himself: 'This is what you lust after – take your fill'. And he remained with the stench until the struggle ceased.

*

> A monk was travelling with his old mother when they came to a river which the old woman could not get across. So he wrapped up his hands and carried her across. She asked why he wrapped his hands, and he told her: 'The female body is a fire which reminds us of other female bodies – that's why'.

*

> In lower Egypt there was an anchorite who was very famous for his austere way of life. He lived alone in a cell in the desert. Incited by Satan, a certain shameless woman said to the young men of the district, who were jealous of him: 'What will you give me if I cause your anchorite to fall?' They promised her a magnificent recompense. She set out in the evening and came to his cell as if she was lost. She knocked and he came out. He saw her and was troubled. 'Why did you come here?' She said: 'Because I am lost'. And he was full of compassion and brought her into the courtyard and then went into his cell and closed the door. She cried out and said: 'Abbas, the wild beasts will eat me'. He was moved and, fearing the judgment of God, said: 'Why am I so angry and so

hard?' And he asked her in.

Then the Devil tempted him and he, knowing what was happening, said: 'The footpaths of the Enemy are in darkness and the Son of God is Light.' So he got up and lit the lamp. Then, as the desire mounted in him, he said: 'Those who do such things go to torment: so try if you can stand eternal fire'. And he put a finger into the flame and burned it. But his passion was so great that he could not feel the fire as it burned his flesh. He carried on doing this until daybreak and burned all his fingers completely away. Then the unhappy woman, seeing what he had done, was terrified and died of fright.

When the young men came to ask for her they found her dead. But the anchorite revived her and she lived chaste ever after.

*

A monk met some nuns on a road and dashed off to one side. As they passed, the mother superior said: 'If you were a perfect monk, you would not have noticed that we were female.'

There is, perhaps, a clue in the following story as to why sexual frustration was less of a problem to the hermits than we might have expected:

A brother asked an abbas how he coped with the sensual thoughts that torment the monk and the abbas said: 'Since I've been a monk, I've never had my fill of bread nor of water nor of sleep and these privations caused me so much suffering that they didn't leave space for the thoughts that trouble you'.

Similar experiences have been reported by the male victims of the concentration camps during the last war, who said they were always too hungry to think about sex.

Fasting

The Fathers had a clear idea of the virtues of fasting and a genuine distrust both of excess and of regarding the practice as an end in itself. They did not deprive themselves of food and drink because they thought either to be impure. Both are gifts from God and to be enjoyed as such. But the appetites of the body are disordered and their constant demands are a distraction. So they have to be held in check and ordered by self-denial. To hold back from eating our fill reminds us that we are dependent; to sit down to three square meals a day can produce the illusion of self-sufficiency:

'. . . give me neither poverty nor riches; feed me with food convenient for me: Lest I be full and deny thee, and say "Who is the Lord?" '[14]

> Abbas John Colobus said: 'If a king wants to get possession of an enemy town, he first gets his hands on the water supply and the food and so the enemies, dying of hunger, surrender to him. It is the same with the passions of the flesh: if a man lives in fasting and hunger, the passions surrender and have no strength against his soul.'

*

> The abbot of a monastery asked Poemen: 'How can I acquire the fear of God?' Abbas Poemen answered: 'How can we acquire the fear of God when we have inside here skins full of cheeses and pots full of salted meats?'

*

> Abbas Poemen said: 'You can't humble the soul if you don't ration the bread'.

*

> An abbas said: 'He who can master his belly can also master impurity and his tongue'.

*

> A brother asked Abbas Tithoes: 'How can I control my heart?' And he replied: 'How can we control our hearts when our tongues and our stomachs are open?'

*

> Hyperechios said: 'Fasting is the rein for the monk against sin: when he rejects it he becomes again a stallion in rut'. He also said: 'The monk's fast dries up the streams of voluptuousness'.

Poverty

In one of the most striking images in the Bible Jesus told his disciples that it is easier for a camel to pass through the eye of a needle than for the rich young man, whom he loved, to enter the kingdom of God.[15] This was not because the man was comfortably off with his worldly goods but because he refused the invitation to part with them. If possession without attachment were possible, then possession would not be a bar to spiritual growth. But the early

Christians recognised that the human condition is such that, for most people, to possess goods is to be in some measure possessed by them. Those who fled to the desert recognised that the desire to possess, which they called the sin of avarice, was a strong tie to the world they were trying to escape. The remedy was poverty. And that poverty had to be absolute.

Abbas Evagrius said: 'A brother who had nothing else but a copy of the Gospels sold it to feed the poor, saying: "I have sold the word that tells me to sell what I have and give to the poor".'

*

A great personage came from abroad to Scete carrying with him a lot of gold and he asked the abbas if he could give it to the brothers. The abbas said: 'The brothers don't need it'. As the other insisted, he placed a basket full of gold at the door of the church and said: 'Anybody who needs it – take some'. Nobody did. So the abbas told the stranger to take it away to give to the poor.

*

Some brigands came one day to the hermitage of an abbas and they said to him: 'We have come to take everything in your cell'. He said to them: 'My children, take everything you like'. So they took everything in the cell and left. But they forgot a little tool-bag that was hanging on the wall so he ran after them, calling: 'My children take what you have forgotten from the cell'. And they were full of admiration for his resignation so they put everything back and did penitence and said to each other: 'Truly this is a man of God'.

*

One day the Abbas Euprepios gave a helping hand to some robbers who stripped his cell. After they had taken everything he had, he saw a stick which they had left behind. He was upset at this and ran after them to give it to them. But they refused to take it, fearing that something might happen to them. So Euprepios asked some people he met on the road to take it to them as they were going the same way.

Obedience

Although these hermits were often beyond the exercise of the Church's formal structures of authority, they did not think of themselves as individuals each pursuing his own spiritual path as he thought fit. They accepted the guidance of a spiritual father.

And the acceptance was total. This was partly because of the clear benefits to be gained from an experienced guide but it was also because obedience was seen as, in itself, a virtue. Its power for good consisted in the fact that obedience negates the will. Fasting and other ascetic practices are pursued in accordance with the will and can so lead to pride; obedience always engenders humility.

St Antony said: 'Submission and temperance break in the wild horse'.

*

John Colobus stayed with an abbas at Scete who planted a dry stick and told him: 'Water it every day with a bottle of water until it produces fruit'. Now the water was so far away that if you left in the evening to fetch it you didn't return until dawn. After three years the stick came alive and produced fruit. Then the abbas took the fruit to the church and said to the brothers: 'Come and eat the fruit of obedience'.

*

They said of John, a disciple of Abbas Paul, that he had a great obedience. In a certain place of tombs a hyena had its lair. The abbas, having seen its dung, told John to bring it to him. He said 'But what shall I do, Father, with the hyena?' The abbas said jokingly: 'If it attacks you, tie it up and bring it here'. That evening the brother went to the place and the hyena attacked him. He tried to catch it but it ran away and following the word of the abbas he gave chase. Having caught her, he bound her up. Meanwhile the abbas was worried about him but he arrived with the trussed-up hyena. The abbas was filled with admiration but, wishing to humiliate him, said: 'Idiot! That's not a hyena you have there – it's just a stupid dog.' And he untied it and let it go.

Vanity

In our own time, the terms 'vanity' and 'pride' have become synonymous and we have few problems in recognising them both – so long as they are palpable in somebody else. But the Fathers made an important distinction between pride, the first of the deadly sins and cause of the fall of the angels, and vanity, which is simply the desire for the praise of others. Vanity promotes ostentation; pride, which is more insidious, can make a person indifferent to the impression he makes on others. So vanity is easily spotted;

pride often lurks beneath a show of humility and piety.

Abbas Silouan said: 'Woe to the man whose fame is bigger than his works!'

*

Abbas Nestorius was walking with a brother one day in the desert when they came across a serpent. They fled from it. The brother was surprised at this and said to him: 'Father, were you, too, afraid?' The old man replied :'I am not afraid but yet it was useful to me to flee because if I had not I should not have escaped the spirit of vanity.'

There is a story in the collection of anonymous apophthegmata illustrating the dangers of vanity and reflecting, perhaps, the risks to which those appointed to lead the most famous and successful monasteries have always been exposed:

An abbot, head of two hundred monks, had a great reputation in the world and Christ decided to visit him. He approached the porter in the guise of an old and poor man and asked for an audience. The abbot was in conversation when the porter approached him and said he was too busy to see the old man. So Christ waited patiently at the door. At about five o'clock in the afternoon, a rich man arrived and the porter hastened to announce him. The abbot came to the door to greet him and Christ humbly approached saying: 'I wish to speak with you, Father Abbot.' But the abbot did not even reply, but pushed the old man aside and ushered in the rich man to a welcoming feast.

After the meal, the abbot escorted his visitor to the gate and said his farewell then turned and went back inside, forgetting the patient old man who stood there waiting to speak with him.

As night fell, Christ showed himself to the porter and said: 'Say to the abbot: "If you want worldly glory, then because of your past good deeds and the way you have lived I will send to you visitors from the four corners of the earth to flatter and be flattered by you. But as for the riches of my kingdom, you shall not taste them."'

Pride

Pride, which is far more subtle than vanity, can easily be engendered by the practice of virtue. It creeps into the soul of the righteous person who feels the first twinge of satisfaction in having behaved well. And the Desert Fathers were well aware of its subtleties:

Isidorus the Preacher said: 'If you practise your asceticism according to the rules, be careful, when you are fasting, not to get above yourself. If you find yourself feeling proud of your self-denial – eat meat immediately. It is far better to eat meat than to have inflated ideas about yourself.'

*

A brother had lived for many years outside his village and never visited it. He said one day to the brothers: 'I haven't been to the village for many years but you – you're always going there'. The brothers told Abbas Poemen this and he said: 'Me, I'd have dashed over there at night and walked all around the place rather than letting myself feel proud of not going there'.

Humility

The defence against both vanity and pride is humility. Indeed the Desert Fathers thought of humility as the defence against all the sins and root of all the virtues. This may seem unremarkable. Most of the great religions seem to point to the need for checks on our natural urge to self-aggrandisement for the sake of our souls. Even the secular humanism of Western civilisation today teaches us to restrain our natural aggression for the common good. The British, for example, have made an elaborate code of self-restraint which they call 'manners', a feature, perhaps even a fetish, of their educational system. 'Manners' involve a ritual humility; the true gentleman is one who never makes his subordinates aware of their inferiority; and the British Empire, it has been said, was the historical enactment of the biblical teaching that the meek shall inherit the earth.

But the social humility which we have come to accept as a sign of good breeding is not that of the Desert Fathers. Our virtue consists in not making evident a superiority of birth, education or income. Its essence is that those who know themselves to be superior should be at some pains to disguise the fact.

The humility of the Desert Fathers was more deep-seated. For them the first internal consent to the idea that they were making a progress pleasing to God was a backward step. Because that idea came from the Enemy. If a monk had been following a fast of half a loaf a day, Satan would appear to him in the guise of an angel and say that God was well pleased with his efforts and would be even more pleased if he could reduce his intake to half a loaf every two days. The monk who did this and felt some satisfaction in so doing was on the slippery slope. Humility was the only sure way to combat the temptations of the Devil.

> Abbas Theodora said: 'Its not through fasting or vigils or hard work that we can be saved, but only through real humility'. There was once an anchorite who managed to exorcise some demons and, as they came out, he said to them: 'What made you flee, was it the fasting?' 'No,' they said. 'We neither eat nor drink.' 'Was it the long vigils?' 'But we never sleep.' 'The retreat to the desert?' 'But we live in the desert.' 'So what was it, then, that finally made you come out?' 'Nothing can ever conquer us', they said, 'except humility'.

That spontaneous and genuine humility is a proof against the wiles of the Devil is illustrated in the story of the brother who had lived for many years in great holiness alone in the desert. One day Satan decided to undermine his virtue and, realising that extreme measures were called for, disguised himself as an angel of light. He burst into the cell in a blaze of glory and announced to the monk: 'I am Gabriel, sent from God with a message for you.' And the monk, glancing up from his plaiting, said humbly: 'Oh no. Can't be me. You must have the wrong man.' Satan vanished.

> Abbas Matoes said: 'When anybody speaks about anything, don't argue with him. If he speaks well, agree with him. If he speaks ill, say: 'I suppose you know what you're saying' and don't argue with him about what he has said. That is humility.'

In seeking to escape the good opinion of others, the monks were following the Biblical injunction 'Woe to you, when all men speak well of you' (Luke 6:26) and they went to some lengths to avoid a decline into social respectability. Abbas Pambo once said: 'A monk should wear such clothes that, if he leaves them outside his cell for three days, nobody will take them away'. As the Desert Fathers were aware of the dangers of respectability, they were careful to follow the biblical injunctions against being offensively well-behaved:

> One of the old men said: 'The man who makes public his good deeds is like the one who sprinkles seed on the surface of the earth. The birds of the air come and eat it. The man who hides his deeds is like the one who plants in a furrow and the earth multiplies his seeds.'

*

A woman who had a sickness in her breast called cancer heard of Abbas Longin and looked for him. He lived nine miles from Alexandria. Whilst she was searching, it happened that the holy man was picking up wood along the sea shore. Having met him, she said: 'Abbas, where does Abbas Longin, servant of God, live?' She did not know who he was. He said: 'What do you want with that imposter? Don't go near him. What's wrong with you?' The woman showed him her illness. Having made the sign of the cross over the place, he said farewell to her, saying: 'Go and God will heal you. Longin can't do anything for you.' The woman, believing him, went away and was healed on the instant. Later, having told others of the story and described the Abbas, she realised that it was Abbas Longin .

*

One day at Kellia there was a feast and the brothers all ate in the church. Now one of them said quietly to a servant: 'I eat nothing cooked, only a little salt'. And the servant shouted across to another, in front of everybody: 'This brother doesn't eat cooked foods. Just bring him salt'. One of the old men got up and said: 'It would have been better for you to eat meat today in your cell than to hear such a thing in front of everybody'.

*

They say that Abbas Macarius had a rule when he was with the brothers: 'If there is wine, drink it because of the brothers. But for every glass of wine, spend a day without water.' The brothers, to raise his spirits, gave him wine and he took it with pleasure to mortify himself but his disciple, knowing what was going on, said to the brothers: 'In the name of the Lord, don't give him any more, otherwise he'll die of thirst in his cell'. And they stopped.

Humility only became a problem when the monks tried, with hilarious ineptitude, the experiment of behaving as other men:

Two brothers had lived together for many years and never had a quarrel. One day, the first said: 'Lets have a quarrel like men in the world outside do'. The second replied: 'But I don't know how to have a quarrel'. So the first said: 'Look, I'll put down a brick between us and I'll say: "It's mine". Then you must reply: "No, it's mine". And so the quarrel will begin. So they found a brick and put it between them and the first said: 'It's mine', and the second said: 'No, it's mine'. So the first replied: 'Oh well then, if it's yours, take it'. And so they did not succeed in having a quarrel.

Discernment

This is the most valuable of the virtues. Many are given humility, many have love, but without discernment they can harm themselves and others. It is a sort of sanctified common sense but goes by the name of spiritual discernment. It sees the humorous side of exaggeration and affectation.

Its overriding importance is recorded by Cassian, celebrated recluse and one of the earliest chroniclers of Egyptian monasticism. He tells the story of a congress of leading monks on St Antony's mountain called to discuss perfection and how to achieve it. Some thought it came from fasting and vigils, some from solitude, some from humility. St Antony said that many monks practised all these things and still didn't make spiritual progress because of the want of discretion. 'Nor can any other reason for their falling off be discovered except', he records, 'that, as they were not sufficiently instructed by their elders, they could not obtain judgement and discretion, which, passing by excess on either side, teaches a monk always to walk along the Royal Road, and does not suffer him to be puffed up, on the one hand by virtue, i.e from excess of zeal to transgress the bounds of moderation in foolish presumption, nor allows him to be enamoured of slackness on the other hand'.

The delights of discernment are in the pricking of pomposity; its serious significance is that it counterbalances the fanaticism of which the Desert Fathers often stand accused.

> Abbas Antony said: 'Some destroy their bodies in asceticism but, lacking discernment, are far from God'.

Those who feel themselves to be on the right spiritual path are always in danger of stumbling into self-righteousness. Discernment showed the Fathers how to cope – to extinguish self-righteousness in themselves and others, often with sly humour:

> The brothers of a community went off to visit an anchorite in the desert. He received them with joy and, as is the custom with the hermits, seeing that they were tired, set the table before the right time and brought what he had for them to eat. As evening fell, they recited the twelve psalms and similarly at night. As the abbas was awake at his vigil, he heard them say to each other: 'The anchorites in the desert have a softer life than we do in the communities'. In the morning, hearing that they were going to visit another hermit in the

neighbourhood, he said to them: 'Give him my greetings and tell him not to water the vegetables'. So they did.

Understanding the cryptic message, the hermit kept them working until the evening without food. When evening came, he sang the Grand Office and said: 'We will stop there because of you, because you are tired'. And he said: 'We don't usually eat every day but, because of you, let's eat a little'. He brought them dry bread and salt. Then he said: 'Because of you, we must have a feast'. And he poured a little vinegar onto the salt.

As they were about to eat, he got up from the table, and began to sing the Little Office. This went on until the small hours. Then he said to them: 'Because of you we can't perform the whole of our rule. You must eat a little, as you come from afar.' They ate a little.

The next morning they wanted to leave but he begged them to stay, saying: 'Stay with us a little. At least three days to follow the customs of the desert'. But they, seeing that he would not give them leave, slipped away secretly.

*

John Colobus said one day to his brother: 'I would like to be carefree like the angels who do no work but serve God unceasingly.' And he threw off his cloak and went off into the desert. A week later he came back to his brother and knocked at the door. 'Who are you?' 'I am John, your brother.' 'John has become an angel', he replied, 'and no longer works with men'. And though he cried out, his brother did not let him in until he had fretted outside all night. Then he opened the door saying: 'You are a man and you must work to eat'. John, having been taught discernment, made a bow saying: 'Forgive me'.

*

A brother came to Abbas Silvain on Mount Sinai and, seeing that the brothers were working, turned to the Abbas and loftily quoted the scriptures to him: 'Do not work for the food which perishes' (John 6:27) and followed it with: 'Mary has chosen the best part' (Luke 10:42). The Abbas said to his disciple: 'Zacharie, give the brother a book and put him in an empty cell'.

When the ninth hour arrived, the brother sat in his cell, his eyes fixed on the door, waiting to be called to eat. But, as nobody called him, he went to find the Abbas and said: 'Have the brothers not eaten today, Abbas?' The Abbas said: 'Yes'. So he asked: 'Why did you not call me?' The Abbas said: 'Because you are a spiritual man and do not need this sort of food; but we are fleshly and so we need to eat and that is why we work. You have chosen the best part: you read all day and do not want to eat fleshly food.' Having heard this, the brother apologised and said: 'Forgive me'. The Abbas said to him: 'Surely Mary had need of Martha, and it is thanks to Martha that Mary is praised'.

*

A brother went to see Abbas Macarius and said: 'Father, for thirty years I have not eaten meat and I am still tempted to do so'. The old man said: 'Don't tell me, my child, that you've spent thirty years without eating meat. But tell me the truth: How many days have you spent without speaking ill of your brother? Without judging your neighbour? Without letting useless words pass your lips?' The brother bowed and said: 'Pray for me, Father so I can begin again'.

*

Bishop Epiphanius sent one day to Abbas Hilarion: 'Come, so that we can see each other before we die'. They met and, while they were eating, someone brought in a chicken. Epiphanius gave it to Abbas Hilarion, who refused it, saying: 'Excuse me, but ever since I put on the habit I have never eaten meat'. Then the Bishop answered: 'And ever since I put on the habit I have never allowed anybody to go to bed if he had anything against me, and I have never myself gone to bed with a resentment against anybody'. The Abbas replied: 'Forgive me, your practice is better than mine'.

Although the Desert Fathers were widely acclaimed for the ferocity of their ascetic practices and the heroism of their self-denial, there are many stories which promote the need for moderation. They remembered how Moses sent a message to the King of Edom to say that his people would pass through the land turning aside neither to left nor to right but following the Royal Road, the King's Highway (Numbers 20:17). This became a symbol of the *via media*, the road between extremes which is the better way:

Abbas Joseph asked Abbas Poemen: 'How should I fast?' The Abbas told him: 'Me, I prefer to eat a little every day but not to eat my fill'. Abbas Joseph said to him: 'When you were young, didn't you spend one day in two without eating?' The Abbas said: 'Ah yes. To tell the truth, when I was young I could fast for three or four days and even a whole week. But all of the Fathers went through that experience and, powerful as they were, they found it preferable to eat a little every day. They have passed on to us the Royal Road, the King's Highway, and it is moderate.'

*

They say that Abbas Megethios was always very humble. He was brought up by the Egyptians and had stayed with a lot of the Fathers, among others Sisoes and Poemen. He lived at Sinai close to the river. He himself told the story that one of the saints came to see him and said: 'How do you live, brother, in the desert?' He replied: 'I only eat one day in two, and only one piece of bread'. And the saint said: 'If you'll take my advice, eat half the piece of bread every day'. He did this and his spiritual progress improved .

*

One of the Fathers told a story of Abbas Sisoes: that one day, wishing to conquer sleep, he had himself hung over the precipice at Petra. But an angel came and untied him and told him never to do this again and never to give such an example to the others.

*

A brother said to Abbas Sarmatas: 'My thoughts keep urging me not to eat, drink or sleep'. The Abbas said to him: 'When you are hungry, eat. When you are thirsty, drink. When you are sleepy, sleep.' Another abbas, when he heard of this, said to the brother: 'This is what the Abbas Sarmatas meant: When you are very hungry and you have a thirst you can't contain, eat and drink. And when you have accumulated vigil after vigil and you are sleepy, then sleep. Thats what the Abbas wanted to tell you'.

*

It is told of Abbas Netras, disciple of Silouan, that when he stayed in his cell on Mount Sinai he treated himself with moderation in his asceticism, but when he became Bishop of Pharan he practised a far more severe regimen. When asked why, he explained: 'Down there was the desert, solitude and poverty and I wanted to treat my body in such a way that I should not become ill; but here is the world with its enticements, and if I fall ill there is somebody to take care of me. So I must here act in such a way that I do not lose the monk in me.'

*

The brothers went one day to visit an abbas and found outside his hermitage some children who were watching over the grazing animals and who were shouting indecent words. After the brothers had told him their thoughts and received his advice, they said to the abbas: 'How can you put up with these children and not order them not to call out such things?' And the abbas said to them: 'Truly, brothers, there are days when I want to go out and give them such an order, but then I reproach myself, saying: If I can't put up with such a small inconvenience, how am I going to cope with a really big temptation, if it should come along? That's why I say nothing: so I'll get used to putting up with whatever happens.'

*

One of the desert hunters visited Father Antony when he was relaxing with the brothers and was scandalised by the levity. The Abbas, wishing to make him understand that it was necessary from time to time to indulge the brothers, said to him: 'Put an arrow in your bow and draw it'. He did so and the Abbas said: 'Draw it a little further'. And he did so. The Abbas said again: 'Draw it further', and the hunter replied: 'If I draw my bow too far it will break'. Then the Abbas said: 'So it is with the work of God. If we stretch the brothers too much, they will quickly break. So we must, from time to time, relax and indulge them.'

But discernment was not always in the direction of relaxing the rules:

Abbas Silvain and his disciple, Zacharie, called at a monastery one day. They were given food to eat before they set out to leave. On the road, the disciple came across a pool of water and wanted to drink. The Abbas said: 'Zacharie, today is a fast day'. He said: 'But, Father, we have already eaten'. The Abbas replied. 'What we ate was out of love [for others]; but now we must, between us, keep our fast'.

Many of the stories show how discernment can step in between an accused person and his accusers:

One day a monk was expelled from the monastery of Abbas Elia for yielding to temptation and he stayed for a while with Abbas Antony, who then sent him back. But the brothers chased him away again and he returned to Antony, who sent a message to the brothers saying: 'A ship is wrecked at sea. It has lost all its cargo and with many struggles had just made it to dry land. And you now want to throw back into the sea that which has been saved.' The brothers took the monk back.

*

A brother who had committed a fault was chased out of the church by the priest. So Abbas Bessarion got up and left as well, saying: 'I too am a sinner'.

*

A brother was accused of sinning and the brothers asked Abbas Moses what should be done. He remained silent and then got up and filled a tattered sack with sand. This he took on his back and carried a small sachet of sand in his hands before him. The Fathers asked what this meant and he said: 'The sack on my back is the heap of my sins. I carry it behind me so I can't see it. The sand flows out unnoticed and is lost from sight. This little sachet is the sins of my brother. I hold it before me so I can see it and I spend my time condemning them. Surely this is not the way to act. Should I not rather carry mine in front of me, keeping them always in sight and begging God's pardon?'

*

Some of the old men came to Abbas Poemen and asked him: 'In your opinion, when we see the brothers getting drowsy at the night service, should we shake them to keep them awake during the vigil?' He said to them: 'As for me, when I see a brother getting drowsy, I put his head on my knees and let him rest'.

Compassion

Perhaps the most surprising – and moving – aspect of these stories is the light they throw on the care these hermits had for each other. We tend to feel that those who shut themselves away from human-ity in desert caves and pursue spiritual perfection with fasting and prayer might turn out to be self-absorbed fanatics with little under-standing of or compassion for their fellows. And so the Desert Fathers have been portrayed. But there are constant reminders of their essential humanity and sensitivity towards their brothers:

> There was an abbas at Scete who was very devoted to manual work but not very mentally alert. He came to ask Abbas John Colobos to help him on the subject of forgetfulness. Having received the advice, he returned to his cell but by the time he got there he had forgotten what Abbas John had said. So he went to ask him again and, having received the same reply, went back again to his cell. But by then he had forgotten the advice. And he did this again and again, each time forgetting the advice he had been given about his forgetfulness.
>
> Some time later he met Abbas John and told him that he had forgotten the advice he had received again and again but said he did not return for fear of wearing the Abbas out. Abbas John said: 'Go and light a lamp'. He did so. John said: 'Go and bring other lamps and light them from this one'. He did so. The Abbas then asked: 'Did this lamp suffer any harm from the fact that the other lamps were lit from it?' He said: 'No'. John said: 'It's the same with John. Even if the whole of Scete came to me they could not take away any of the grace of Christ. So, when you want, come without hesitating'.

*

One day, when Abbas John was climbing up to Scete with other brothers, the one who was guiding them lost the way, as it was getting dark. Another brother said to Abbas John: 'What shall we do so that we do not die because the brother has gone astray?' The Abbas said: 'If we tell him, he will be desolated and ashamed. But look, I'm going to pretend to be ill and say I can't go any further, I must rest until dawn.' He did this. The others said: 'We can't go on without you; we shall stay too'. So they sat down until dawn so as not to upset the brother who had lost the way.

*

A brother asked Abbas Poemen: 'Some brothers have come to settle near to me; do you want me to give them orders?' The Abbas said: 'No! You must first act, and then, if they want to live, they will watch you'. The brother then said: 'But they themselves want me to command them'. The Abbas said: 'Not at all! Be a model for them, not a lawgiver'.

*

Abbas Romanos, close to death, his disciples grouped around him asked: 'How shall we behave?' He replied: 'I don't remember ever having told one of you to do anything without having previously made a resolution not to be angry if he didn't do what I said. That's why we have lived the whole of our lives in peace.'

*

He said again: 'If you have spoken ill of your brother and your conscience reproaches you, go and ask his forgiveness and say: "I have spoken ill of you". And take care not to let yourself indulge again in this, because malicious gossip is the death of the soul.'

*

A Father said: 'Do not judge the fornicator if you are chaste. If you do you will be a lawbreaker also, because the one who said: "Do not fornicate" said also: "Do not judge".'

*

Three old men, one of whom had a bad reputation, went to visit Abbas Achilles. One of them said to him: 'Abbas, make me a small fishing net'. He answered: 'I shall not make it'. The second said to him: 'Do this charitable thing for us so we may have a souvenir of you and the hermitage'. But the Abbas said 'I have not the time'. Then the third, the one with the bad reputation, said: 'Make a net for me so that I may have something made by your hands, Abbas'. Straight away, he answered: 'All right. I will do it for you'. Then the others said to him privately: 'Why, when we asked you, you did not want to do it and yet you said to him: "I will do it for you"?' The Abbas answered: 'I said to you I will not do it and you were not upset since I explained that I did not have the time. But for him, if I had not done it he would have said: "It is because of my sin, which he must have heard about, that the Abbas will not do it". And straight away we cut the rope that binds him to us. Now I have perhaps awakened his soul and he is not overcome by guilt.'

*

It is said that Abbas Gelasius had a Bible bound in leather valued at eighteen pieces of silver. It contained both the Old and New Testaments and was kept in the church so that any brother who liked could read it. A foreign brother who had come to visit the Abbas saw it, coveted it, and took it and left. The Abbas did not run after him to take it back, even though he was aware of what had happened. The brother then, having left the town, looked for somebody to sell it to and, having found a dealer, asked him sixteen pieces of silver. The dealer said: 'Leave it with me to examine it and then I will tell you the price'. So he left it

The dealer took it to Abbas Gelasius so that he could examine it, and he told him the price the seller had asked. The Abbas said: 'Buy it for it is beautiful and well worth the price you tell me'. The man went to the seller and said: 'I showed it to Abbas Gelasius and he told me it was expensive and that it is not worth what you ask for it'. Hearing this, the brother said: 'Did the Abbas not say anything else?' He answered: 'No.' So the brother then said: 'I can no longer sell it'. Full of remorse, he went to the Abbas to ask his pardon and beg him to take back the Bible. But the Abbas would not accept it. Then the brother said to him: 'If you do not take it I shall have no rest'. The Abbas said: 'If you have no rest, then I will take it'. And the brother remained, till his death, edified by the conduct of the Abbas.

*

One day Abbas Ammonas went to eat in a place where there was someone with a bad reputation and it happened that a woman arrived and went into this brother's cell. Having heard of this, the inhabitants of the place came together to expel the brother from his cell. Knowing that Ammonas was there, they asked him to go with them. When the brother heard what was happening, he hid the woman in a barrel.

Abbas Ammonas, accompanied by the crowd, came in and realised what had happened but for the sake of God he hid it. He seated himself on the barrel, and then ordered the cell to be searched. And when the people had failed to find the woman, he said to them: 'What is this? May God pardon you all!'

Having prayed, he sent them all out and, taking the hand of the brother, said to him: 'Watch over yourself, brother'. And, having said that, he went away.

*

An ancient said: 'Don't do to somebody else something you detest. If you detest someone who speaks ill of you, don't speak ill of others. If you detest someone who scorns you or injures you, or steals your goods or commits another fault, don't do the same thing to others. It is enough to keep this word to be saved.'

The essential humanity of the Fathers and what Helen Wadell has called their 'heartbreaking courtesy' is well attested in the many stories which demonstrate that hospitality must always take precedence over rules of abstinence:

A brother visited an anchorite who gave him a meal and ate with him. As he left, he said: 'Forgive me, Abbas, for I made you break your rule'. But the other replied: 'My rule is to refresh you and send you away in peace'.

*

Two brothers visited an abbas one day. He had the habit of not eating every day. When he saw the brothers, he rejoiced and said: 'The fast brings its recompense. But he who eats through charity fulfils two precepts: he gives up his own will and he fulfils the demands of charity.' And he fed them.

The form of monastic life lived by the Desert Fathers prevailed in Northern and Middle Egypt until the mid fifth century. The great settlements of hermits were at Nitria and Scete on the left bank of the Nile, those at Nitria tending to settle in small communities and those in an area known as Celia living totally separate lives. None of the hermits lived according to superimposed rules; the solitary calling was usually under the guidance of a spiritual master but subject to no wider authority. To the south, St Pachomius founded the first Christian monastery, inaugurating the Christian cenobitic life at Tabennisi, near Dendara, in about 315–320. Here the monks lived according to a highly organised system of prayer and work. Towards the middle of the fifth century, Egyptian hermits began to decline in numbers and their way of life survived in the Syrian Desert to the north.

In the West, monasticism was reformed and purged of its Oriental asceticism by St Benedict, whose Rule (*c.* 500) was adopted by all the Latin monasteries outside Ireland. It stresses the need for a monk to sink his individuality in the life, of the community. Law and order were introduced into the monastic life, and a stability which bound the monks to their community. The Benedictine would normally live and die within his monastery. Later orders of monks formed in the Middle Ages sought to return to the severity of the original Rule and had little sympathy for the eremitic life. There was a movement in the Western Church in the eleventh century towards establishing small groups of hermits to emulate the Desert Fathers, and this led to the orders of the Camaldose in Italy (*c.* 975) and Carthusians (1084) in France, but monasticism generally in the West was a highly organised and centralised way of life.

In the East the hermits survived in Syria and Armenia and, from the tenth century, on the Holy Mountain of Mount Athos, the rocky peninsula in Northern Greece which kept alive the Orthodox tradition of spirituality as established by the Desert Fathers. It was this tradition which, imported into Russia in the eighteenth century, produced the rich flowering of spiritual descernment and wisdom of the *startsy*, to which we can now turn.

CHAPTER THREE

Lying Low in the Dark Forest: The Russian Startsy

All the books, all the works of the intellect, are not equal in my opinion to the example of a holy Orthodox *starets* in whom I can find a guide, to whom I can impart each of my thoughts, and whose mouth expresses not a more or less private opinion but the very judgement of the holy Fathers. Thanks be to God that there still exist such *startsy* in our Russia.

Ivan Kireevskii,[1] nineteenth-century philosopher

The Holy Mountain

There is a legend that the Virgin Mary, late in life, set out to pay a last visit to Lazarus, who, having been raised from the dead, had joined the clergy and was living as Bishop of Kitium, in Cyprus. A storm blew her ship off course and she took refuge in a bay at the tip of a rocky peninsula jutting out from the coast of Macedonia into the Aegean Sea. She looked up at the grey marble peak that soars over 6,000 feet above the bay and declared it to be, in perpetuity, a holy mountain.

The name of the mountain was Athos. The peninsula which it dominates, is still called in Greek 'Το Αγιον Ορος', the Holy Mountain, and it was first settled, in the Christian era, by hermits following the way of life of the Desert Fathers. By tradition, these appeared in the age of Constantine. The first records of hermits on Mount Athos date from the ninth century, when St Peter the Athonite lived there for thirty-five years alone in a cave. By then the Holy Mountain had such a reputation for sanctity that hundreds lived out their solitary lives on its slopes. In 885, the Emperor Basil the Macedonian emancipated the hermits from the control of a nearby monastery and vested control of Mount Athos in them.

But, as we have seen, sanctity is magnetic. Some of the hermits attracted disciples, who settled in nearby caves and formed communities. These in turn blossomed into monasteries which eventually became the main focus of religious life on the peninsula, though the hermits remained, and remain, a witness to the continuing tradition of the Desert Fathers. They have inspired solitaries all over the world as far distant as the frozen wastes of the northern forests of Russia.

Hermits in Russia

The conversion of Russia was brought about by splendour rather than doctrine. Towards the end of the tenth century, Prince Vladimir of Kiev, so the story goes, sent emissaries to all parts of the world in search of a religion suitable for his people. They were unimpressed by Western Christianity, which they came across in Germany, decided that Judaism would not suit the Russian temperament, and rejected Islam as soon as they heard of the prohibition on alcohol. Then they attended a liturgy at Aghia Sophia, in Constantinople, and reported:

> We knew not whether we were in heaven or on earth, for surely there is no such splendour or beauty anywhere upon earth. We cannot describe it to you; only this we know, that God dwells there among men and that their service surpasses the worship of all other places. For we cannot forget that beauty . . .[2]

Vladimir was converted, married the sister of the Emperor of Byzantium, and introduced Byzantine laws and religion to his people. That tradition imported into Kievan Russia not only the public performance of a highy ritualised and ornate liturgy but also the culture of asceticism involving solitude and austerity.

The first Russian hermit whose name survives was St Antony of Kiev, who set out from his home shortly after Christianity had arrived there to learn more of the new faith. He visited Mount Athos, was tonsured there, and saw, on the Holy Mountain, hermits who were living the lives of the Desert Fathers. When he returned to Russia, he moved into a cave on the side of a hill where he lived on dry bread and water, spending each day in manual labour and prayer. His asceticism and renunciation of the world proved a lure to others, who began to call on him for a blessing. He welcomed all, rich or poor, boyar or slave. People began to settle near him. They enlarged his cave into a crypt and dug out a church surrounded by little cells where other hermits could settle. But Antony needed his solitude. He left the place where he had become so popular to dig out another cave on a more remote hill, where he was left to end his days in silence and prayer. He died in 1073. Little else is known about his life, and he left no wise words, but his example inspired many thousands in later centuries to follow the calling of the solitary.

The Tartar invasions of the thirteenth century destroyed many of the towns and monasteries of Russia and gave rise to a new movement of hermits who are called the *pustniki*, from the word *pustyn*, which means desert. The 'desert' into which they fled was the vast forest to the north, where, remote from human settlement, surrounded by mud in the summer and the hard frozen earth of winter, they emulated the Desert Fathers by seeking solitude in the wasteland.

> This new Russian monastic asceticism, which can be dated from the second quarter of the 14th century, is essentially different from that of ancient Russia. It is the monasticism of the 'desert' . . . most of the saints of the age left the towns for the virgin forests . . . this new trend . . . reflects the difficult and turbulent life in the cities which were still subject to occasional devastation from new Tartar raids. On the other hand, however, the very decadence of the urban monastic houses prompted a zealous search for new ways, ways that were already indicated in the classical tradition of the desert monasticism of Egypt and Syria. Russia did not have any 'desert' in the literal sense; but monks could still escape both men and civilisation: the vast northern forest thus became the 'desert' of the Russian monks. In their fervent choice of the wilderness these pioneers revealed a greater detatchment from the world and its destinies than the monks of Kiev. . . In taking upon themselves the harder task – one necessarily connected with contemplative prayer – they elevated spiritual life to a height not yet achieved in Russia.[3]

Not only did these *pustniki* have an influence on the spiritual life of Russia, ironically they boosted the prosperity of the society they fled by stimulating the colonisation of the forests. The pattern of events was that a lone hermit would flee the company of men and travel deep into the forest in search of solitude. He would cut down the first trees to build his hut and then clear another patch for the vegetable garden. Then, as his reputation for sanctity spread, other would-be hermits would come to settle near him and clear their own patches of woodland. The peasants would follow, and the solitary hermit would end up as the abbot of a large and flourishing monastery owning villages and great stretches of agricultural land.

The First Startsy

The Byzantine Church which established itself in Russia had evolved a dual approach to maintaining the truth of its traditions. The performance of the liturgy, which the Orthodox Church sees as the fundamental reason for its existence, is a public event in which the words and gestures of the priest, familiar to all, are repeated before the eyes of the faithful; any variation or deviation can be recognised. The deep spiritual truths of the Faith, on the other hand, were communicated to individuals by spiritual fathers who had prepared themselves through long periods of solitude and prayer. They were and are the chain of transmission of the wisdom of the Desert Fathers down the centuries.

Whoever sets out to climb a mountain for the first time needs a guide who has already made the ascent and knows the route and the pitfalls.[4] This was the role of the Desert Fathers, and we have seen with what sensitivity and discretion they were able to carry it out. In the Orthodox Church, the tradition has been treasured of seeking guidance from a spiritual father, called in Greek *geron* and in Russian *starets* (plural *startsy*). Because, as has been said, religion is caught and not taught, it is through direct human contact with these persons, rather than by formal instruction, that the faith has been kept alive.

The *startsy* are not appointed. They are recognised. The spiritual gifts they display are acquired in a long period of preparation, almost always in solitude. Hermits were common throughout the lands of Eastern Orthodoxy, living in deserts or forests or close to a village or monastery. The highest calling of the monk is, in Orthodoxy, that of the solitary rather than the cenobitic. St Isaac the Syrian said: 'The glory of Christ's Church is the life of the solitaries'.

But frequently the solitude was not a permanent separation from society but a preparation for taking an active part in it. St Antony of Egypt spent his first fifty-five years seeking greater seclusion in the desert until he finally succeeded in spending over twenty years in complete solitude in the desert fort. But, after his friends had broken down the door, he emerged to become the great spiritual father of many, available to all. This was the pattern of life followed by many of the hermits of the East and the *startsy* of Russia.

The most famous and best-loved of these is St Sergius of Radonezh, who, at the age of twenty, settled in the forest to live a life of solitude and prayer. For twenty-three years, according to the traditions, he faced the rigours of the northern winters, sustained by roots and berries from the forest and the occasional crust of bread from the monastery of Khotkov, ten versts (about six and a half miles) away, which he shared with the visiting bears. When he was discovered by the local peasants they began to visit him regularly to ask for his advice. A few decided to stay close to him in the forest. Gradually, his isolation brought fame, and fame brought disciples, so that he ended up as the abbot of the lavra of the Trinity, established by the authority of the Patriarch of Constantinople.

But Sergius, through all the years of fame and prosperity, was careful to keep his monks to their vows of poverty. He insisted that they refuse all offers of donations and would not even allow them to beg. They had to live from the produce of their own labour. Monks were allowed no private property, not even a basin in their cells for their own use. So in spite of the growing numbers, the ideals of renunciation and asceticism which drew men to the desert were maintained. Even their solitude was protected: they lived alone in separate huts, coming together only for communal work and meals.

The fame of Sergius spread all over Russia and people from all classes flocked to him for advice. Having served his time as a solitary, he emerged as a *starets* available to all. He put an end to four civil wars between Russian princes, and inspired Prince Dimitri to the first Russian victory over the Khans of the Golden Horde at Kulikovo in 1380. In spite of his prestige, Sergius refused advancement in the Church and turned down the proposal that he should succeed Alexis as Metropolitan of Moscow. He was canonised before 1449 and remains Russia's greatest saint.

The inspiration of St Sergius drew many thousands to the northern forests in what became known as the 'Northern Thebaid', the Russian counterpart of the Egyptian Thebaid where the Desert Fathers lived.[5] They left the society of their day for much the same reasons as those which drove the Fathers of Egypt to the desert, and they consciously tried to maintain the same traditions as the Desert Fathers in asceticism, solitude, prayer and the transmission of spiritual truths from a *starets* to his spiritual children. Some lived totally solitary lives and left no memorial; others came together to form monastic communities which, as we have seen, became powerful and influential. There was also a middle way, the skete.

The Sketes

From the earliest times in the Christian world, the cenobitic, or communal, monastic institutions gradually assumed a greater importance than the individual hermits who had preceded them. In the West, a passion for organisation and categorisation produced Rules for the monasteries and eventually different Orders of monks following different Rules. Eastern Christianity has always been less concerned with legalism and has no Orders of monks. There is also a recognition of the fact that monasteries are a great hindrance to the solitude and contemplation of the individual monk. So a form of solitary life evolved in which hermits take up residence out of sight of each other but close enough to come together from time to time in communal worship. These loose communities of solitaries are known as sketes (from the Greek σκητης or ασκητης, a monk or hermit). They began in the desert, were established on Mount Athos, and were imported from there to Russia, where they produced generations of the most influential *startsy*. The disciples of St Sergius lived in an early skete. The most famous skete in all Russia became so influential that, in the nineteenth century, men and women of all classes travelled from all over the land to seek the guidance of its *startsy*.

Optina Pustyn – the Beginning

The origins of Russia's most famous skete lie in the dark days of the 'Enlightenment'. Peter the Great, uncritical enthusiast for Western ways, began the destruction of the Church's authority by abolishing the Moscow Patriarchate and setting up a synod subordinate to the Tsar to rule in its place. His successors – his widow, his grandson, his niece and his daughter – shared his indifference to religion and increased the influence of Western rationalism in Russia. In 1721, monks were forbidden to live as hermits; in 1724, monasteries were changed by decree into refuges for sick soldiers; in 1734, it was forbidden to tonsure anyone but widowed priests and retired soldiers. Catherine the Great, whose views on Christianity were shaped by her regular correspondence with Voltaire and the *Encyclopédistes*, appropriated monastic property and assigned a government salary to the monks. Of the 953 monasteries then existing, 568 were closed down entirely and 160 were left without income. Court prelates became prominent among the higher clergy; men like Ambrose, Archbishop of Moscow and Kaluga, who, at his death in 1771, left, among many other possessions, 252 shirts of fine linen and nine eye-glasses framed in gold.[6]

Spiritual life in Russia during the eighteenth century was at a low ebb; the seductions of French intellectuals captivated the upper classes, and religion came to be thought of as a way of indulging the superstitions of the peasantry. It had no place in the intelligent and sophisticated environment of the cities and was thought to be properly situated amongst the peasants and other wild life of the northern forests from whose benighted conditions polite society had evolved.

The man who revived the authority of the *startsy* and became the inspiration of the most famous skete in Russia was Paissii Velichkovsky, who, having studied at the Academy of Kiev, was dissatisfied with the Latin scholasticism he found there and went in search of true Orthodox traditions. Failing to find a spiritual director in Russia, he settled on Mount Athos in 1746 to live the solitary life and study the works of the Fathers. Paissii translated into Slavic the most important collection of patristic texts on prayer, asceticism and mysticism known as the *Philokalia*. He established a skete on Mount Athos where he gave instruction to his disciples on the contemplative life. He left Mount Athos with his followers to settle in Moldavia, from where his influence reached into all parts of Russia as many monks crossed the border to visit him and returned inspired by his example. That influence became focused at Optina.

The monastery of Optina, two miles from the town of Kozelsk, not far from Moscow, was founded, according to tradition, in the fifteenth century by a reformed robber called Opta who became a hermit, and eventually it grew to be the centre of a small community. Records date back to 1598, and the monastery was never large or influential: there were only sixteen monks when Peter the

Great closed the place down in 1709. It opened again and survived the secularisation process of Catherine the Great on the condition that it should never house more than seven monks. In 1800, a monk called Theophanes, a pupil of Paissii, settled there to join the three resident monks, one of whom was blind. When several other admirers of Paissii arrived, keen to propagate their teacher's ideals, the Metropolitan of Moscow, also a sympathiser, appointed one of them as abbot and, in 1821, the Optina Pustyn was founded. Under the influence of its three great *startsy*, Leonid (1798–1841), Macarius (1788–1860) and Ambrose (1812–91), it rose to the peak of its fame.

Starets Leonid[7]

Leonid was called Lev Danilovitch Nagolkine by his family. Born in 1768, as a young man he travelled all over Russia working as a commercial traveller and gaining the first insights into the anfractuosities of human nature which he was later to demonstrate as a *starets*. There are no reliable indications of his inner development at this time but, at the age of twenty-nine, he made the decision to become a religious and began his life as novice in the Optina Pustyn.

He stayed only two years and went on to the monastery of St Cyril on the White Lake, where he met a monk who inspired him to the life of solitude and prayer. Theodorus had been a disciple of Paissii and had spent many years with him in Moldavia. On his return to Russia, he was sought out by those who wanted to re-establish there the tradition of the spiritual fathers. When he arrived at White Lake, Leonid had been elected abbot but, in 1808, the two of them left the monastery to live in a hermitage over a mile away in the forest. Here they were visited by pilgrims and soon became so famous in the district that their solitude was disturbed every day by crowds seeking their blessing.

So they moved deeper into the forests to the north, following the paths and the way of life of the fourteenth-century hermits, but by this time the hermitages were known and had become accessible so they went to a remote skete near the monastery of Valaam situated on the islands of Lake Ladoga, the largest lake in Europe, which divides Russia from Finland. For a time they found peace there, but before long they had become the centre of the spiritual life and again attracted crowds. It had become clear that flight was impossible and that the *starets* had to choose another way to preserve his peace of mind. Leonid by this time had found one. When asked one day by a young and pious monk how he could allow his solitude to be destroyed every day by so many people, he replied that his love for his neighbour was so great that he could converse with one for two days together and still not allow the conversation to interrupt his interior prayer.

The Abbot of Valaam was irritated that the crowds were drawn to his monastery by hermits who lived outside it and he complained to the Metropolitan of St Petersburg that the influence of the three *startsy* interfered with his authority. It happened that the office was held at that time by Philaret, later to become famous as Metropolitan of Moscow, a scholar who knew well the importance to the Church of the tradition which the hermits were seeking to revive. So he supported them. But the hermits felt that the peace of the monastic community should be protected and so, in 1817, they left and settled at the monastery of Svirsk, where they were visited by the Tsar Alexander I.

Here Theodorus died in 1822 and Leonid decided to find a skete where he could settle to spend the rest of his life alone. He went for about six months to Ploschank hermitage, situated at an almost equal distance between the towns of Dimitrov and Sevsk. But the Abbot of Optina, Father Moses, had just organised the construction there of a new skete and invited Leonid to occupy it.

In 1829, accompanied by six disciples, Leonid returned to Optina, where his monastic life had begun. He was at this time an imposing but unascetic figure: very tall and heavily built, given to obesity. He was very strong and could easily lift more than 400 pounds. His head was said to be like a lion's, with a greying yellow mane and grey piercing eyes. His presence, claimed the pilgrims, brought peace, tranquillity and interior joy to all the people he met. Nobody ever saw him to be sad, irritated or impatient. He had a very strong moral authority, but this never betrayed him into the unctuous expressions of conventional piety. He spoke in popular and colourful language, always with a streak of humour, and did his best to put visitors at their ease by making jokes.

Leonid initiated at Optina a system in which leadership is given to those with the gift of the *starets*: a gift for revealing thoughts. Philaret of Moscow, who had supported the hermits against the

Abbot of Valaam, once said: 'Our visible but unreal virtues impede us from fighting against our invisible but real sins'. We all create artificial personalities for ourselves which we present to the world, and often this mask replaces our true selves and we end up believing it. The *starets* sees behind the mask. He sees us as God sees us. Leonid taught that this should happen during confession. Too often, he said, confession is an impersonal and formal exercise. The confessor asks a few questions and deals with a general situation involving abstract sins which does not touch the person in front of him. The *starets*, he said, must address himself to a human being with a unique destiny, with his own peculiar vocation and needs. To do this he needs more than a long experience of human nature: he needs the gift of discernment and a vision of the true nature of the penitent. A person's true nature, he said, can only be known through a revelation.

From the time that Leonid established himself at Optina, the monastic way of life there changed. His cell became the centre of spiritual life. The Abbot and all the brothers went to him to reveal their thoughts and seek his counsels. Soon, crowds of people from outside came to what had come to be known as a new source of spiritual grace. The skete which he organised allowed for solitude in a monastic environment:

> For those who are unfamiliar with the structure of Optino and of monastic life in general we would remark that, compared to regular monastic life, life in a skit is stricter and more solitary. Apart from the fact that in the skit there is not such a multitude of pilgrims as in the monastery, the skit brothers live in far greater solitude than those of the monastery . . . The monks perform the rule of prayer in their own cells in which in general they spend the greater part of their time in solitary contemplation of God and in the reading of spiritual literature. On entering the skit, the visitor will very rarely meet any of the skit dwellers, and the skit produces the impression of a deep wilderness. For recreation the skit dwellers work with their hands binding books, making covers, doing woodwork, making spoons and copying . . . The inhabitants of the skit fast the whole year except for Christmas, Easter, and the weeks requiring no fast. To keep a check on themselves spiritually the skit dwellers are required to go as often as possible to a staretz in order to confess their thoughts to him in great detail.[8]

Leonid's life at the skete was a strictly ordered one. He never slept for more than three hours. He got up at two each morning to say his prayers, and that was the only free time he allowed himself.

For the rest of the day he received visitors without ever interrupting his manual work. He would talk to them as he sat on his bed plaiting belts. He ate twice a day, conversing with the monks at table. After the evening meal, his disciples would gather in his cell for prayer or reading. He took communion twice a month at the monastery church.

Unlike his successors, Leonid was not a great letter-writer and we have few records of his insights. The impression he made on people seems to have been the effect of his total personality rather than specific advice, though, as he was careful to make this personal and addressed directly to individuals, most of whom were illiterate, little has survived. He took some delight in scandalising the sanctimonious, who were affronted by the coarseness of his dress, the vulgarity of his speech and his physical bulk. This last seems to have been possibly due to some glandular malfunction, since Leonid ate frugally all his life as a monk but remained fat.

A pilgrim who went to see him at Optina has left a vivid memory of him. Seated on the bed dressed in white, he was plaiting and talking to a crowd of pilgrims who knelt on the ground around him. A merchant came in and Leonid asked him why he had come. 'I come in search of your counsel, Father'. 'Have you followed what I told you last time?' 'I'm sorry, Father, I could not do it.' The *starets* told his disciples to throw the man out. When they asked him why he had been so severe, he replied: 'That man came to see me a long time ago and I told him to stop smoking. He promised me that he would. Now he doesn't want to. Let him do what I told him before he comes for more advice.'

One of his disciples went to see him after the daily crowds had left and said he noticed a great difference in attitude among the visitors. Some arrived first but were content to wait patiently until other had been seen before coming forward; others waited a little and then pushed their way to the front; yet others refused to wait at all and insisted on being seen immediately. Were these different attitudes important? The *starets* replied: 'Yes, they are important. Those who try to come first can never remember what I tell them. They ask again and again and keep forgetting. But those who wait patiently, allowing others to go before them because they consider others better than themselves, keep my words firmly in their heart. They remember as long as they live what I have said.'[9]

Another brother often came to Leonid protesting that he earnestly desired to be a martyr. Leonid replied that no one should seek martyrdom, though it may come unsought for. The monk insisted, so one night, when there was a particularly vicious storm raging outside, Leonid told him to go on an errand from the skete to the monastery. The monk objected, saying that the high winds in the great forest terrified him. 'Miserable man,' said the *starets*.'You keep asking for martyrdom and here I give you the chance. The wolves outside would almost certainly kill and eat you in the storm and you would be a martyr for holy obedience and yet you turn down the opportunity!' And the monk was ashamed and never said another word about his ambition.

Then there were the brothers who yearned for the more theatrical forms of self-inflicted penance. One kept asking for permission to wear chains, and finally Leonid decided to silence him. The *starets* called for the monastery blacksmith and said: 'When a certain brother comes to you and asks you to make chains for him, slap him across the face and ask him why'. Then he told the brother that he had permision to wear chains. The brother went to the smith and was slapped across the face. They fought, and when they came before the *starets* he said to the brother: 'How can you dare to wear chains when you can't even put up with a slap on the face?'[10]

To Father Anthony Bochkov, a spiritual son who was later to become abbot of a large monastery, Leonid once described the way in which grace can most easily enter our hearts: 'If you were as simple in heart as the Apostles were you would not hide your human faults, would not appear pious and would live without hypocrisy. This way, which seems so simple and easy, is not given to or understood by many. Yet it is the shortest way to salvation and attracts grace . . . Unless you become as little children, you canot enter the Kingdom of God.'[11]

Starets Macarius[12]

The second *starets* of Optina, who was an intimate friend of Leonid and known as his 'other half', seems to have had little in common with him. Leonid was a man of the people, jovial, uncultured and with little education, but with rude health and practical common sense. Macarius was of noble birth, refined, scholarly, much given to study and contemplation, but with a delicate constitution.

He was born in 1788 on his parents' estate near Kaluga. His family name was Mikhail Nikolaevich Ivanov. As a child, he rarely left his mother's side, was delicate, sensitive and an insomniac. He lost his mother when he was eight years old and was privately educated at the house of his aunt. When he was only fourteen he took the job of bookkeeper in the District Treasury and did it so well that three years later he was given an official position in the Treasury Department. The duties were not onerous and he spent much of his time reading and playing the violin, until the death of his father in 1806, when a family gathering agreed to hand over the estate to him.

He saw this as an opportunity to spend even more time reading and playing the violin, which he did with far greater care and attention than he gave to the estate. The peasants, seeing there was no supervision, took to stealing the produce. When Michael was told of this, he quoted Holy Scripture at them without effecting any change of behaviour. His brothers sought to introduce a pragmatic influence into his life by marrying him off to a local girl, but they failed to follow the customary procedure in such matters, which was strictly observed in provincial towns, and, to Michael's relief, the prospective in-laws refused the proposal.

In October 1810 he went for a retreat to the Ploschank hermitage, far from human habitation and deep in the forest, and suddenly decided never to return. From there he wrote to his brothers, handing over to them the whole estate on the sole condition that they would donate 1,000 roubles for the erection of a church in the village where his father was buried.

Ploschank hermitage was rich only in the quality of its spiritual life. It had barely enough money to clothe the brothers, who wore threadbare homespun and worked the land. After a five-year noviciate, Michael was accepted as a monk, taking the name Macarius after the Desert Father, Macarius of Egypt, and two years later he was ordained priest. He enjoyed the deprivations after a life of luxury and later recalled how he even liked the bast shoes, which were woven from dried reeds, because they were the humble footwear of Russia's humble peasants, who were, he said, 'the most Christian'. He did admit that his own shoes were slightly different: 'To me, as a man of lesser nobility', he said, 'were given not crude bast shoes, but some kind of footwear, also made of bast, but made skilfully, called "bakhirs".'[13]

The rule of life at the hermitage was strict on matters of church attendance, fasting, communal prayer and work. But little attention was paid to the inner spiritual life and Macarius was much relieved when one Father Athanasius, visiting the hermitage, dislocated a joint in his leg and decided to stay there. Athanasius had been an officer in the Hussars before entering a monastery in Moldavia, where he was tonsured by Paissii and lived for seven years, absorbing the traditions of the spiritual life brought from Mount Athos. He had returned to Russia to become one of the propagators of the tradition of *starchestvo* and had also brought with him the manuscripts of patristic texts which, under the inspiration of Paissii, he was translating. Macarius was delighted to join him in this work, and a number of books dealing with prayer and the contemplative life, on which they had both worked, were later published at Optina.

But Athanasius died in 1825 and Macarius prayed for a spiritual father to take his place. It was at this time that Leonid spent his six months at the Ploschank hermitage before settling at Optina, and Macarius felt his prayers had been answered. They kept up a correspondence and, in 1834, Macarius went to join Leonid in the skete at Optina. There he helped Leonid in giving spiritual counsel and busied himself with the gardens and forests around the hermitage. He had a special love for the forests, and wrote:

> Man finds peace of mind and benefit for his soul in forests. We see that in former times people used to withdraw into thick forests and there, away from worldly vanity, through prayer and ascetic labour, sought salvation. Just one look at the evergreen conifers of our homeland gladdens the eyes, portraying a symbol of our hope for eternal life which people go to the deserts to seek . . . The forests which surround our monasteries should be preserved from destruction by all means in order to prevent the word 'wilderness' from finally losing its meaning.[14]

Macarius at this time was small, very weak and rather ugly. He had problems with his breathing, which, together with difficulties in his speech, made it difficult for him to sing in church, but his knowledge of music made him careful to insist that all the chanting was correctly done. Although his poor health deprived him of energy, he had a lively nature and taught his disciples that they should never be idle. He introduced handicrafts into the skete, such as lathe work, bookbinding, the making of wooden boxes and the carving of spoons. The brothers who were skilled in calligraphy were kept busy copying patristic texts. When they brought their work to him for approval, he would encourage them by what were known as 'consolations': gifts of a quarter-pound of tea, one or two pounds of sugar, a handkerchief or a prayer rope or a book.

For twenty years, Macarius lived in a small cell about fourteen feet long and nine feet wide, with one window facing south which looked on to the path to the church. Under the window, which was covered by a green blind, stood a simple wooden table painted white. On the table was an old oil-cloth with a glass inkstand and a wooden sandbox which he had made himself. The table had drawers in which were writing materials and little icons, crosses, prayer ropes and belts for distributing to visitors. On either side of it were the piles of letters: one requiring immediate answer, another which could wait; another which had not yet been read. There were usually religious periodicals, of which Macarius received a regular supply. Then there were always one or two books by the Fathers of the Church from which, as he said, he drew his 'life and breath'.

The south-east corner of the cell and most of its southern wall were covered by icons of various sizes painted on wood and glass, icons of enamel and mother of pearl, and crosses painted on wood or carved from cypress, mother of pearl or ivory. In the centre hung the icon he most cherished, that of the Vladimir Mother of God, with a lamp constantly burning before it.[15]

From this small cell Macarius exercised a spiritual influence all over Russia as *starets* not only to the hundreds of visitors who came each day to Optina but also as spiritual director of three monasteries for men and over twenty monasteries for women. His life was regulated. He followed the middle path of asceticism. His health was so poor that he allowed himself to eat all foods, but in very small quantities and frequently. Every day he got up at two o'clock to pray for several hours and then, at six o'clock, he would drink a little tea and sit at his desk to write letters or prepare texts for publication. (After his death his letters filled five volumes.) As he wrote, visitors started to arrive and ask their questions. At 11 a.m. he went to the refectory to take a meal with the brothers. After this, he reserved for himself a free hour in which he walked alone in the garden. He would pause for a long time to admire each flower. From 2 p.m., in the guest house of the monastery, he would receive the crowds of men and women who came to visit him. A short figure with grey hair, wearing in summer a worn white cassock and in winter an ancient fur coat covered with dark green wool felt, he walked with a cane in one hand and a prayer rope in the other. He had a short nose and eyes that always seemed to be half closed in concentration.

In the evening he would return to his cell so worn out that he couldn't speak a word. Then, pretending to rest, he said prayers before going to the evening meeting with the brothers. After supper and the evening prayers, his light would be seen burning late into the night.

Macarius was a diplomat. When people came to see him out of mere curiosity he would say little and avoid discussing spiritual matters. This seemed to be mere tact, but it was also realistic in that he did not speak of matters that were beyond the limits of the spiritual understanding of his hearer. To the questions of rationalist intellectuals who would occasionally join the pilgrims to make fun of the occasion, he would reply: 'You know best of course. I am an uneducated man' and would turn the conversation to trivial matters which he called 'fluff'. To those who seemed to be honestly in search of a truth they could not find he would say: 'Don't try to understand everything – take on board as much as you can and try to make it work for you. Then the things that are hidden will be made clear to you.'

Under his guidance, the spiritual influence of Optina became more universal. Leonid spoke to the peasants and Macarius to the intellectuals. In 1846, the life of Paissii was published and, following that, a stream of spiritual works which appealed to the erudite world of Moscow. Macarius and his pupils, encouraged by Metropolitan Philaret of Moscow, published many writings of Christian mystics and the early Fathers with annotations explaining difficult passages.

The idea for editing the early Fathers was given to Macarius by one of his friends and spiritual sons, the philosopher Ivan Kireevskii, whose links with Optina are very significant. He had studied philosophy in Berlin and Munich under Hegel and Schelling, but, although he was impressed by the intellectual power of Western philosophical romanticism, decided that it was spiritually bankrupt. Under the influence of his wife, he was converted to Orthodoxy and, to his astonishment, discovered in the Fathers of the Church what he had sought for in vain among the philosophers. He wrote:

The cold analysis of many centuries has destroyed the foundations upon which, from the very beginning of its development, European enlightenment has rested. As a consequence, its own basic principles (i.e. those of Christianity) have become strange and alien to it. And this analysis which has destroyed its roots . . . this despotic rationality, this logical activity – is cut off from all man's other cognitive powers.[16]

When Macarius visited the Kireevskiis at their estate of Dolbino in 1847, he mentioned that the pressure of visitors at Optina made him aware of his lack of solitude. So the following year they built for him a small house in a birch grove half a mile from the estate house, and he was able to leave the monastery from time to time and find there the seclusion he sought.

Macarius died on 7 September 1860. Pious memorials record that his corpse, like that of Leonid, remained intact, with no smell of putrefaction. The cortège which took his body from the skete to the monastery had nothing funereal about it. It was more like an Easter procession.

The letters of Macarius[17] which have survived contain a wealth of advice given to people from all sections of society – nobles, peasants, intellectuals, soldiers – and they show clearly how it was possible for an Orthodox *starets* to maintain a tradition and yet deal with contemporary problems. Although he makes clear that the advice he gives applies only to the person to whom he writes, the situations faced by people in nineteenth-century Russia are part of the human condition we all share and the remedies Macarius suggests are based on universal truths.

> What I write to you, I write for you alone, and I must ask you to refrain from passing it on to others as a general rule of conduct for all. It is nothing of the kind. My advice to you is fashioned according to your inner and outward circumstances. Hence, it can be right only for you.

> *

> I cannot possibly give her any guidance unless she herself asks for it. And even if she did, I am doubtful whether I could: her mind is divided, she is quite uncertain as to what it is she wants; and at times she doubts if she wants anything at all.

> *

> I can only answer direct, sincere and simple questions put with simple faith. God himself sees that such questions receive the right

answer. An insincere question, put half-heartedly, is no question at all. Confronted by it, I can get no help. I should not know how to answer it. As to your playing the piano, that has nothing to do with your spiritual life and I have nothing to say on the matter.

*

I do not like the way you have of repeatedly exclaiming that after I have read this letter of yours I shall be disgusted with you. Nor do I like these assurances that it has cost you much and that you are smarting with shame. I think, by now, you yourself will clearly have seen from what source all this uneasiness and anxiety spring.

*

I am very much to blame for having offended you with my unwise letter. You are right, I was indeed at my wits end, torn between visitors, my work and my immense correspondence. Besides, I was feeling so ill, so weak, that I could not find in my empty and shallow mind suitable answers to all the problems that came pouring in.

But you must not conclude that I had rather you did not describe your difficulties to me. Tell me all about them; but pray that the Lord may grant me the wisdom to find the right words for your consolation and guidance. And, in order to make things a little easier, perhaps you could underline the *questions*, thus singling them out from the rest of the text.

*

As to this life insurance, since I have read nothing on the matter in the Scriptures or the Fathers, I can say nothing about it. Knowing nothing at all about such matters I can neither permit nor forbid your taking this step. Nor can I give you my blessing for it nor even offer advice. But read Matthew 6: 34. [*Take therefore no thought for the morrow: for the morrow shall take thought for itself.*]

*

I have told you nothing that is an invention of my own. All of what I say comes from the writings of the Fathers. Mine is only the humble work of choosing passages suitable to your particular case. And this humble work has been of the greatest profit to me, since it has freshened up much that was growing dim in my constantly weakening memory. so you see that there is no occasion at all for you to thank me so extravagantly.

As the Desert Fathers had insisted, Macarius consistently maintained that the most fundamental essential to spiritual progress and the solvent of most spiritual problems is humility:

You are distressed to find that whenever you now examine your conscience you see yourself as bad; whereas formerly, when you were young, such examination showed that, on the whole, you were good rather than bad. What an extraordinary reason for distress!

It is infinitely better for us to see ourselves as bad than good. In the first case, we acquire humility and find the door to forgiveness, the door to grace; in the second we grow proud, and pride blocks the way to grace.

*

You certainly have my deepest sympathy, but your own attitude to your misfortune will, in the long run, prove to be more helpful towards your regaining your poise than any feelings of mine could be. You are right: it is, of course, you yourself who have made the cross which you must now carry. A saintly man once said: 'The wood of the cross that now breaks your back first grew in the soil of your heart.' He was right.

*

Your digressions about pride and humility and your wordy self-justifications wander far from the point. John Climacus writes: 'Wherever we can note a fall, we can be certain that pride preceded it'.

Not one of us can boast of having acquired humility: our actions, the whole of our life, prove the contrary. And where there is a lack of humility, pride is always present. When light is wanting, darkness reigns.

*

Can you really think that the inner peace you are seeking depends on the locality you finally choose to live in? Surely, inner peace is only acquired by humbly living in accordance with the commandments. *Learn of me; for I am meek and lowly of heart; and ye shall find rest unto your souls* (Matthew 11:29).

Where you do it is beside the question . . . In constant intercourse with other people, we can sooner come to see our defects than we should in solitude.

*

It is wrong to draw particular attention to oneself during public prayer through excessive kneeling or mistimed bowing. Bowing and prostrations should only be performed during those parts of the service where they are customary. Then most of the people present will be doing likewise and no one will pay any attention to you.

*

As to your asking forgiveness (of those whom you have hurt) when you know that they will only mock and abuse you for doing so before going to confession, do not approach the matter so formally. The first thing for you to aim at is a clear perception of your own misdeed. By the time you have attained to this, and true penance has matured within your soul, these people may also have experienced a change of heart. But if you know that they have not, and that they really will mock and abuse you, you should beg forgiveness of God in your prayers, and of them in your hushed heart. Then consider the subject closed and rest in peace.

The Desert Fathers had taught that discernment was essential to detect those spiritual practices which are misguided but appeal to the emotionally extreme. The Russian temperament was especially susceptible:

Your so-called 'daring', your gesture of writing with your blood a declaration always to serve God and the Community, is simply absurd.

*

Living in the world, surrounded by your family, you cannot possibly give away all your possessions. So you must aim at finding the golden mean and strive to keep to it: never turn your back on the world but see to it that the world does not engross you. All things that your children require you should carefully keep for them. Any surplus of any kind give to the needy.

*

Your impulse to help these poor people whose houses have been destroyed by fire is good. But it will remain good only if you temper your impulse with reason. And, although your help must be kept within reasonable limits, give your mite with a feeling of deep compassion. But, above all, be reasonable.

Even if you gave all you have, you could not possibly alleviate the intense misery of them all. On the other hand, you have your family to care for and must strive to keep them comfortable, although it is right to dispense with all luxury for yourself and for them. But beware of the temptation to be unreasonably lavish. Besides, if you should follow this impulse on the spur of the moment, you would regret it later when it becomes clear that your children were doing without bare necessities. Then you would be well caught in the cauldron of a great and hopeless agitation.

Humble yourself and find peace.

There is a more subtle form of discernment shown to those who are sincerely trying to lead a Christian life among the complexities of the modern world:

> Do not limit yourself to striving for the right outward order: fasting and prayer. Strive also for greater inward order, only to be attained through intensified love and deep humility.
>
> You say that the longing for obedience has pierced your heart, and you ask: 'How can I attain it?' Shall I tell you?
>
> In the world you live in, Princess, you must have seen how long it takes for an artist to train for his art and how much effort he must devote to it. Is it not natural that the art of arts should exact even more time and even greater effort?
>
> Pray that you may be granted the grace to read the Fathers with the right understanding, the grace to live up to the standards they set before you, and the grace clearly to see your own frailty. You will not long be left wanting and waiting. God will give you help.
>
> In the meantime, carefully examine the movements of your heart, the pattern of your thoughts, the intention of all your words and actions. In your case it may be good to do this in writing. It may help to make more clear to you your utter poverty; it may humble your pride of mind.

*

It is excellent that you should have found work as tutor to the sons of so influential a family. Passing on to others the knowledge God has permitted you to acquire, you double your talent.

Have recourse to God in all your difficulties: in discipline, ordinary teaching and the teaching of divinity. Your clumsiness in society and your inability to gain the love of your charges provide lessons in the art of living and are good for you as a counterweight to your preoccupation with theories. You are still very young and only beginning to try your wings in the great flight. Life itself must teach you, in one way and another, what is wrong and what is right. Use your mistakes to encourage and develop your humility and to increase your perspicacity and discrimination. Employ most of your spare time in reading the Greek and our own Fathers. No art is acquired easily or without much diligent study and practice. Could it be otherwise with the greatest art of all – the art of arts – the spiritual life, the soul's salvation?

*

Since you clearly want me to be quite outspoken, I have to tell you frankly that I cannot think it right for you to leave the Service and restrict your activities to the peaceful, uneventful occupation of organising and improving the life of a hundred men or so. Remember the parable of the talents.

Considering the benevolence that our Monarch is pleased to show you, who can doubt that you may be of much greater use to humanity remaining where you are?

You say: 'At Court vainglory may seize me.' It is good that you should fear this; but do not let fear grow into panic. Accept promotions gladly, though humbly – not as food for pride but as an occasion to help others – listening carefully all the while to the voice of conscience resounding in your heart. God will not refuse His help.

As to this girl who has so much impressed you, why not marry her? You say you seek neither beauty nor riches but gentleness, intelligence and devotion to the faith. The lady in whose house you met confirms your impression that she has all these qualities, and says she is well educated too. No mean advantage in a wife.

But, not daring to influence you in so important a matter, I can only recommend you to God. Pray that you may learn to read His will and, having read it, you may accept it.

If this marriage is agreeable to Him, your eagerness will increase after prayer. Then have a church service said, requesting the special blessing of our Lord and our Lady and tackle the business straight away.

But if, after prayer, your eagerness wanes, accept this as a sign that God does not approve. Then drop the matter.

*

There is no occasion to be afraid of praise; we must only guard ourselves against feeling gratified by it. St Isaac tells us that such gratification, whenever felt by us, is in itself our full reward. But praise to which we are indifferent is harmless.

And do not agitate yourself over your resolution to read a litany daily at a fixed hour: this resolution which, you say, you now find impossible to carry out. To your question, 'When it has been impossible to do so at the appointed hour, may I read it later, while knitting and minding the children?' I answer: No! This would be quite wrong. Our pledges are not debts owed to a harsh master who wants them carried out to the letter and cares for little else. The Lord does not wish to enslave us. He wants us free.

When you really cannot carry out a resolution, make a penance, thinking of yourself as a humbled debtor. If you then refrain from the temptation of feeling agitated, it will be of greater profit than half-hearted mumblings followed by self-satisfaction and the pride of having kept your pledge in spite of all difficulties.

*

The moral qualities of the individual beggar have nothing to do with it: that is Christ's concern and not yours. Who are you to judge your brother? Christ is using His hand and mouth to test your compassion of Himself. Will you fail Him?

But, rather than cut down your allowances to your poor relations, I should recommend a careful examination of your own expenses, with a view to cutting down a multitude of unnecessary little luxuries. There is a large margin between this and 'failing to live up to the requirements of your station', which is certainly not what you should aim at. This, a self-righteous form of shirking of your responsibilities, would be quite wrong.

Macarius , in the traditionof the greatest of the *startsy*, managed to combine the most refined spirituality with the most basic common sense:

When you see F. Y. give him my warmest greetings and best wishes for a speedy recovery. Tell him too that, even if his hope and faith are strong, he should not despise the help of a physician. God is the creator of all men and all things: not of the patient only but also of the physician, the physician's wisdom, medicinal plants and their curative power.

*

God bless your decision to move into a new house, and may all go well with you there. But I cannot approve of this passion for smoking cigars. Just think, until recently you could call yourself a free woman, but now you are a slave, in bondage to a silly fad. Think, too, how much money you squander on it.

Mind you, I do not forbid this indulgence; you must do as you choose. But my advice is: leave off. Leave off for your own good.

*

Truly I have nothing at all to say to your lengthy description of our Monarch's graciousness to you and your family, your gift of the icon, the incident with the portrait of the *starets*, or to your opinion of the Bishop of Kiev. All these matters are far beyond the scope of a humble monk, weighed down with age, harassed by bodily and mental shortcomings, preoccupied by a ceaseless stream of ordinary hard work.

As to your daughter's wish, discuss it with her, not me. She is old enough to know her own mind. Question her, noting most carefully how she answers you. If her desire remains steadfast, if the sequence of her thoughts on this subject is unmuddled, and if she maintains perfect serenity throughout the whole discussion, you should look upon all this as true signs that God has stamped her desire with His seal. You should then definitely refrain from raising any more objections. Far from creating difficulties, you should give her your blessing.

*

I am sorry indeed that your wife should be suffering from insomnia. This comes of her worrying so much about everything. Having myself been at one time subject to sleeplessness, I know how thoroughly exhausted it leaves you. The only certain remedy is to thrust away the whole lot of harassing thoughts and consciously to put everything in the hand of God, accepting His will in all.

But, since this is more easily said than done, some simple devices may prove helpful: let her drink a glass of water before getting into bed, and put some bread near the bedstead – the smell of rye is very soothing. A good prayer to recite at such times is the prayer of the Seven Sleepers of Ephesus.

*

I cannot approve of your intention to send your son to B. Nor can I understand why you should attach so much importance to the special commercial training he would get there. What is the point of learning how to make greater profits?

As I see it, he can very well be trained at home in everything that really is important. He need not leave home to become a good Christian, a kindly man, a respectful son. Nor need anyone wander abroad to learn prayer, and respect for the Church and for the servants of the altar. Are we more likely to acquire, far from home, the wish to work for the profit of our own soul and for the profit of the souls of others? Or to learn to love our neighbour? Or to be sober in all things? Or to lead a pure life? Or to resolve never to hurt another's feelings? Or to keep our humility alive and active?

You are quite rich enough as it is: your land not only provides an honest income for yourself and your family, but makes it possible for you to extend your charity to the needy. The tilling of the soil was blessed by God at the beginning of time. Be satisfied with the profit He sends you for your honest toil.

And, finally, it is perhaps surprising to note that Starets Macarius, so steeped in the traditions of Orthodoxy and so faithful to the spirit of the Desert Fathers, can look with tolerance on the free-thinkers of his own time:

I was very glad to hear that you are so happy and so much at peace with yourself and others, now that you have become a member of our Church which has kept the Apostolic Tradition unbroken and unadulterated.

As to those people who are good and kind but are not believers, we cannot and must not judge them. The ways of the Lord are inscrutable; let us leave these good people entirely to His judgement and the grace of His Providence. He alone knows why He has built the argosy of humanity and the small boat of each one of us, such as it is.

Refrain from heated discussions on religious matters, there is no good in them.

Starets Ambrose[18]

Alexander Mikhailovich Grenkov was born into a clerical family in a small village in the province of Tambov, Russia. His grandfather was a priest, his father a sexton. He was the least pious of three brothers and seemed destined by his natural ebullience, wit and gaiety for a noisy, secular life. He graduated from the Tambov Theological Seminary[19] in 1836 in the first rank of students and was popular and sociable, but immediately fell so seriously ill that he promised God he would enter a monastery if he recovered.

Once he was fit again, the promise seems to have slipped down his list of priorities and he took a job as tutor to the children of a nearby landowner. His teaching duties were slight but he put in a good deal of spadework in preparation for his future as a *starets* by patching up the marital quarrels of his employer. He left these behind after a year and a half to take a teaching post at the local school, where his social life blossomed and he was a great favourite of the teaching staff.

In the summer of 1839, he was spending a holiday at the estate of a friend when they decided to make a trip to see a famous local hermit and ask what they should do with their lives. Whether this was a serious quest or something in the nature of consulting an astrological columnist is not known. The hermit told Alexander quite simply: 'Go to Optina', adding the enigmatic words 'You are needed there'.

But Alexander found life at the school very agreeable and he went back there and continued enjoying his social activities. One evening in late September he left a particularly successful party feeling he had outshone himself in repartee but, on arriving home, was suddenly beset by feelings of self-disgust. The next day he told his friends he would leave immediately for Optina and, in spite of their protests and the opposition of the school authorities, he did so.

He arrived on 8 October 1839, and was immediately upset by his first meeting with Leonid, who was sitting on his bed joking with visitors and looking fat and jovial. But he soon discovered that his first impressions had been misleading and asked to be accepted as a postulant. Leonid first gave him the job of copying a manuscript entitled 'The Salvation of Sinners' so that his character would be improved by its contents and his patience by the task of copying them. He then served for a time as cell-servant[20] to Leonid, then moved to the bakery where, for a year, he perfected his skills at making altar bread.

On the death of Leonid, in 1841, Macarius took Alexander to be his cell-servant and a year later he was tonsured with the name Ambrose, after St Ambrose of Milan.[21] Ambrose was then thirty years old. Two years later he was ordained a hieromonk and his close friendship with Macarius made it seem likely that he was being groomed for spiritual direction, but in 1846 he became so ill that he had to be relieved of all duties. He seemed to be close to death. For two years he was immobile, and only in the summer of 1848 was he able to move around with the help of a cane. He had lost all his upper teeth and could not chew his food without embarrassment, so he was given permission to eat alone.

He spent much of his time alone. The abbot of the monastery wrote: 'As far as I could tell, Fr. Amvrosy lived at that time in complete silence. I went to him almost every day to confess my thoughts and almost always found him reading Patristic books.'[22] His daily reading of the Fathers was to ensure that any spiritual advice he gave should be in accordance with their traditions. Indeed, at the time the only spiritual help he offered to those who came to him for confession was to read and then discuss a chapter from the Patristic writing. It was only when he felt that his own ideas were completely at one with the Fathers that Ambrose put them forward to help others.

In 1860, on the death of Macarius, Ambrose took over the guidance of his spiritual children, and in 1865 he was accepted as the sole *starets* of Optina. His daily life during the thirty years he held that position varied little and was similar to but even more arduous than that of his predecessors. He got up at about four o'clock and read the morning prayers with his cell-servants. These were followed by the twelve psalms and the first, third and sixth hours. He would then wash, usually helped by his cell-servants, who began the day's petitions by asking for advice or blessings on behalf of others. After washing, Ambrose would take tea, during which time he began dictating replies to letters. He sat at one table to eat while a scribe sat close by at a writing desk to take down what he said. But already the day's challenges were gathering outside:

> While the *starets* dictated a letter, visitors would begin little-by-little to approach his quarters. From within would come men and from without those of the female sex. He would not even succeed in finishing a needed letter before the crowd had begun to knock at the door and ring the little bell which he had installed outside his cell. The cell-servant would come out to them. They would ask to be announced and he would usually answer: 'The *starets* is busy.' Soon the impatient visitors would begin ringing and knocking again; again would come the same request and again the same answer. But the more they waited the more the impatience of the visitors would increase and they would begin to murmur.[23]

At ten o'clock Ambrose was ready to face them, and his morning session lasted for two hours, after which he would take a break:

> Without dismissing his visitors, Ambrose would go to the cell adjoining his. There, half-lying at the table because of exhaustion, he would eat a meal which consisted of two dishes – fish soup made from fresh fish, not very fatty, and *kissel* [a sort of blancmange] made from potato flour with cranberry sauce. With this was served either white bread or *sitnik* [sieved wheat bread] . . . The *starets* never ate more food than could be eaten by a three-year-old child. His dinner would last ten or fifteen minutes during which time his cell-servants would continue to ask questions about various persons and receive answers.[24]

After eating, Ambrose would rest for a while and then by three o'clock would walk out again to meet the visitors. He received them in the afternoon, in a cell, lying on a cot where he would drink tea at five o'clock and continue receiving and discussing. This went on until the evening:

> The *starets* had dinner at about eight o clock. The same things were served as for lunch. During dinner, the cell-servants would again query the *starets* about someone or something and he did not cease from answering them. Or he would get someone to read something. Shortly after dinner the *starets*, if his health gave out completely,

would limit himself to the granting of a common blessing. If, however, his strength had not completely abandoned him, he would begin the usual receptions and talks which would sometimes continue until eleven o'clock at night.[25]

However late it was, Ambrose never neglected the evening prayers, which included a canon to his guardian angel, after which he would ask forgiveness of those around him, give a blessing to his cell-servants, and go to bed. It was usually as the clock tolled twelve. Four hours later another day began.

Ambrose was, as we have seen, unsparing of himself in his daily routine and firm in his allegiance to the traditions of Orthodoxy, but he could be surprisingly flexible in his relations with the public:

> Once a group of young society ladies came to the *starets* for a blessing; only curiosity brought them. While waiting with us in the hut for Batiushka's[26] arrival, they complained of their surrounding and, speaking among themselves in French, they constantly mocked both us and the *starets*, saying, amongst other thing: 'What are we waiting for? What could we possibly hear from Fr. Amvrosy that would be interesting? What does *he* understand?' Suddenly the door of the hut opened and Batiushka entered with his usual smile; his attention was first of all attracted by the newly-arrived visitors.
>
> Having blessed them and without asking who they were or where they were from, he immediately began to discuss their wardrobe; he discussed their parasols, the feathers in their hats, and engaged in a long conversation with them about women's fashions. He talked in this way for a long time; we listened and the ladies, recognising the emptiness of their usual conversations for which the *starets* was so wisely censuring them, became embarrassed. They became extremely humble and afterwards acted very respectfully towards the *starets* from whom they had not expected anything special.[27]

There are many stories of visitors to Ambrose being impressed by the warmth of his personality rather than by any specific remembered formula of words, and it is part of the Orthodox tradition that religious truth is more easily communicated by an unspoken interaction between people than by learning a catechism. One very striking example is the visit of an intellectual who had lost his faith through the influence of the general culture of materialism that pervaded urban Russia in the mid nineteenth century. He had studied much, conversed with those who had pretensions to understand the meaning of life – including Tolstoy –

and finally called at Optina:

> He told Batiushka that he had come to have a look at him. 'Well, look!' answered the *starets*. He got up from his bed, stretched to his full height and looked at the man with a clear gaze. From this look there flowed into the man's soul a kind of warmth which was something similar to reconciliation. The unbeliever settled down near Batiushka and every day held a long conversation with him. A long time passed. Then one morning he informed Batiushka: 'I have come to believe'.[28]

The teachings of the Desert Fathers on vainglory and pride were among their most numerous, and Ambrose kept up the tradition with an image from his own time:

> Recently I was given a rug on which ducks were beautifully depicted. I regretted that they had neglected to put in geese as well, since there was a lot of room left on the rug.
>
> Such a thought occurred to me because the characteristics and actions of ducks and geese well depict the characteristics and actions of the passions of vainglory and pride.
>
> Although vainglory and pride are of the same vintage and have the same characteristics, their action and distinguishing marks are different. Vainglory tries to snare the praise of men and for this reason often lowers itself and makes itself pleasing to men; but pride breathes forth a despising and lack of respect for others although it too loves praise.
>
> The vainglorious man, if he has an attractive and handsome appearance, beautifies himself and shows off his good looks like a gander, though he is often as baggy and clumsy as a gander is. If the man overcome by vainglory does not have an attractive appearance and other good qualities, then to snatch praise he licks up to others and cries out like a duck: 'That's right! That's right!' [in Russian *Tak! Tak!*] . . .
>
> The goose, if everything is not going his way, raises his wings and cries '*Kaga! Kago!*' In the same way the proud man, if he has any importance in his own circle, often raises his voice, screams, argues, objects, insists on his own opinion. But if the man who suffers from pride happens to have no influence or rights in a given circumstance, then he hisses at others out of inner wrath like a goose sitting on its eggs. And whoever he can bite, he bites.[29]

The Fathers had insisted that the only safeguard against vainglory and pride, as against all sins and aberrations, was humility, and Ambrose, in castigating the ducks and the geese for their insistent noise, was mindful of the words of St Isaac the Syrian: 'Not every quiet man is humble, but every humble man is quiet'.

Ambrose, like his predecessors, had to cope with the effects of the Russian temperament on the religious lives of those who sought his help. There were dreams, visions, mystical voices in abundance:

You write that you once experienced an attack of the enemy and that when you kissed the icon of the Mother of God in church you smelled a fragrance coming out of it; and previously you once sensed how a fiery flame came out of this icon. According to the counsel of St Mark the Ascetic, such things should be left without significance and no trust should be put in them . . .

*

You describe what happened to you on the night of the 13th August. This had such a powerful effect on you because you, I think, have become accustomed to believe both your dreams and that which you see or hear during the time of prayer; pure prayer consists in not accepting any external thought during the time of prayer and in not accepting anything that you may see or hear, i.e. the changing of icons or the hearing of any voices. But if you persist in believing your dreams, or in anything similar, it is possible that you will go out of your mind.[30]

*

You complain that a storm of various thoughts during the reading of the twelve psalms or after their reading. Whether or not thoughts come to us does not depend on our will. But whether or not we accept them – that depends on us.[31]

But as well as questions dealing with the spiritual journey, Ambrose, like all the *startsy*, was often consulted on decisions relating to family or business affairs. The subject of marriage was often raised and his advice was always based on the conviction that, next to the monastic state, marriage is to be recommended. Bachelors and spinsters have nothing to temper their self-absorption:

You write that your sister's eldest son wants to marry a rich Greek. Let him get married. That's better than living as a bachelor.

On the question of bringing up children, Ambrose warned against the prevailing materialism which insisted on an education to produce a high income. It is more important to be right than to be rich:

I do not advise you to educate your children, especially the girls, after the demands of the present age. It would be more useful for them to be uneducated in the worldly sense of the word and to live in poverty than to be governesses in the homes of others with the accompanying loss of everything which is Christian. Therefore care more about giving your children a religious education than about giving them either great or small wealth.[32]

But Ambrose did not have that high-minded scorn for money which can come easily to those who live in the security of an ancient monastery:

Money by itself, or rather by the purpose which was designed for it by God, is a very useful thing. It takes the place of the lack of simplicity and love between men. Without money, how could men be reckoned? There would be eternal arguments and disputes and even fights to the death. Little pieces of money and even insignificant pieces of paper, however, free men from all this even if they do not understand it. The harm is not from money but from foolish greed or stinginess or from evil use. Perhaps also from unjust neglect.[33]

Ambrose was not above giving very direct and practical advice on business matters:

In your letter you explain that it was proposed to you that you buy the land which is next to your estate of N. The price at the present time is not cheap – 120 roubles a *desiatina* [about 2.7 acres] but you write that the quality of the land is very good and that what is most convenient of all is that all this land will be under one direction so that the land can be distributed to the peasants for a good price – 12 roubles a *desiatina* from their spring crops. If you find it profitable and convenient for yourself, then may God bless you not to let this estate get away.[34]

The *starets* was also ready to help others, not only in the salvation of their immortal souls, but in getting a job:

The conveyer of this letter is a civil servant who has lost his position because of drink. But it is now already the eighth month since he has stopped drinking and he has promised not to drink in the future . . . Could you not show him the kindness of hiring him, at least on a trial basis as a scribe or try him out in some other place on the same condition? It is good to give help to a man in extreme need. If, however, he is careless, then he himself will be guilty.[35]

On wider philosophical and social issues, Ambrose was not afraid to speak out against the prevailing nineteenth-century notion of the progress of humanity:

Progress or improvement is only in external human affairs, in the comforts of life. For example, we use railroads and telegraph which previously did not exist; coal is mined which had previously been hidden in the depths of the earth etc. In the Christian or moral sense, however, there is no progress. At all times there have been men who attained a high degree of Christian and moral perfection . . . At all times there have been men who gave themselves up to various sins and lawlessness. . .

Moral perfection on earth (which is imperfect) is not attained by mankind as a whole but rather by the individual believer . . . The desire to work for the welfare of mankind is very commendable but is not put in the proper perspective. The prophet King David says, *'First depart from evil, then do good'* [Psalm 34]. But with modern men the situation is just the opposite.[36]

When modern man sought to improve himself by his own efforts, in the ways which were recommended by the popular press and often from the pulpit, he was departing from the only path to spiritual progress:

In your first letter you mention the books *Self-Help* and *Independent Action*. I have not yet seen these books and do not know what is contained in them. Old-timers used to say: 'Without God you can't enter a house [*Bez Boga ne do poroga*]' . . . But the new wise men, as is evident from the titles of these books, think otherwise . . .

In conclusion, I will say the following: advise your son not to confuse external human affairs with spiritual and moral ones. In the former let him find progress, as in inventions and the sciences. But in the moral and Christian sense, I repeat, there is no general progress in humanity. By the way, in many sciences or branches of knowledge no progress is apparent. I do not think, for example, that our modern scholars know and understand mythology and, in general, classical antiquity as well as Basil the Great and Gregory the Theologian knew and understood them.[37]

Ambrose wrote most extensively in reply to the thousands of letters he received; but he also occasionally penned a few general words on a topic which struck him as being enlightening, such as the contrast in the way we care for our bodies and our souls:

To the service of the body are consecrated the most blossoming years of our life and to the eternal salvation of the soul only the final minutes of a decrepit old age. The body is daily toasted, as at the feast of a rich man, with overflowing cups and sumptuous dishes; but the soul barely manages to collect the crumbs of the Divine word from the threshold of the house of God ...

For the health and preservation of the body, air and dwelling place are changed, the most learned and distant physicians are called, food and drink are refrained from, the most bitter medicines are taken, we allow ourselves to be burned and cut; but for the welfare of the soul, for the avoidance of temptations, for our removal from sinful contagion, not a single step is taken. We remain in the same air, in the same evil company ... and we refrain from seeking a doctor of souls or we choose an unknown and inexperienced doctor and hide from him that which is already known to both heaven and hell and of which we ourselves boast in society.[38]

It was in the wide sweep of subjects on which these *startsy* gave advice, as well as the nature of that advice, that they maintained the traditions of the Desert Fathers. Thousands of people of all classes flocked to Optina during the nineteenth century, not only peasants, but officials, writers, intellectuals and political leaders. Tolstoy visited Optina in 1877 and pronounced himself impressed by the wisdom of Ambrose. He called again in 1881 and said, after his conversation with the *starets*: 'That Fr. Ambrose is a completely holy man. I talked with him and somehow my soul felt light and gay. When one talks with such a man one feels the nearness of God'.[39] In 1890, Tolstoy called again and discussed several faiths with Ambrose, emerging from the discussion with the words 'I am shaken, shaken'.[40]

In 1878, Dostoevsky went to visit Ambrose after the death of his son. His wife recalled: 'Our youngest son Alyosha passed away ... Fyodor was terribly aggrieved by the death ... He saw the famous *starets* Amvrosy three times ... The *starets*'s conversations left a deep and penetrating impression on him. .. The *starets* asked him to convey his blessing to me and also those words which Staretz Zossima later said to the grieving mother in [*The Brothers Karamazov*].'[41]

It was in Dostoevsky's last and greatest novel that the image of the Russian *starets* was projected for the world to admire. In the character of Starets Zossima he speaks of the value to the world of those who retire from it:

Fathers and teachers, what is a monk? Among the educated this word is nowadays uttered with derision, and some even use it as a term of abuse ... It is true, alas, it is true that there are many parasites, gluttons, voluptuaries and insolent tramps among the monks. Educated men of the world point this out: 'You are idlers and useless members of society,' they say. 'You live on the labour of others. You are shameless beggars.' And yet think of the many meek and humble monks there are, monks who long for solitude and fervent prayer in peace and quiet. These attract their attention less and less . . . and how surprised they would be if I told them that the salvation of Russia would perhaps once more come from these meek monks who long for solitary prayer! . . . In their solitude they keep the image of Christ pure . . . in the purity of God's truth, which they received from the Fathers of old, the apostles and martyrs, and when the time comes they will reveal it to the wavering righteousness of the world. That is a great thought. That star will shine forth from the East.[42]

Ornamental Hermits:
an Interlude

There has never been universal agreement that the state of solitude is to be preferred to sociability. In the mid eighteenth century, when Russian monks were struggling to keep alive the true spirit of the Desert Fathers by setting themselves apart in the northern forests, a distinguished Frenchman, one of the most intelligent and informed of his day, penned the following:

> This is the effect of solitude. Man is born for society. Separate him, isolate him and his ideas will become disjointed, his character will change, a thousand ridiculous emotions will rise in his heart, extravagant thoughts will rise in his spirit like brambles in waste land. Put a man in a forest and he becomes wild there; in a cloister where the idea of inevitability joins that of servitude and it's still worse: you can leave a forest but you can never leave a cloister. You need, perhaps, greater strength of soul to resist solitude than to resist misery; misery degrades; solitude depraves. Is it better to live in abjection than madness? That I can't decide; but we should avoid both.[1]

Denis Diderot was the founder of the *Encyclopédie ou Dictionnaire Raisonné des Sciences, des Arts et des Métiers*, the textbook of the Age of Reason. His thoughts on solitude were in sympathy with those of great men with talent for sociability down the ages: Dr Johnson famously declared that 'a man who is tired of London is tired of life', and Sydney Smith described the countryside as 'a healthy grave'. But at the same time as Diderot was castigating the solitaries, Rousseau was penning his *Discourses* - his apologia for romanticism based on sensitivity to the impulses of the natural world. The one found human fulfilment in agreeable salon conversations; the other in solitary contemplation of the beauties of nature.

So the intelligent man of sensibility during the second half of the eighteenth century found himself at the centre of conflicting pressures. To convince his neighbours that he was cultivated he must be seen at the London theatre to applaud the latest Goldsmith or Sheridan satire, employ the brothers Adam to give his house a refined sense of proportion, hang a Chardin or a Joshua Reynolds on its walls, and have it furnished by Thomas Chippendale. He should then fill it with polite society and be able to discuss the latest volume from Gibbon or Adam Smith. But, on the other hand, if he was truly and fashionably a man of sensibility, he would have to put it about that he was spending a certain amount of his time alone, being melancholy on a mountain.

There was a way out of this impasse for the men of means. Since they believed there is no point in doing anything for yourself if you can pay somebody to do it for you, they employed people to be melancholy on their behalf. These latter were the ornamental hermits. They flourished fitfully during the late eighteenth and early nineteenth centuries around the gardens of the English landed gentry.

Ornamental hermits had to be presented in a congruous setting, and landscape architects of the time were ready with their inspirations. *Grotesque Architecture or rural amusement* by William Wrighte was published in 1767.[2] It contains a range of detailed suggestions for housing hermits, from the least expensive 'Hut . . . intended to represent the primitive state of the Doric Order' which was a mere 10 ft 9 ins square, made of trees and lined with moss, right up to the top of the range, 'Gothic Grotto', which has six rooms lined with shells. There is a 'Hermitic Retreat', made of trees that are twined with ivy, and a 'Hermit's Cell', with seating alcoves on either side and a skull over the door as a *memento mori*. A seasonal note is struck by the 'Summer Hermitage', a simple affair with a floor 'paved with sheeps' marrowbones placed upright, or any other pretty device' and an owl stuck on the roof, by contrast with the 'Winter Hermitage', which is 'lined with wool or other warm substance intermixed with moss'. For the exotically inclined, there is the 'Chinese Hermitage', a complicated structure built around a central tree which protrudes through the roof like a chimney brush. Its roof is in the Chinese style and it is furnished with a tablet in Arabic, a couch and seats of retirement. Middle of the range are the 'Augustan Hermitage', in classical style, and the 'Rural Hermitage' made of trees with a fitted gazebo above.

In some of these retreats the owner might occasionally choose to pass a sombre hour. The personal grotto of the poet Alexander Pope at Twickenham became celebrated, though Dr Johnson is rather dimissive about it: 'being under the necessity of making a subterraneous passage to a garden on the other side of the road, he adorned it with fossil bodies and dignified it with the title of a grotto; a place of silence and retreat from which he endeavoured to persuade his friends and himself that all cares and passions could be excluded'.

But the majority of country gentry who indulged themselves in the folly of constructing hermitages in their gardens preferred to staff them with employees. Mr Hamilton, who owned a country house at Payne's Hill, in Surrey, advertised for a hermit to occupy his grotto.[3] He seems to have been unaffected by the doubt so cogently expressed by a fictional contemporary of ours that 'a hermit who takes a newspaper is not a hermit in whom one can have complete confidence'.[4] The conditions specified in the advertisement were that the successful applicant should continue in the hermitage for seven years, where he should be provided with a Bible, optical glasses, a mat for his bed, a hassock for his pillow, an hourglass for his timepiece, water for his beverage, food from the house, but never to exchange a syllable with the servants. He was to wear a camlet robe, never to cut his hair or nails nor ever to stray beyond the limit of the grounds. If he lived there, under all these restrictions, until the end of the term, he was to receive 700 guineas. But on breach of any of them, or if he quitted the place at any time before the end of that term, the whole was to be forfeited. One person attempted it, but after three weeks he was caught going down to the local pub and lost his position as a recluse.

Mr Powys of Marcham, near Preston in Lancashire, was more successful. He advertised 'a reward of 50 pounds a year for life to any man who would undertake to live seven years under ground without seeing anything human; and to let his toe and finger nails grow with his hair and beard, during the whole time'.[5] Apartments were prepared under ground: 'very commodious, with a cold bath, a chamber organ, as many books as the occupier pleased, and provisions served from his own table'. Whenever the recluse wanted any convenience he was to ring a bell and it was provided for him. Although this would seem to have been an Elysian Field for anyone with a taste for his own company, it seems that nobody managed to stay solitary in the commodious grotto of Mr Powys for more than four years.

Archibald Hamilton, later Duke of Hamilton, according to a report by his daughter, Lady Dunmore,[6] advertised for a hermit as an ornament to his pleasure grounds, on the slightly more lenient conditions that his beard should be shaved once a year 'and that only partially'. She did not record what success he had, but Sir Richard Hill did rather well with the occupant of his grotto at Hawkstone in Shropshire. There is a record in *Blackwood's Magazine* for April 1830 referring to the editor of another magazine who had been 'for fourteen years Hermit to Lord Hill's father; and sate in a cave in that worthy baronet's grounds with an hour glass in one hand and a beard once belonging to an old goat from sunrise to sunset with orders to accept no half-crowns from visitors, but to behave like Giordano Bruno'.[7] However contented the literary hermit might have been with his isolation, the popular conscience would not permit him to enjoy it: there was a movement in the locality against the 'slavery' at Hawkstone which forced the good baronet to dismiss the real hermit and substitute a stuffed one. He attempted to conceal the deception from visitors by bathing the hunched figure in a dim religious light, according to regulars, but the effect was not the same.

The practice of advertising for hermits has been called in question on the ground that the true recluse does not purchase newspapers, let alone scour the 'positions vacant' columns, but the would-be solitary could, with more confidence, advertise for a position:

> A young man, who wishes to retire from the world and live as an hermit in some convenient spot in England, is willing to engage with any nobleman or gentleman who may be desirous of having one. Any letter directed to S. Lawrence (post paid) to be left at Mr Otton's, No 6, Colman's Lane, Plymouth mentioning what gratuity will be given, and other particulars, will be attended to. [*Courier*, 11 January 1810]

Ornamental hermits had a long vogue. They came into fashion in the 1740s, and there is a record by Miss Cynthia Aldburgham who remembers as a child early this century that visitors used to tour the grounds of her house and be shown a hermit who sat in a cave fondling a skull.[8]

CHAPTER FOUR

By Walden Pond:
Henry David Thoreau

In the year 1845, over the north-western states of America, the industrial revolution was in full swing. Steamboats were running, railroads were crossing the prairies, the electric telegraph was being extended, people were getting richer. Progress and prosperity were evident on all sides. Confidence in humanity was running high.

In March of that year, a 28-year-old graduate of Harvard College left his town house, borrowed an axe, chopped down a few pine trees, and built a log cabin on the shores of a lake in New England. He had decided to opt out of society and try the experiment of living alone as a hermit. Henry David Thoreau wrote a book called *Walden* about the experience. It aroused little interest. He was thought, during his lifetime, to be a harmless eccentric, a 'Yankee Diogenes' whose views were of interest only to a minority of antisocial cranks. Thoreau is now considered by some to be one of America's greatest writers.[1]

His influence has been widespread among many different classes of people. During the Depression years, Thoreau was said to be the only writer a man could read without a nickel in his pocket and not feel insulted. The poet W.B. Yeats wrote his most famous poem, 'The Lake Isle of Innisfree', inspired by Thoreau. The boxer Gene Tunney read Thoreau during his training for the last defence of his world heavyweight title and said 'the spirit of Thoreau lends its luminous wisdom to man and nature whenever they meet'.[2] Tunney retired undefeated.

Thoreau's views on civil liberties were required reading among the British Fabians in the early days of the Labour Party. Gandhi said that he found inspiration in Thoreau's books to fight for civil rights in South Africa and recommended Thoreau to all his friends who were struggling for independence in India. Tolstoy often mentions Thoreau in his correspondence and once formally thanked the American people for the help which Thoreau, among other American writers, had given him. And Lin Yutang, explaining in *The Importance of Living* that Thoreau was the most Chinese of American writers, wrote: 'I could translate many passages of Thoreau into my own language and pass them off as original writing by a Chinese poet without raising any suspicion'. The way discovered by Thoreau in his personal experiment with the hermit life was heading in the same direction as the Way of Tao.

Thoreau has been claimed by a wide variety of lobbies since his death: by the Marxists for his analysis of the destructive effects on humanity of the capitalist system; by the vegetarians for his poetic apologia for their creed;[3] by nudists because, as one study puts it, 'he had the courage of his convictions to challenge the "code of morals" which required him to hide his body from the sight of man, the sight of the sun, and even the sight of himself'. Even the gay lobby have recruited him posthumously into their ranks and he finds a place in the *Gay American History*,[4] where his creative genius is put down to the conflict between his sexuality and the repressive elements in the New England society of his day. On 4 July each year the US radio station Voice of America has taken to broadcasting extracts from Thoreau to the world in celebration of the achievement of nationhood.

Henry David Thoreau was born in Concord, Massachusetts, on 12 July 1817. There was, at the time, stretching northward from the city, a sparsely settled area of woodland from which the beaver had only recently been exterminated but where the muskrat and mink were still to be seen. Henry and his brother John went there often to hunt and to pick nuts and berries. If it seems fanciful to attribute his later preoccupation with nature to these childhood experiences, it is an attribution he would have supported. Childhood memories were central to his experience of life: 'We seem but to linger in manhood', he wrote in his journal, 'to tell the dreams of our childhood, and they vanish out of memory ere we learn the language'.

After school in Concord, Henry went to Harvard College on a scholarship at the age of sixteen – a not unusual age at the time – and studied the Latin and Greek classics as well as English poetry. He never rose above a moderate position in his class, partly because he tended to ignore the curriculum and follow his own tastes in reading. When he graduated, in 1837, he took a job as teacher in the Concord Academy. But after only a few weeks there he decided that the discipline he was paid to impose along with the learning he was paid to impart was not to his taste so he opened a private school with his brother John. Here there was no whipping. Pupils went for long nature walks with the teachers. The school did well but had to close when John's health broke down.

In 1841, Henry moved into the house of the poet and essayist Ralph Waldo Emerson, where he was employed to look after the garden and keep the woodpile stacked. He stayed there not out of a need to exercise his skills as a handyman but because of a deep affection and admiration for Emerson and his ideals. He became so caught up by the famous spell-binding charm of the Sage of Concord and the magic of his philosophy that, his friends noted, Thoreau was falling into the habit of adopting Emerson's mannerisms and even his ways of speaking.

Emerson and the Transcendentalists

Emerson had an inspired and inspiring view of human possibilities and was not won over by the glories of the industrial revolution:

> Things are in the saddle
> And ride mankind

he wrote, as a warning against the aggressive material prosperity which was sweeping America. He had been a Unitarian minister in Concord but resigned when it became obvious from his sermons that his views on Christianity had swung away beyond the limits of what even the progressive churches of New England found permissible. His religion was an intuitive one, as was his philosophy, woven out of the essays of Coleridge, the mysticism of Swedenborg and the nature poetry of Wordsworth. It came to be known as Transcendentalism.

At the end of the seventeenth century, Locke had proposed a theory of knowledge in his *Essay Concerning Human Understanding* which assumed that the mind of a new-born infant is a *tabula rasa*. We are all born, he claimed, in a state of total ignorance. All our knowledge comes to us, as we grow, through the senses of sight, hearing, touch, smell and taste. It follows that the only valid knowledge is that which is verifiable by the senses. On this empirical assumption were built the great scientific advances of the time and it lay at the heart of eighteenth-century rationalism.

But, in reaction to it, the philosophers Kant and Hegel claimed that there is a body of knowledge which is innate in human beings and that this knowledge transcends the senses – hence transcendentalism. Some said that this knowledge was the voice of God within Man – his conscience, inner light, moral sense or 'over-soul'. A child is born, according to this view, with a capacity to judge right from wrong; but his moral sense is often calloused by sense impressions received from the world outside. So the duty of the good citizen and the road to enlightenment for the adult was to return once more to childish innocence and listen to the voice of God within.

These ideas were brought to England by Coleridge, especially in his essay *Aids to Reflection*, published in 1825. By the 1830s, they had reached New England. When a group of Harvard alumni adopted them and decided to meet regularly to promote their advancement, it was natural that they should come together in the Concord house of the most eminent Coleridge enthusiast, Emerson. They became known as the 'Transcendentalists', and Thoreau joined them in the autumn of 1837.

This was the great age of social experiment. In 1841 – the year in which Thoreau moved in on the Emerson household – Nathaniel Hawthorne, novelist and short-story writer, invested his money and settled in a Transcendentalist agricultural community at Brook Farm, near West Roxbury, Massachusetts. Here members shared equally the work and remuneration. The declared intention of the community was 'to ensure a more natural union between intellectual and manual labour than now exists; to combine the thinker and worker, as far as possible, in the same individual; to guarantee the highest mental freedom by providing all with labour adapted to their tastes and talents and securing to them the fruits of their industry'.[5] Hawthorne soon found the communal living at Brook Farm not to his taste and he moved with his bride into the Old Manse at Concord, where he became the friend and supporter of Thoreau.

Strangely, Emerson, the inspiration of these experiments in social organisation and new trends in philosophy, distanced himself from them all. Of Brook Farm, he wrote that it was 'a perpetual picnic; a French revolution in small; an age of reason in a patty pan'. Having tried the experiment of manual labour he discovered that hard work in the fields meant poor work in the study and came to the conclusion that 'The writer shall not dig'.[6]

As for the Transcendentalist school, Emerson, although clearly its inspiration in New England, refused to be identified with it. He disclaimed allegiance to any formal or consistent philosophy. He thought consistency of opinion was a sign of small-mindedness. A man should never be afraid today to say something he believes in simply because he may contradict it tomorrow. 'A foolish consistency', he wrote, 'is the hobgoblin of little minds adored by little statesmen and philosophers and divines. With consistency a great soul simply has nothing to do'.[7]

The great soul was above all independent and individualistic. 'Whoso would be a man must be non-conformist.' 'Insist on yourself. Never imitate'. Self-reliance was the key to the good life because the divine spirit was self-reliant, and people – its embodiments – were good insofar as they share this attribute. If self-reliance became universally practised it would bring about a regeneration of society. Indeed, the reform of individuals is the only way to bring about that regeneration: 'with the appearance of the wise man, the State expires. The appearance of character makes the State unnecessary'.[8]

Emerson's insights came to him in flashes. He never attempted to back up his opinions by argument. He once said: 'I do not know what arguments mean in reference to any expression of a thought'.[9] His philosophy was impressionistic, intuitive, conveying a strong personal vision unsupported by logical argument. When asked how he knew the truth of an assertion, he replied: 'We know truth when we see it from opinion as we know when we are awake that we are awake'.[10]

Those who met Emerson fell under his spell. He pronounced his gnomic utterances with total sincerity in a thrillingly modulated voice, his face radiant with conviction. Thoreau was entranced and became a close family friend. In 1843 he went to Staten Island as tutor to the children of William Emerson, Ralph's elder brother. He was trying out the possibilities of making a living as a writer at the time and met Horace Greeley, founder of the *New York Tribune*, which had a soft spot for radicals. Greeley helped him publish a few articles, but it soon became clear that Thoreau was not going to be able to support himself by his writing and he retired, in the summer of 1845, to solitude at Walden Pond.

94

At Walden Pond

There has been much speculation as to why Thoreau went off to live as a hermit. The most obvious reason is that he was disappointed by his failure to win recognition as a creative writer and wanted to withdraw from a society that had proved unresponsive. Others have suggested that he was not moving away from society so much as towards nature and independence. His own explanation, set down after the event, is: 'I went to the woods because I wished to live deliberately, to front only the essential facts of life, and see if I could not learn what it had to teach and not, when I came to die, discover that I had not lived'.[11]

He had often toyed with the idea of a solitary life in communion with nature, having absorbed the romantic poets directly and through the transforming genius of Emerson. In his journal dated March 1841, he wrote: 'It is a great relief when, for a few moments in the day, we can retire to our chamber and be completely true to ourselves.' And by December of the same year he is writing: 'I want to go soon and live away by the pond where I shall hear only the wind whispering among the reeds. It will be a success if I shall have left myself behind. But my friends ask what will I do when I get there. Will it not be employment enough to watch the progress of the seasons?'[12]

Three years and three months later, Thoreau went to Walden Pond, which is a small lake about three-quarters of a mile long and half a mile wide situated two miles south of Concord. On its banks was a piece of land owned by Emerson. Thoreau had his permission to build and occupy a cabin on it. He had no very clear idea of how long he would stay.

He tackled the business of settling in there as an experiment in living out his economic philosophy. This was a nineteenth-century expansion and articulation of much that lay behind the thinking of hermits of all persuasions down the ages. He distinguished between the activities necessary to maintain life and those on which a free individual would choose to spend his time. The former were drudgery, the latter worthwhile. The good life should be organised to maximize free time and minimise drudgery. In fact his declared aim was to reverse the biblical injunction and labour for one day only, saving the other six for 'free time'.

The richest person was not the one with the greatest accumulation of goods but the one with the largest amount of free time.

Thoreau saw that the luxuries and comforts of modern living had become its necessities and that people were making slaves of themselves in order to pay for them. His solution, which goes back to Socrates, was to see how many things he could live without. Certain items had to be purchased in exchange for the produce of a person's labour; their worth should be assessed on how much free time had to be given up to acquire them. It was spiritually as well as economically prudent to surrender as little as possible of free time, therefore the best solution was usually not to purchase but to make them.

So, one day in late March 1845, he cut down the first pine trees at Walden Pond with his borrowed axe and hewed the main timbers for his house: 'six inches square, most of the studs on two sides only and the rafters and floor timbers on one side, leaving the rest of the bark on so that they were just as straight and much stronger than sawed ones'. Three weeks later he had jointed together the whole frame of the house. He bought an old shack from a neighbour for $4.25 and spread its boards in the sun 'to bleach and warp back again' and he dug a cellar 'six feet square and seven feet deep where potatoes would not freeze in any winter'.[13]

The pioneering tradition was that neighbours gave a hand with the erection of the frame and putting on the roof, and Thoreau managed to suppress his urge for independence enough to follow this. In early May, 'with the help of some of my acquaintances, rather to improve so good an occasion for neighborliness than from any necessity, I set up the frame of my house'.[14] It was ten feet wide by fifteen feet long. It had cost exactly $28. 12½ cents. He noted that 'the student who wishes for a shelter can obtain one for a lifetime at an expense not greater than the rent which he now pays annually'.[15]

The benefits of building for himself were not just financial:

> There is some of the same fitness in a man's building his own house as there is in a bird's building its own nest. Who knows but if men constructed their own dwelling with their own hands, and provided food for themselves and families simply and honestly enough, the poetic faculty would be universally developed, as birds universally sing when they are so engaged? . . . I never in all my walks came across a man engaged in so simple and natural an occupation as building his house.[16]

Thoreau took up occupation of this physical symbol of independence on the most fitting day of the year: 4 July 1845.[17] He carted his furniture to the cabin in a hay rig and settled in with a cane bed, a table with three chairs, a desk, a mirror three inches in diameter and a pair of tongs for the fire. For eating, he had three plates, two knives and forks, one spoon and two jugs (one for oil and one for molasses). He cooked in a long-handled pan, a frying pan and a kettle, he served with a ladle and had a bowl for washing up. He was careful to guard against adding to these objects. When somebody offered to give him a mat for the floor he declared he could spare neither the space to put it down nor the time to shake it out. 'I declined it', he wrote later, 'preferring to wipe my feet on the sod before my door. It is best to avoid the beginnings of evil.'[18]

To feed himself with a minimum of expenditure, he planted a vegetable garden whose most notable feature was a series of bean rows totalling seven miles in length. Since he spent the hours from 5 a.m. till noon in the growing season hoeing his beans and confessed that he was 'by nature a Pythagorean, so far as beans are concerned' (i.e. he wouldn't eat them), the beans had to be the subject of special pleading in his economic scheme. He decided that time spent hoeing was 'free time' and hoeing a chosen activity because he had come to love his beans and they 'attached me to the earth, and so I got strength like Antaeus'.[19] Not only did he feel a spiritual charge from his daily contact with the soil, he was able to indulge in private reveries of ancient and modern history:

> As I drew a still fresher soil about the rows with my hoe, I disturbed the ashes of unchronicled nations who in primeval years lived under these heavens, and their small implement of war and hunting were brought to the light of this modern day. They lay mingled with other natural stones, some of which bore the marks of having been burned with Indian fires and some by the sun, and also bits of pottery and glass brought hither by the recent cultivators of the soil.[20]

As a bonus to the spiritual and imaginative benefits of his hoeing, Thoreau worked out that, over the year, he made a net profit from his bean rows of $8. 71½ cents.

He was not, of course, self-sufficient in all things at Walden and took odd jobs from time to time as a gardener, fence-builder, stonemason or surveyor to bring in a little cash. But he did not feel himself extended by these activities and wrote to Horace Greeley: 'I am convinced, both by faith and experience, that to maintain oneself on this earth is not a hardship but a passtime if we will live simply and wisely . . . It is not necessary that a man should earn his living by the sweat of his brow, unless he sweats easier than I do.'[21]

The idyll of life at Walden was briefly interrupted when Thoreau spent a night in the local jail. This was to be one of the most significant events in his life. He had gone into Concord to collect a shoe which he had left for repair at the cobbler's shop. Meeting the local constable, tax collector and jailer, one Sam Staples, in the street, Thoreau greeted him and, after an exchange of pleasantries, was reminded that his poll tax was overdue. 'If you're hard up, Henry', Sam went on, 'I'll pay your tax.'

Thoreau was not well off at the time, but that was not the reason for his refusing to pay the tax. The Transcendentalists encouraged individuality in such matters, and Thoreau had no intention of contributing to the maintenance of a system of government of which he disapproved. He was an abolitionist and the State supported slavery; furthermore the Mexican War had just started and it was clear that Mexico had been provoked into aggression so that more land could be grabbed for the extension of slavery. He explained to the constable that he had the money, but refused as a matter of principle to hand it over. 'Henry, if you don't pay', said Sam Staples, maintaining the light touch, 'I shall have to lock you up pretty soon.' But Thoreau saw an opportunity: 'As well now as at any time, Sam', he replied. And Sam took him off to jail.

The next day, much to Thoreau's annoyance, somebody – probably his aunt – paid the tax and he was released. Sam Staples, who had a distant respect for the Transcendentalists,[22] showed him the door with some deference, and Thoreau objected, saying that as he hadn't paid the tax he had the right to stay in jail. But Sam said simply that if he didn't leave he would be thrown out. So he left. In his journal he wrote at the time: 'The only highwayman I ever met was the State itself. When I have refused to pay the tax it demanded for that protection I did not want, itself has robbed me. When I have asserted that freedom it declared, it has imprisoned me, I love mankind. I hate the institutions of their forefathers.'[23]

He went back to his cabin on Walden pond and stayed there until 6 September 1847. He said later: 'I went there because I was ready to go; I left it for the same reason'.

Life in Concord

Having spent his time in solitude, Thoreau, in the tradition of the hermits who retire in order to return, settled back in Concord and helped out in the family business of making lead pencils. The townspeople were curious as to why a respectable citizen should have chosen to go to jail rather than pay his taxes, and Thoreau gave a lecture to explain his motive at the Concord Lyceum on 26 January 1848. This was the basis of his famous essay on civil disobedience, which has inspired so many leaders of movements for political and civil rights. Its fundamental principle is that the ultimate arbiter of all human behaviour must be the law of the individual conscience, which carries a greater authority than any civil law. When the two are in conflict, it is the clear duty of the citizen, however loyal, to obey his conscience rather than the laws of the society to which he belongs.

> Unjust laws exist; shall we be content to obey them, or shall we endeavour to amend them, and obey them until we have succeeded, or shall we transgress them at once? Men generally, under such a government as this, think that they ought to wait until they have persuaded the majority to alter them. They think that, if they should resist, the remedy would be worse than the evil. But it is the fault of the government itself that the remedy *is* worse than the evil. *It* makes it worse.[24]

To the objection that, in a democracy, the will of the majority – even of one – must prevail, Thoreau answers grandly that 'any man more right than his neighbors constitutes a majority of one already'.[25] The plain duty of the just citizen is to resist, to passively impede the machinery of an unjust government: 'A minority is powerless while it conforms to the majority; it is not even a minority then; but it is irresistible when it clogs by its own weight'.[26] The democracy practised in his country he saw as only a stage in the improvement of society from a state of absolute monarchy to total individual freedom, and he looked forward to a future in which the State could afford to be just to all men:

> There will never be a really free and enlightened State until the State comes to recognise the individual as a higher and independent power, from which all its own power and authority are derived, and treats him accordingly.[27]

Thoreau saw the possibilities of arousing the consciences of enough people to passive resistance against an unjust law so that the machinery of government – the courts and the prisons – became clogged and overflowing. Sadly, his aunt had made it impossible for him to demonstrate this over the matter of his poll tax. But Gandhi and Martin Luther King have both proved since that civil disobedience can be effective.

There has been a tendency to think of Thoreau as a rather truculent and self-indulgent theorist who was cautious enough to suffer no more than a night in jail for his political views, but, in his opposition to slavery and his support for the abolitionist movement, he was open and far from prudent. In 1857, old John Brown of Kansas – he whose body lies a-mouldering in the grave – visited Concord looking for support and he took meals with Thoreau at his house. Two years later, in October 1859, he returned to Concord collecting funds for the movement and then went straight on, with a force of eighteen men, to capture the Federal arsenal at Harper's Ferry. Two days later the arsenal was recaptured by a force of US troops under Robert E. Lee. John Brown surrendered, after which he was seriously wounded and put on trial for treason. The press attacked him as a dangerous and insane fanatic.

It was at this time that Thoreau addressed meetings in Concord and then at Boston and Worcester, with a powerful defence of Brown's character. He was taking a stand against public opinion by doing this and in some danger of deflecting the national passions against Brown on to himself and his family. Brown was hanged.

In 1859, on the death of his father, Thoreau took over the graphite pencil business and improved it into one which sold graphite mixture for printing, but his health was now breaking down and he spent the next two years slowly dying of tuberculosis. By early 1862, *Walden,* after eight years in print arousing only a sluggish interest, had at last sold out and the success which had eluded him all his life approached with the end of it. He was depressed by the Civil War, and, when asked by a visiting friend how he envisaged the next world, could only reply: 'One world at a time'. Another asked him if he had made his peace with God, to which he answered: 'I did not know we had ever quarrelled.' He died on 6 May 1862.

Emerson said, in a deeply felt eulogy: 'His soul was made for the noblest society; he had in a short life exhausted the capabilities of the world; wherever there is knowledge, wherever there is virtue;

wherever there is beauty, he will find a home.'

Insights

Thoreau's insights came to him in surges of inspiration. He was not a writer to spend time polishing his prose but one who felt that all really worthwhile writing had to come from a natural overflow of a powerful intuition. This can make him difficult to follow at times – easy writing makes hard reading – but also, occasionally, as quotable as La Rochefoucauld. His basic stance as a communicator, learned from Emerson, was a truculent individualism which he not only lived out but preached:

> Age is no better, hardly so well, qualified for an instructor as youth, for it has not profited so much as it has lost. One may almost doubt if the wisest man has learned anything of absolute value by living. Practically, the old have no very important advice to give to the young, their own experience has been so partial, and their lives have been such miserable failures . . . and they are only less young than they were. I have lived some thirty years on this planet, and I have yet to hear the first valuable or even earnest advice from my seniors.[28]

*

> The greater part of what my neighbors call good I believe in my soul to be bad, and if I repent of anything, it is very likely to be my good behaviour.[29]

*

> If I knew for a certainty that a man was coming to my house with the conscious design of doing me good, I should run for my life . . .[30]

His economic theories spelled out the need to conserve free time by owning fewer things. But he was also aware that the impulse to asceticism has deeper roots:

> Most of the luxuries, and many of the so-called comforts of life, are not only not indispensable, but positive hindrances to the elevation of mankind. With respect to the luxuries and comforts, the wisest have ever lived a more simple and meagre life than the poor. The ancient philosophers, Chinese, Hindoo, Persian and Greek, were a class than which none has ever been poorer in outward riches, none so rich in inward . . . The same is true of the modern reformers and benefactors of their race. None can be an impartial or wise observer

of human life but from the vantage ground of what *we* should call voluntary poverty.[31]

The largest single expenditure in the life of a modern individual is the family home. This has long been accepted as the inevitable consequence of our improvement in living standards over those of our more primitive ancestors. The Russian *startsy* had challenged the notion of progress by admitting it in the economic, but denying it in the spiritual field. Thoreau, surrounded by enthusiasm for the most rapid technological advances the world had so far seen, used an economic argument to question material progress:

> If it is asserted that civilisation is a real advance in the condition of man – and I think that it is, although only the wise improve their advantages – it must be shown that it has produced better dwellings without making them more costly; and the cost of a thing is the amount of what I will call life which is required to be exchanged for it, immediately or in the long run. An average house in this neighborhood costs perhaps eight hundred dollars, and to lay up this sum will take from ten to fifteen years of a laborer's life . . . so that he must have spent more than half his life commonly before *his* wigwam will be earned . . . Would the savage have been wise to exchange his wigwam for a palace on these terms?[32]

As for that other item of conspicuous consumption in social interchanges down the ages – expensive clothing – Thoreau had the sane and balanced view of the outsider:

> Let him who has work to do recollect that the object of clothing is, first, to retain the vital heat, and secondly, in this state of society, to cover nakedness, and he may judge how much of any necessary or important work may be accomplished without adding to his wardrobe. Kings and queens who wear a suit but once though made by some tailor or dressmaker to their majesties, cannot know the comfort of wearing a suit that fits. They are no better than wooden horses to hang the clean clothes on. Every day our garments become more assimilated to ourselves, receiving the impress of the wearer's character . . .[33]

*

I say, beware of all enterprises that require new clothes . . .[34]

Solitude

Thoreau, like the rest of the hermits we have met, sought solitude not out of simple misanthropy but because he felt the need to free

By Walden Pond

himself from distractions so as to get to know himself better. He was capable of close friendship: his ties with his family were important to him, and his intimacy with his brother was so great that, when John died of tetanus, Henry developed, for a time, the same symptoms. He wrote, possibly following the lead of Emerson, an essay on friendship. Emerson was pragmatic: 'We must be our own before we can be another's' and 'The soul environs itself with friends that it may enter into conversation or society.'[35] But Thoreau was more poetic: 'There are passages of affection in our intercourse with mortal men and women . . . which transcend our earthly life and anticipate Heaven for us'.[36] These sentiments, however, may well have been confined to the intellect of an imaginative writer rather than issue in his relationships with others. Certainly Thoreau was never a warm and tactile person. The intellectual Elizabeth Hoar once said: 'I love Henry but I cannot like him; and as for taking his arm, I should as soon think of taking the arm of an elm tree'.[37]

He makes much of his desire for solitude in *Walden*, but when he discovered true hermits in Maine woods living miles from any neighbour he was appalled by their squalor. He wanted merely to be alone when he felt like being by himself, not to dwell in complete solitude. He maintained close ties with his family and with the Transcendentalist fellow-travellers. The first entry on the first page of his journal (22 October 1837) reads: 'Solitude – To be alone I find it necessary to escape the present – I avoid myself. How could I be alone in the Roman emperor's chamber of mirrors? I seek a garret. The spiders must not be disturbed nor the floor swept, nor the lumber arranged . . .' On 13 March 1841 he writes in his journal: 'How alone must our life be lived – We dwell on the sea shore and none between us and the sea – Men are my merry companions – my fellow pilgrims who beguile the way but leave me at the first turn in the road – for none are travelling *one* road so far as myself.'

On 20 March, 1841 he wrote: 'It is a great relief when, for a few moments in the day we can retire to our chamber and be completely true to ourselves. It leavens the rest of our hours.' And, at Walden, he writes in his journal of 18 April 1846:

I have never felt lonely or in the least oppressed by a sense of solitude but once, and that was a few weeks after I came here to live when for an hour I doubted if the near neighborhood of man was not essential to the healthy life – to be alone was something. But I was at the same time conscious of a slight insanity and seemed to foresee my recovery – in the midst of a gentle rain while these thoughts prevailed – There suddenly seemed such sweet and beneficent society in nature – and the very pattering of the drops and in every sight and sound around my house – as made the fancied advantage of a human neighborhood insignificant.

In *Walden* the musings of the hermit have a more rounded, literary quality:

I love a broad margin to my life. Sometimes, in a summer morning, having taken my accustomed bath, I sat in my sunny doorway from sunrise till noon, rapt in a revery, amidst the pines and hickories and sumachs, in undisturbed solitude and stillness, while the birds sang around or flitted noiselessly through the house, until by the sun falling in at my west window, or the noise of some traveller's wagon on the distant highway, I was reminded of the lapse of time. I grew in those seasons like corn in the night and they were far better than any work of the hands would have been.[38]

*

I have my horizon bounded by woods all to myself; a distant view of the railroad where it touches the pond on the one hand, and of the fence which skirts the woodland road on the other. But for the most part it is as solitary where I live as on the prairies. It is as much Asia or Africa as New England. I have, as it were, my own sun and moon and stars, and a little world all to myself.[39]

*

Yet I experienced sometimes that the most sweet and tender, the most encouraging society may be found in any natural object, even for the poor misanthrope and most melancholy man. There can be no very black melancholy to him who lives in the midst of nature and has his senses still. There never was such a storm but it was Aeolian music to a healthy and innocent ear ... The gentle rain which waters my beans and keeps me in the house today is not drear and melancholy but good for me too.

*

What sort of space is that which separates a man from his fellows and makes him solitary? I have found that no exertion of the legs can bring two minds much nearer to one another. What do we want most to dwell near to? Not to many men, surely, the depot, the meeting house, the school house, the grocery, Beacon Hill or the five points where most men congregate, but to the perennial source of our life, whence in all our experience we have found that to issue, as the willow stands near the water and sends out its shoots in that direction. This will vary with different natures, but this is the place where a wise man will dig his cellar.[40]

*

I find it wholesome to be alone the greater part of the time. To be in company, even with the best, is soon wearisome and dissipating. I love to be alone. I never found the companion that was so companionable as solitude. We are for the most part more lonely when we go abroad among men than when we stay in our chambers.

*

A man thinking or working is always alone. Solitude is not measured by the miles of space that intervene between a man and his fellows. The really diligent student in one of the crowded hives of Cambridge College is as solitary as a dervis in the desert.[41]

*

God is alone – but the devil, he is far from being alone; he sees a great deal of company; he is legion. I am no more lonely than a single mullein or dandelion in a pasture, or a bean leaf, or a sorrel, or a horse fly or a humble bee. I am no more lonely than the Mill Brook, or a weather cock, or the north star, or the south wind, or an April shower, or a January thaw, or the first spider in a new house.[42]

Human relations

One characteristic of the hermit which is constantly cropping up is his tendency to see the foibles of society from the perspective of distance with a clarity denied to the sociable:

> Society is commonly too cheap. We meet at very short intervals, not having had time to acquire any new value for each other. We meet at meals three times a day and give each other a new taste of that old musty cheese that we are. We have had to agree on a certain set of rules, called etiquette and politeness to make this frequent meeting tolerable and that we need not come to open war.[43]

*

> I had three chairs in my house; one for solitude, two for friendship, three for society.[44]

*

One inconvenience I sometimes experienced in so small a house, the difficulty of getting to a sufficient distance from my guest when we began to utter the big thought in big words. You want room for your thoughts to get into sailing trim and run a course or two before they make their port . . . As the conversation began to assume a loftier and grander tone, we gradually shoved our chairs further apart till they touched the wall in opposite directions, and then commonly there was not room enough.[45]

*

I had more visitors while I lived in the woods than at any other period in my life; I mean that I had some . . . But fewer came to see me on trivial business. In this respect, my company was winnowed by my mere distance from town.[46]

Nature

Thoreau's human relationships were diminished, he felt, by his preoccupation with nature. He once wrote: 'If I am too cold for human friendship I trust I shall not soon be too cold for natural influences. It appears to be a law that you cannot have a deep sympathy with both man and nature. Those qualities which bring you near to the one estrange you from the other.'[47] He certainly had an intense enthusiasm for the natural world and a friend once remarked that Thoreau could get more out of ten minutes with a chickadee than most men could get out of a night with Cleopatra.

Like many a nature lover brought up or forced to live in town, he thought of the countryside as a therapeutic influence on the illnesses generated by urban living. 'In society you will not find health, but in nature. You must converse much with the fields and woods if you would imbibe such health into your mind and spirit as you covet for your body.'[48] And he practised this communing with nature throughout his life from his boyhood. He frequently expressed views such as: 'I think that I cannot preserve my health and spirits unless I spend four hours a day at least – and it is commonly more then that – sauntering through the woods and over the hills and fields absolutely free from worldly engagements.'[49]

He looked for the ideal men who should have the right relationship with nature; 'It is the marriage of the soul with nature that makes the intellect fruitful that gives birth to imagination.'[50] He sought for these ideal men in the early pioneers, because they had been forced into a closer contact with nature than the men of his

time; but he failed to find it. Then he turned to the American
Indians and felt that the Indian could teach the white man, who
was pathetically involved in his self-created civilisation, the necessity of a more congenial rapport with a natural environment. As a
child, Thoreau had collected Indian relics and filled many notebooks with observations about their culture. For a time, he saw
himself as following the Indian way of life in his living wild and
free on the fruits of the earth, predicting the weather, handling his
canoe, Indian-style, with one paddle. But he became disillusioned,
because it seemed to him that the Indian was making no attempt
to cultivate his spiritual side, and he wrote: 'In the case of the
savage, the accompaniment of simplicity is idleness with its atten-
dant vices, but in the case of the philosopher it is the highest
employment and development.'[51]

In their close attention to detail, there are passages describing
the natural world in *Walden* which echo the most scrupulous writing of Gilbert White. Thoreau records the appearance and
characteristics of plants animals and birds on Walden Pond as well
as the pleasure they gave him and the reassurance that in their
company he could never feel alone.

But, though some of his writing on nature comes perilously
close to pathetic fallacy, he could be at times clear-eyed and un-
sentimental. He writes in one of his letters: 'I see, at Martial
Miles's, two young woodchucks, taken sixteen days ago when
they were perhaps a fortnight old. There were four in all and they
were dug out with the aid of a dog. *The mother successively
pushed out the little ones to save herself,* and one was at once
killed by the dog.' And he records having seen a dead turtle lying
on its back, its entrails having been eaten by a bird with a long
slender bill: 'Such is Nature, who gave one creature a taste or
yearning for another's entrails as a favorite tid-bit!'[52]

He had hunted with enthusiasm in his boyhood and, as he lived
his solitary life at Walden, he continued for a time to find his food
in the woods:

> Once or twice . . . while I lived at the pond, I found myself ranging
> the woods like a half-starved hound with a strange abandonment,
> seeking some kind of venison which I might devour, and no morsel
> could have been too savage for me . . . I found in myself, and still
> find, an instinct toward a higher, or, as it is named, spiritual life,
> and another toward a primitive rank and savage one, and I
> reverence them both. I love the wild not less than the good.[53]

But it seems that the wildness in him was tamed to a degree by living close to nature, and he writes:

> I have found repeatedly, of late years, that I cannot fish without falling a little in self-respect, I have tried it again and again. I have skill at it and, like many of my fellows, a certain instinct for it, which revives from time to time, but always when I have done I feel it would have been better if I had not fished. It is a faint intimation, yet so are the first streaks of morning.[54]

*

> Our village life would stagnate if it were not for the unexplored forests and meadows which surround it. We need the tonic of wildness – to wade sometimes in marshes where the bittern and the meadow-hen lurk and hear the booming of the snipe; to smell the whispering sedge where only some wilder and more solitary fowl builds her nest. At the same time that we are earnest to explore and learn all things, we require that all things be mysterious and unexplorable, that land and sea be infinitely wild, unsurveyed and unfathomed by us because unfathomable. We can never have enough of nature.[55]

Philosophy of Living

Thoreau was no more a consistent philosopher than his mentor, Emerson. He was suspicious of systems and respectful of instinct. He was against all ideologies which set out to improve mankind, believing that all improvements must come from within the individual and cannot be imposed. All a man can do to help others is to find his own self-fulfilment and then encourage them by his example. All societies, however well intentioned, warp their members. When sticks prop one another up, only one of them stands erect.

In writing *Walden*, he made the point that he was not addressing himself to everybody, particularly not to those of a strong and valiant nature, who were content with their lives, but to the mass of men who, he affirmed, 'lead lives of quiet desperation'.[56]

> I also have in mind that seemingly wealthy but most terribly impoverished class of all, who have accumulated dross, but know not how to use it, or get rid of it, and thus have forged their own golden or silver fetters.[57]

He also stresses that he is not urging that everybody follow his example:

I would not have anybody adopt *my* mode of living on any account; for, besides that before he has fairly learned it I may have found out another for myself, I desire that there may be as many different persons in the world as possible; but I would have each one be very careful to find out and pursue *his own* way and not his father's or his mother's or his neighbor's instead.[58]

How far Thoreau may be classified as a Transcendentalist has been much debated. In the sense that he believed that one can and should go beyond Locke in believing that all knowledge is acquired through the senses, that to attain the ultimate in knowledge one must go beyond the senses, he remained one all his life. But the emphasis changed. 'It is not the invitation which I hear, but which I feel, that I obey'[59] and 'My genius makes distinctions which my understanding can't and which my senses do not report'.[60] Up to 1850, his journals are full of Transcendental avowals. The 'Higher Laws' chapter of *Walden* is one of most explicit statements of his beliefs. As he grew older he transcended his senses less frequently. He was aware of and lamented this change. In the early 1850s, he wrote: 'I fear that the character of my knowledge is from year to year becoming more distinct and scientific . . . I see details, not wholes nor the shadow of the whole. I count some parts, and say, "I know." '[61]

Although his later journals contain more direct observation and fewer transcendental experiences, he never abandoned Transcendentalism for purely scientific observation. In the journal for 1856 he wrote: 'It is by obeying the suggestions of a higher light within you that you escape from yourself and . . . travel totally new paths'.[62] And 'In all important crises, one can only consult his genius.[63]

Thoreau had a basic and unchanging foundation for a philosophy of living in his belief that the good life is one of poverty and material asceticism. All the real obstructions to human happiness come from a fancied dependence on things which are not necessities: too much food, money, fancy clothes or houses. 'If a man has spent all his days about some business by which he has merely got to be rich as it is called: i.e. has got much money, many houses and barns and wood lots, then his life has been a failure, I think'.[64]

Although he felt strongly that a man should follow his own impulses and not ask for advice, his writing is studded with insights into the human condition for the benefit of other searchers. For example, that intuition is the basis of all morality:

Any man knows when he is justified and not all the wits in the world can enlighten him on that point. If one hesitates in his path, let him not proceed. Let him respect his doubts, for doubts, too, may have some divinity in them. That we have but little faith is not sad, but that we have little faithfulness. By faithfulness, faith is earned.

And that real goodness is undeliberate and unconscious:

I want the flower and fruit of a man; that some fragrance be wafted over from him to me, and some ripeness flavor our intercourse. His goodness must not be a partial and transitory act, but a constant superfluity which costs him nothing and of which he is unconscious.

*

Morning is when I am awake and there is a dawn in me. Moral reform is the effort to throw off sleep . . . To be awake is to be alive. I have never yet met a man who was quite awake. . . I know of no more encouraging fact than the unquestionable ability of man to elevate his life by a conscious endeavor. It is something to be able to paint a particular picture, or to carve a statue and to make a few objects beautiful; but it is far more glorious to carve and paint the very atmosphere and medium though which we look, which morally we can do. To affect the quality of the day, that is the highest of the arts.[65]

*

I am sure that I never read any memorable news in a newspaper. If we read of one man robbed, or murdered, or killed by accident, or one house burned or one vessel wrecked . . . we need never read of another. One is enough. If you are acquainted with the principle, what do you care for a myriad instances and applications? To a philosopher, all *news,* as it is called, is gossip and they who edit and read it are old women over their tea.

*

When we are unhurried and wise, we perceive that only great and worthy things have any permanent and absolute existence, that petty fears and petty pleasures are but the shadow of the reality. This is always exhilarating and sublime. By closing the eyes and slumbering, and consenting to be deceived by shows, men establish and confirm their daily life of routine and habit everywhere, which is built on purely illusory foundations . . . We think that *is* which *appears* to be.[66]

*

God himself culminates in the present moment, and will never be more divine in all the lapse of the ages. And we are enabled to apprehend at all what is sublime and noble only by the perpetual instilling[? *sic* does he mean 'stilling'?] and drenching of the reality that surrounds us. [67]

*

I learned this, at least, by my experiment: that if one advances confidently in the direction of his dreams, and endeavors to live the life which he has imagined, he will meet with a success unexpected in common hours. He will put some things behind, will pass an invisible boundary; new universal and liberal laws will begin to establish themselves around and within him; or the old laws be expanded and interpreted in his favor in a more liberal sense, and he will live with the license of a higher order of beings. In proportion as he simplifies his life, the laws of the universe will appear less complex and will not be solitude, nor poverty poverty nor weakness weakness. If you have built castles in the air, your work need not be lost; that is where they should be. Now put the foundations under them.[68]

*

If a man does not keep pace with his companions, perhaps it is because he hears a different drummer. Let him step to the music which he hears, however measured or far away.[69]

Religion

There is a story that an elderly lady used to make a pilgrimage to Sleepy Hollow Cemetery every spring and lay flowers on the graves of Emerson and Hawthorne before turning and shaking a fist at the grave of Thoreau with the words: 'None for you, you dirty little atheist'. But Thoreau has also been widely hailed as a spiritual genius, and he certainly valued what he himself would have called the spiritual dimension in his life.

His early and formal education had not predisposed him to a taste for spirituality. At Harvard, the Professor of Divinity, Henry Ware, was of a practical temperament. Two textbooks used by him were Paley's *Evidences* and Butler's *Analogy*. Both deal with the journey through life and the need to overcome its inevitable hardships. They approach religion through the intellect, and were not to likely to strike sparks from an intuitive and impetuous youth such as Thoreau. Their analysis of the human condition is basically unenthusiastic. They do, however, share a concept which

Thoreau was to accept: that the natural and the moral and spiritual elements of human life are linked.

Thoreau grew to hate all organised religion and its ministers. When asked to deliver a lecture in the basement of a Congregational church, he said he 'trusted he helped to undermine it'. He despised the complacency of established Christians: 'The church! It is eminently the timid institution, and the heads and pillars of it are constitutionally and by principle the greatest cowards in the community.'[70] He wished that 'the ministers were a little more *dangerous*'. [71]

He was critical of the effect of Christianity on his contemporaries and thought it was often a 'blast' on youth that prevented their full development.[72] His religious interests were nourished by Emerson, who had a strong leaning towards the mysticism of the East. There are references to Hindu texts in Emerson's journals from the early 1930s, and the famous lecture at Harvard in 1838, which finally made public his distance from the organised Christianity of the time, expressed belief in the divine element in man, akin to the Atman.[73] Thoreau read Hindu, Chinese and Persian scriptures in Emerson's library, and his journals attest an enthusiasm for Manu, Confucius, Zoroaster and the great masters of Eastern spirituality: 'Arabia, Persia, Hindostan are the native lands of contemplation. If the Roman, the Greek and the Jew have a character in history – so has the hindoo. He may help to balance Asia which is all too one-sided with its Palestine.'[74]

He tells the story of Alexander's meeting with the gymnosophists[75] with enthusiasm: 'It was not an unfilling nor unpleasing contrast that the impetuous Macedonian should be met – at this which he thought the eastern boundary of the world – by the calm philosophy of the Brahmens'.[76]

He was interested in a universal religion made up of the high points of all the scriptures. He wrote: 'To the philosophers, all sects, all nations are alike. I like Brahma, Hari, Buddha, the Great Spirit as well as God.'[77] He suggested to Emerson a 'joint Bible' of the Asiatic scriptures: 'Chinese, Hindu, Persian, Hebrew, to carry to the ends of the earth'. He read to Emerson from his writing for *Week on the Concord* an enthusiastic eulogy of the *Bhagavad Gita* and he experimented with austerities during his time at Walden Pond which he recognised were Hindu in their inspiration. His sitting in rapt revery from dawn to noon has a mystic contemplative quality and he seems to have had knowledge of yoga, because he wrote to his friend Harrison Blake in 1849: 'To some extent and at rare intervals, even I am a yogi.' When an English visitor, Thomas Cholmondley, sent him a present of forty-four volumes of Hindu scriptures, the gift was clearly to feed rather than to awaken an interest. He adopted as his motto '*Ex Oriente Lux*' – Light comes from the East.[78] To the bearers of that light we can now turn.

CHAPTER FIVE

Light from the East: Ramakrishna

The role of the hermit in the West has always been that of the out-sider: the individual who chooses solitude because he hears a different drummer. Even when large numbers have withdrawn from Western society to seek a life of asceticism and isolation, as in the age of the Desert Fathers, they have been seen as a distinct and particular order: they are not as other men are. In the more ancient civilisations of the East, however, the condition of the her-mit has long been held to be the natural and proper culmination of all human life.

In the Upanishads, the Sanskrit writings which underpin Hindu philosophy, the ascetic calling is obligatory and all men are expected, at a certain stage in life, to abandon their homes and pos-sessions and to retire to the forest. Life, for the Hindu, was divided into four stages: the first stage, of *bramacarya,* is the period of apprenticeship when the student had to live in the house of the teacher and learn the sciences and arts. The teacher would live in a hermitage in the forest not far from a town. The student saw the teacher as spiritual father and learned through word of mouth and by contact with nature. The second stage, of *garhastha*, or house-holder, is that of shouldering the responsibilities of life, marriage and children. The duty of the householder is to acquire wealth and dispose of it justly.

The next stage is of *vanaprastha*, the forest dweller or ascetic: 'When the householder sees wrinkles [in his skin] and greyness [in his hair] and the son of his son, let him retire to the forest.'[1] He relinquishes the responsibilities which restrict his life and sets off on a spiritual path. This is to prepare him for the final stage of *san-nyasa*, the life of renunciation. The *sannyasin* is the ideal man who has renounced all worldly cares to attain the supreme goal of enlightenment.

The hermit was so generally accepted a feature of Indian society that the Laws of Manu[2] set out in detail regulations covering his way of life and economic responsibilities:

> . . . let him live without a fire, without a house, wholly silent, subsisting on roots and fruit . . . chaste, sleeping on the bare ground, dwelling at the roots of trees.

> A potsherd [for an alms bowl] , the roots of trees [for a dwelling], coarse, worn-out garments, life in solitude and indifference towards everything are the marks of one who has attained liberation.

> An ascetic, a hermit in the forest and Brahmanas who are students of the Veda shall not be made to pay a toll at a ferry.

> For secret converse with female ascetics, a small fine is payable.

> Eight mouthfuls are the meal of an ascetic, sixteen that of a hermit in the woods, thirty-two that of a householder, and an unlimited quantity that of a student.[3]

The *sannyasin*, then, is the ideal to which all can – and should – aspire. He lives a life of complete independence and solitude, without possessions, pondering on the mysteries of life and wandering the world as the spiritual sentinel of the human race. He is highly respected in society but is indifferent to praise or blame, success or failure. He is the ideal but he occupies a stage in life's journey through which we must all pass. In the words of the first guru of the modern age: 'The last part of Life's road has to be walked in single file.'

Those words were spoken by Sri Ramakrishna, who was described by Pandit Jawaharlal Nehru, the first Prime Minister of India, as 'completely beyond the average run of men. He appears, rather, to belong to the tradition of the great rishis of India who have come, from time to time, to turn our attention to the higher things of life and of the spirit.'[4] His appearance in India coincided with a high tide of secularising pressures from the West. It was becoming the fashion for the more affluent youth of Calcutta to abandon traditional ways and adopt the eating of beef and drinking whisky as emblematic of a more evolved civilisation when Ramakrishna began his spiritual disciplines in the solitude of a nearby temple. His teachings were to make him famous throughout India and across the seas in America and Europe. He revived an interest in the ancient truths of Hinduism within his own culture and then was the most influential of the gurus who

introduced nineteenth-century Europe and America to the spiritual
treasures of the East.

Life of Ramakrishna

He was born the son of a poor but orthodox Brahman on 20
February 1833 in the village of Kamarpukur, which is in the Hugli
district of Bengal.

There was a pilgrim road to Puri passing the outskirts of the village, and a rest house for pilgrims in the village where ascetics and
religious men would stay. As a boy, Ramakrishna used to spend
time with them, hearing about their travels and their faith. He
loved the religious dramas and used to organise the children of the
village to act them out in the fields. He was familiar at a very early
age – his biographer Max Müller[5] claims at six years old – with the
great Hindu epics of the Ramayana, the Mahabharata and the
Puranas, which he learned from a class of men who travel about
reading them to the illiterate peasantry.

At the age of sixteen, his father took him to visit his elder
brother, Ramkumar, who ran a school in Calcutta. The idea was
that he should settle there for a while to be educated, but he was
very soon disillusioned with formal education. He found that there
was much rarefied talk of religious matters, of the nature of being
and non-being and of the liberation of the soul, but the scholars
who spent their time discussing such matters were as aggressive,
acquisitive, competitive and malicious as academics anywhere. He
decided against education. He would seek alone for a direct experience of God.

On the banks of the Ganges, about five miles north of Calcutta,
is the temple of the goddess Kali at Dakshinervara. Here
Ramakrishna came to settle as an assistant to another brother,
who was chief priest. Shortly afterwards, his brother became too
ill to carry out his duties and asked Ramakrishna to take his place.
He did so and quickly came to see himself as priest and worship-
per of the goddess.

Because Kali became so central to the life of Ramakrishna, it is
important to try to understand her significance. This is not easy for
the Westerner. Her statues are gruesome and terrifying. She is
usually depicted with a girdle of severed arms and a necklace of
skulls. She is black, with blood-red palms to her hands. She sticks

out her tongue in a grimace interpreted as lapping up blood. She has four arms: one holds a decapitated head, one a bloody sword, one confers blessings, and one is raised in a gesture which means 'be without fear'. So Kali is the bringing together of contradictions. She is the universal mother and the universal destroyer – the one who gives life and death, blessings and curses, pleasures and pains.

Ramakrishna became obsessed by the desire to see the reality which lay behind the image of Kali which he tended every day at the temple, and he fasted and prayed continuously. To humble himself, he cleaned out the temple privies with his bare hands and ate the remains of food which had been left by the beggars. He then swept and washed clean their eating place. He cultivated an indifference to worldly goods which he would express by taking a pile of coins in one hand and earth in the other, shouting 'Money is dirt! dirt is money!' before throwing both into the Ganges.

In his search for direct religious experience, he frequently fell into trances from which it became more and more difficult to revive him. He would weep for hours when he came round. His parents thought him ill or possessed. They consulted doctors who gave him medicines, and priests who performed exorcisms, but all to no effect. Finally, they decided that he should get married, hoping this would bring him down to earth; but he lived alone after the ceremony and continued his ascetic practices.

Then came his period of life as a hermit. He set out, in fact, on a vision quest, searching, through solitude and asceticism, for a direct vision of the goddess. To the north of the temple was a patch of forest covered in thick undergrowth which had once been a burial ground. It was avoided by everybody for fear of ghosts, but Ramakrishna began to spend his nights there in prayer and meditation. Eventually he gave up his duties at the temple and lived alone in this area for twelve years.

The various lives of Ramakrishna[6] have different versions of his life in solitude. Some say that he prayed and meditated continually while the birds sat on his head and pecked his hair for grains of food. Snakes crawled over his body. Neither the birds nor the snakes nor Ramakrishna was aware of the presence of the others.

There are two traditional Hindu approaches to ultimate reality for the seeker: the way of discrimination and the way of devotion. The choice depends on temperament. The first is through the rejection of all that is not Brahman. This is the way of the Buddha. He looks at phenomena and says 'not this, not this' rejecting all that is impermanent. In this way he passes through life constantly reminding himself that all he sees around him is fleeting and unreal. The only permanent reality is unseen. This is the way of discrimination. The way of devotion is by saying 'this, this', in recognition of the fact that all is Brahman. This way recognises the reality behind the phenomena. This was the way of Ramakrishna. He practised the different yogic disciplines at this time under the guidance of a Brahmin holy woman and began to develop psychic powers. These were commonly demonstrated in India by holy men as a sign of their sanctity. They were the most eye-catching feature of Indian religious life and spiced many travellers' tales; but Ramakrishna was wary of them. He said that psychic powers were an obstacle to enlightenment, because aspirants to spiritual progress would often be distracted by having developed and then becoming inordinately proud of them. He was echoing the experience of the Desert Fathers and, like them, had a story to demonstrate his thesis:

> A man had two sons. The elder left home while he was still young and became a monk. The younger got his education and became learned and virtuous. He married and settled down to fulfil his duties as a householder. After twelve years the monk came to visit his brother, who was overjoyed. When they had eaten together, the younger said: 'Brother, you have given up our worldly pleasures and wandered around as a monk all these years. Please tell me why. What have you gained by it?' The elder brother said: 'You want to see what I have gained? Come with me!' So he took his brother to the bank of a neighbouring river and said: 'Watch!', and then he stepped out on the water and crossed the river, walking on the surface. When he reached the other bank he called to his brother: 'Did you see that?' But the brother had paid half a penny to the ferryman to row him across and he went up to his brother and said: 'Didn't you see *me* cross the river by paying half a penny? Is that all you've gained by all your austerities?' Hearing his brother's words the elder understood his mistake. And he began to set his mind to realise God.[7]

In 1865 a wandering ascetic called Tota Pura arrived to visit Ramakrishna for the customary three days' stay – a wandering monk must travel on continuously like a wandering stream without attachment. He was of the Naga sect of naked religious beggars and had been the head of a monastery before taking to the road. He saw the special quality of Ramakrishna and stayed with him for eleven months, during which time he initiated him as a *san-*

nyasin. Then he left and was never seen again. After his departure, it is said that Ramakrishna stayed in a continuous state of trance for six months, being fed by a holy man who would strike him with a stick so as to bring him close enough to consciousness to be able to take food.

When he recovered he set out to understand other faiths. He went to live with an Islamic holy man and adopted his dress and way of life. Then he had a vision of Jesus, after which he could not speak for three days. These experiences confirmed his belief that all religions are true: they are simply different paths to the same end.

By the early 1870s he was becoming famous and became influential in the revival of Hinduism which was then taking place. One consequence of the Christian missionary activity in India was that young educated Hindus, while rejecting missionary claims, took a closer look at their own faith. They decided that Hinduism could be purged of its superstitions and obsolete customs and, as they saw it, brought into line with other world religions. This would bring the religious systems of India into the modern world. Some used the beliefs of Hinduism as a unifying force in the nationalist movement. They said that spirituality had always been the great strength of India and it was time to reassert her spirituality as a first step to regaining political freedom.

Ramakrishna influenced but kept apart from these reforming movements. His diagnosis of the human malady was that it was spiritual. Only when men came to realise God dwelling within them could society improve. Human relationships could find their true meaning only through the knowledge of men's relationship with God. The only true foundation for ethics was a realisation of the oneness of existence and the solidarity of mankind. During the last seven years of his life he talked constantly with his visitors but never wrote anything. His disciples made notes of his sayings in Bengali, and these were later published. In 1885 he developed throat cancer and was advised by his physicians to stop talking. He refused and, on 15 March 1886, fell into a trance from which he never recovered.

Ramakrishna lived a very simple life without possessions. He had an aversion to gold and silver so great that, if he were to touch them, the mere contact, even when asleep, would make him shake convulsively. He had no formal education; he knew no Sanskrit or English or even scholarly Bengali. As he was not trained in systematic philosophy or theology, he picked up all he knew from holy men and prayer. He never claimed to found a new faith but simply to teach the old one.

His faith was simply that God, the ultimate reality, is unknowable and beyond the reach of human intelligence. On the other hand, every human being is a manifestation of God and contains the indwelling Spirit. These beliefs he shared with traditional Christianity. His affinity with the Desert Fathers and with the mystical theology of Eastern Orthodoxy extends to the teaching that religious experience is the only way to become fully aware of religious truths; that the divinity that lies within us can best be contacted through asceticism; and that to set out securely on a spiritual journey we need the company of a spiritual guide.

Ramakrishna's religious insights were passed on to his followers in simple language and they have been preserved by them like the apophthegmata of the Desert Fathers. When we read them today they take us straight to the heart of Hinduism, away from the more colourful and even violent manifestations of particular sects or gurus, to that centre of religious understanding which is the great treasure of India. Max Müller, who first edited these stories of Ramakrishna for a Western readership, explained to a Cambridge audience in 1882 his life-long championship of Hinduism:

> If I were asked under what sky the human mind has most fully developed some of its choicest gifts, has most deeply pondered on the greatest problems of life and has found solutions of some of them which deserve the attention even of those who have studied Plato and Kant – I should point to India. And if I were to ask myself from what literature we here in Europe, we who have been nurtured almost exclusively on the thoughts of Greeks and Romans and of one Semitic race, the Jewish, may draw that corrective which is most wanted in order to make our inner life more perfect, more comprehensive, more universal, in fact more truly human, a life not for this life only, but a transfigured and eternal life – again I should point to India.[8]

The Sayings of Ramakrishna

At the heart of Hinduism is the basic conviction that the nature of the ultimate reality is and will remain a mystery, and that the beginnings of wisdom lie in the recognition of this fact. As the Desert Fathers had insisted, the Scriptures can point to but never elucidate this mystery. Ramakrishna told a story which echoes closely their teaching:

> A man had two sons. The father sent them to a teacher to learn the knowledge of Brahman. After a few years they returned from the teacher's house and bowed low before their father. Wanting to find out what they had learned, he first questioned the elder: 'My child, you have studied all the scriptures, now tell me what is the nature of Brahman?' The boy began to explain by reciting texts from the Vedas. The father did not say anything. Then he asked the younger son the same question. But the boy was silent and stood with downcast eyes. No word escaped his lips. The father was pleased and said to him: 'You have understood a little of what the Brahman is. It cannot be expressed in words.'[9]

But it is also true that we all have a need for an awareness of that ultimate reality:

> As the lamp does not burn without oil, so man cannot live without God.

*

> He who has faith has all; he who lacks faith lacks all.

So we should all set out on the spiritual journey; but we are held back by our worldliness:

> So long as the iron is in the furnace it is red hot, but it becomes black as soon as it is taken out of the fire. So it is with the worldly man. As long as he is in church or with pious people he glows with religious emotion; but removed from these associations he loses them all.

*

> Flies sit at times on the sweetmeats that are exposed for sale in the shop of a confectioner; but as soon as the sweeper passes by with his basket of filth the flies leave the sweetmeats to settle on it. The honey bee never sits on filth but only on flowers. Worldly men are like flies. They may get a taste of the Divine Sweetness but their natural tendency towards dirt soon brings them back to the dunghill of the world. The good man is always absorbed in the contemplation of divine beauty.

*

> A group of fisherwomen were on their way home from an afternoon market when they were overtaken by a heavy storm as night fell. They came to the house of a florist who let them in to sleep in one

of his store rooms where bunches of flowers were kept. The sweet-smelling atmosphere of the room was too much for the fisherwomen, who could not sleep until one of them suggested: 'Let us each keep her empty fish basket close to her nose so as to prevent this troublesome smell of flowers from attacking our nostrils and killing our sleep.' They all agreed and soon began to snore contentedly. Such is the influence of bad habits on those who are addicted to them.

*

If you move a bound soul to a spiritual environment, he will pine away. The worm surrounded in filth is perfectly happy there. It thrives on dirt. It will die if you put it in a pot of rice.

*

A boat should stay in the water but water should not stay in the boat. So an aspirant may live in the world but the world should not live in him.

But Ramakrishna, too, understood that human kind cannot bear very much reality:

Ornaments cannot be made of pure gold. Some alloy must be mixed with it. A man totally devoid of Maya [illusion] will not survive more than twenty-one days. So long as the man has body, he must have some Maya, however small, to carry on the bodily functions.

In the search for enlightenment, we all need a guru or spiritual father to point the way:

Many roads lead to Calcutta. A certain man set out from his village for the metropolis. On the road he asked a man: 'Which way must I follow to reach Calcutta quickly?' The man said: 'Follow this road'. After a time he met another man and asked him: 'Is this the shortest way to Calcutta?' 'Oh no,' said the man. 'You must retrace your steps and take the road to your left'. He did so. After a short distance on the new road he met a third man who pointed out yet another road as being the shortest to Calcutta. So the traveller made no progress but spent the entire day changing one road for another. He should have followed consistently the road shown by the first man. So those who want to find God should follow one and only one guide.

On the importance of choosing the right guru:

One day as I was . . . on my way to the pine grove I heard a bull frog croaking. After a while, on my way back, I could still hear it croaking so I looked to see what was the matter and found that a water snake had seized it. The snake could neither swallow it nor give it up so there was no end to its suffering. I thought that if it had been seized by a cobra it would have been silenced after three croaks at the most. As it was only a water snake, both of them had to go through this agony. A man's ego is destroyed after three croaks if he gets into the hands of a real teacher. But if the teacher if an 'unripe' one, then both the teacher and the disciple go through endless suffering.

The greatest obstacle to spiritual progress is vanity and the concern for the self:

The sun can give heat and light to the whole world but it can do nothing when there are clouds in the sky which shut out its rays. So long as there is egoism in the soul, God cannot shine upon the heart.

*

The cup which has held garlic juice keeps the smell even though it is cleaned and scoured hundreds of times. So the odour of egoism never completely leaves us.

*

Water appears to be divided into two parts if one puts a stick across it. But, in reality, there is only one water. It appears as two because of the stick. The 'I' is the stick. Remove the stick and there is only one water as before.

*

A disciple had faith in the infinite power of his guru. So he walked across a river by just pronouncing his name. The guru saw this and said to himself: 'If there is such power in my name, I must be a great and powerful man.' And he set out across the river shouting 'I, I, I!' He sank and was drowned. Faith can achieve miracles but vanity and egoism is the death of man.

*

A tree laden with fruit bends low. So, if you want to be great, be meek.

On the journey, we can only recognise spiritual truths if we have developed a spiritual sensitivity:

A man with 'green' bhakti [love of God] cannot assimilate spiritual talk and instruction, but a man with 'ripe' bhakti can. The image that falls on a photographic plate covered with black film [silver nitrate] is retained. On the other hand, thousands of images may be reflected on a bare piece of glass but not one of them is retained. As the object moves away, the glass becomes the same as it was before. One cannot assimilate spiritual instruction unless one has already developed love of God.

But God gives to those who really search for him the awareness that they need:

As a king who intends to visit the house of one of his subjects sends from his own stores the necessary seats, ornaments, food etc., so that his servant may properly receive him, so, before the Lord comes, he sends into our hearts the love, reverence, faith and yearning.

And one other prerequisite for wisdom which is widely echoed in many faiths:

As long as you are not simple like a child you will not be illumined. Forget all worldly knowledge and become as ignorant as a child and you will know the Truth.

Related to this universal truth is the teaching that we can only stop falling over and bumping into things on our spiritual journey when we have come to acknowledge our complete dependence on God:

The young of the monkey clasps and clings to its mother. The young kitten cannot clasp its mother, so it mews piteously whenever it is near her. If the young monkey lets go, it falls and is hurt. This is because it relies on its own strength to hang on; but the young kitten runs no such risk, because the mother carries it about from place to place. Such is the difference between self-reliance and complete resignation to the will of God.

The sign that real understanding has been achieved is not a missionary sermon but silence:

So long as a bee is outside the petals of the lotus and has not tasted its honey, it hovers around the flower buzzing. But when it is inside the flower it drinks the nectar silently. So long as a man quarrels about doctrines and dogmas, he has not tasted the nectar of true faith; once he has tasted it he becomes still.

*

If you throw an unbaked cake of flour into hot ghee, it will make a bubbling noise. The more it is fried, the less the noise becomes, and when it is fully fried the bubbling ceases. So long as a man has little knowledge he goes about lecturing and preaching, but when he has attained knowledge he stops making vain displays.

*

And one of the effects of illumination is that we can live on in a worldly society without contamination:

Milk and water, when brought into contact, are sure to mix so that the milk cannot be separated again. So if the young man mixes indiscriminately with all sorts of worldly men he not only loses his ideals, but also his faith, love and enthusiasm die away imperceptibly. But when you convert milk into butter it no longer mixes with the water but floats on top. Similarly, when a soul once attains Godhead it may live in any company without being affected by evil influences.

*

The wind carries the smell of sandalwood as well as that of ordure but does not mix with either. Similarly, a perfect man lives in the world but does not mix with it.

*

An aquatic bird like the pelican dives into the water but the water does not wet its plumage; so the perfect man lives in the world, which does not touch him.

Another effect of enlightenment:

Once a holy man, while passing through a crowded street, accidentally trod upon the toe of a wicked person. The wicked person, furious with rage, beat the sadhu mercilessly till he fell to the ground in a faint. His disciples comforted him and when he had recovered a little said to him: 'Sir, do you recognise who is looking after you?' The sadhu replied: 'Yes. He who beat me'. A true sadhu finds no distinction between friend and foe.

But this high spiritual state is not for everyone, and Ramakrishna has some practical advice for the would-be *sannyasin*:

A lover of God and a knower of God were once passing through a forest. They saw a tiger at a distance. The knower of God said: 'There is no need to flee; God will protect us.' The lover of God said: 'No, brother. Let us run away. Why should we trouble the Lord to do what we can accomplish by our own exertions?'

*

It is true that God is even in the tiger, but we must not go and face the animal. So it is true that God dwells even in the most wicked, but it is not meet that we should associate with the wicked.

God tells the thief to go steal and at the same time warns the householder against the thief.

Religion must be experienced and not just discussed or read about:

It is easy to pronounce 'do re mi fa so la' but more difficult to sing or to play the notes on an instrument. So it is easy to talk about religion but difficult to act it out.

But the outward forms of religious ritual are important:

Although the germ in a grain of paddy is the important bit for growth, the husk being of no use, yet if you plant a husked grain it will not grow. To get the crop you must sow the grain with the husk on. So rites and ceremonies are necessary for the growth and perpetuation of religion. They are the receptacles which contain the seed of truth; every person must perform them before he can reach the central truth.

That central truth, the reality of God, can only be reached if God himself takes a hand. And it is for this that we should pray:

A police sergeant goes his rounds in the dark of night with a bull's-eye lantern in his hands. [N.B. these lanterns had dark glass on three sides.] No one sees his face, but with the help of that light the sergeant sees everybody's face, and others too can see one another. If you want to see the sergeant, however, you must pray to him: 'Sir, please turn the light on your own face. Let me see you.' In the same way one must pray to God: 'O Lord, be gracious and turn the light of knowledge on thyself so that I may see thy face.'

But even when God reveals himself, we can only know what our perceptions permit:

Once a man went into a wood and saw an animal on a tree. He came back and told another man he had seen an animal with a beautiful red colour on a certain tree. The second man said: 'When I went into the woods I saw that animal. But why do you call it red? It's green'. Another man who was there contradicted them both and said it was yellow. Then others arrived and they began to argue, some saying it was grey, violet, blue and so on. To settle the argument they all went to the tree. They saw a man sitting under it. When they asked him, he said: 'Yes, I live under this tree and I know the animal very well. You are all correct. Sometimes it appears red, or green – violet, grey or blue. It's a chameleon. Sometimes it has no colour at all.

In the same way, somebody who constantly thinks of God knows his nature. He can reveal himself to others in various forms and aspects. Then again, sometimes God has attributes, sometimes he has none. Only the man who lives under the tree knows this. The others suffer from the agony of futile argument.

*

Once some blind men chanced to come across an animal that people told them was an elephant. They were asked what the elephant was like, so they began to feel its body. One of them said the elephant was like a pillar – he had touched its leg; another that it was like a winnowing fan – he had touched its ear; others, touching the tail or belly, gave their different versions. Just so, a man who has seen only one aspect of God limits God to that alone. He cannot see that God can be anything else.

It has always been the practice of religion to stress the greater importance of inner thought over outer practices:

Once two friends were walking along the street when they saw some people listening to a reading of the Bhagavata. One said to the other: 'Come, friend, let us hear the sacred book'. And he went in and sat down. The second peeped in and then went away to visit a brothel. But soon he felt disgusted with what he had done, 'Shame on me!' he said to himself. 'My friend has been listening to the sacred words of Hari and see where I am!' But his friend, listening to the Bhagavata, was also disgusted. 'What a fool I am!' he said to himself. 'I have been listening to this fellow's blah-blah and my friend is having a rare old time!' In the course of time they both died and the messenger of Death came for the soul of the one who had listened to the Bhagavata and dragged it off to hell. The messenger of God came for the one who had been at the brothel and led him off to heaven. Verily, the Lord looks into a man's heart and does not judge him by what he does or where he lives.

Only God knows our true self, the one we search for in solitude, and we tend to cultivate a false self, shaped by the expectations of the society we live in:

Once a tigress attacked a flock of goats. As she sprang on her prey, she gave birth to a cub and died. The cub grew up with the goats, and when they ate grass the cub did so. When they bleated, the cub bleated too. It grew to be a big tiger. One day the flock was attacked by a tiger, who was amazed to see a grass-eating tiger grazing with them. The wild tiger seized the grass-eating one, which began to bleat. So the wild tiger dragged it to the water and said: 'Look at your face in the water – it's just like mine. Stop eating grass, try a little meat.' And it thrust some meat into its mouth. But the grass-eating tiger spat it out and began to bleat. Gradually, however, it got the taste for meat and would accept small pieces from the wild tiger. Then the wild tiger said: 'Now you see there is no difference between you and me. Come away with me into the forest.' So the guru will let you know what your true nature is.

Ramakrishna was fond of pointing out what was true and important knowledge and what was irrelevant:

Once several men were crossing the Ganges by boat. One of them, a pundit, was making great display of his erudition, saying that he had studied the great books: the Vedas, the Vedanta and the six systems of philosophy. He asked a fellow passenger: 'Do you know the Vedanta?' 'No, Reverend Sir'. 'The Samkhya and the Patanjala?' 'No, Reverend Sir?' 'Have you read no philosophy whatever?' 'No, Reverend Sir.' The pundit went on talking in this way and the passenger sat in silence when a great storm rose and the boat began to sink. The passenger said to the pundit: 'Sir, can you swim?' 'No,' replied the pundit. The passenger said: 'I don't know the Samkhya and the Patanjala, but I can swim.'

But his greatest contribution to world religions was the perception that they are all, at heart, a search for the same God. He once said:

A lake has several ghats. At one the Hindus take water in pitchers and call it 'jal'; at another the Mussulmans take water in leather bags and call it 'pani'. At a third the Christians call it 'water'. Can we imagine it is not 'jal' but only 'pani' or 'water'? How ridiculous! The substance is one under different names and everyone is seeking the same substance; only climate, temperament and names create differences. Let each man follow his own path.

*

It is not good to feel that my religion alone is true and other religions are false. The correct attitude is this: 'My religion is right but I do not know whether other religions are right or wrong, true or false.' I say this because one cannot know the true nature of God unless one realises Him.

After the death of Ramakrishna, a group of his disciples decided to devote their lives to spreading his teachings. Their leader was Narendra Nath Dutt, who took the name of Vivekananda and attended the Parliament of World Religions in Chicago in September 1903. He then lectured in America for two years and visited France and England. He was the first Indian to persuade British and Americans to accept him as a teacher. He was the precursor of many gurus who have carried from India a message which was seen as a revelation in the West. The story of the gradual corruption of that message into a charter for self-indulgence is one of the clichés of our age.

The religious insights of Ramakrishna remain.

CHAPTER SIX

Hermit of the Sahara:
Charles de Foucauld

We turn to the hermits for the insights they have gained in their solitude. By and large it is what they say rather than what they do that makes them important: the solitary life tends to be uneventful. But Charles de Foucauld is different. His life was colourful, exciting and full of challenges; it was in his response to these challenges that his perceptions sharpened and his insights deepened into the nature and value of solitude. He felt strongly, after his conversion, the calling to be a hermit: he dressed as he thought a hermit should dress; he called himself a hermit; he built hermitages in ever more remote parts of the Sahara desert; but his search for solitude led him into deeper intimacy with remote peoples he felt called to serve. His principal legacy to the world is an order of men and women who are committed to living closely alongside and in community with the poorest workers, wearing the same clothes, living in the same houses, doing the same jobs. The ideal of dedication to service which they follow was conceived by Charles de Foucauld out of an experience of solitude. As a desert hermit in the remotest depths of the Sahara, he inspired a way of life which is followed by hundreds of witnesses all over the world and in the inner cities of today.

He was born in Strasbourg on 15 September 1858. His father was from the Périgord and descended from a noble family stretching back to the tenth century which included courtiers, crusaders and at least one official martyr of the Catholic Church. Above all, it was a family of professional soldiers – proud, patriotic and resolute: the family motto was *'Jamais Arrière'* (Never Retreat). His mother's family were also military, and both families had provided leaders of men who had died gloriously at the head of their regiments in battle for the greater glory of France.[1]

Charles was the eldest child and had one sister, Marie, who was three years younger and known as Mimi. Both were adopted when their parents died in 1864 by their maternal grandfather, Colonel de Morlet, who was by then rather elderly and set in his ways. He minimised the friction of having children about the place by the usual strategy of indulging them. A photograph of Charles taken at the time shows a rather plump and not particularly amiable child who stares into the camera lens with an incurious disdain.

In 1870 came the Franco-Prussian war and France lost the territory of Alsace to Germany. It was unthinkable that a patriotic ex-soldier should continue to live in Strasbourg so the Colonel settled with the two children in Nancy, where Charles went to school and took his first communion. When he left school at sixteen, he received a report describing his work there as 'very fair' . This was to be the highest praise he ever received during his period of formal education.

He had come to realise by this time that a vast fortune awaited him and that it would be foolish to wear out his youth in study when life was short and so many pleasures lay in store. The context in which he could most agreeably indulge his appetites was, he decided, the fashionable and undemanding career of a cavalry officer, so he proposed to attend the military school at St-Cyr. There were a few modest entrance requirements and the Colonel, anticipating that some cramming might be necessary, sent Charles to meet with his first taste of formal discipline, with the Jesuits in the rue des Postes, Paris. The regime was a severe shock. Charles was expected to rise each day at 4.40 a.m. and to work hard on a frugal diet, and he was not even allowed Christmas holidays. He wrote repeatedly to the Colonel pleading to be taken away, and eventually the Jesuits, who had long given up hope of reforming him, sent him home in March 1876 on the grounds of ill health. He was fat, lazy, and had lost his faith.

This rejection of religion was not entirely individual and hormonal. The climate of the times was against piety. Darwin and Auguste Comte had dethroned God and replaced him by the religion of Humanity; Renan's humanist *Life of Jesus* (1863) had secularised Christ; Emile Littré, the scientific positivist philosopher, who had been refused election to the Académie Française because of his atheism, published his *Dictionnaire de la Langue Française* between 1863 and 1872. Charles argued his way out of faith by using his reason. He wrote to a friend that the fact that so many diverse religions existed condemned them all, and that, so far as Christianity was concerned, he 'rejected the illogicality of 1 = 3'. Mankind, he decided, had for too long been a victim of its own fears and superstitions. Unless and until the resurrection of Christ could be scientifically demonstrated to him, he would stay with the prudent realism of the disciples of Auguste Comte.[2]

In June 1876, he took the entrance exam for St-Cyr and passed 82nd out of 412 candidates, but almost failed to gain admission because he was too fat. He presented himself there on 30 October 1876 and discovered that none of the uniforms available would fit him. For ten days he had to wear civilian clothes incongruously topped by a distinctive kepi, before a tailor could cover his ample form with the cadet uniform. The atmosphere of St-Cyr was reactionary and royalist. Charles found a special friend there in the Marquis de Mores, who was to become Duke of Vallombrosa, and he embarked on a relaxed attitude to his studies which resulted in his passing out 333rd of 386. He had also collected forty-five punishments for disobedience and laziness.

The cavalry school at Saumur, pleasantly situated on the banks of the Loire, with a long tradition of catering for affluent and aristocratic young men, was even more to his taste. Here he shared an apartment, No. 82, with de Mores. They cleared out all the furniture and replaced it with *ameublements* more *sympathiques*: expensive carpets, elegant chaises-longues and English aquatints on the walls. Charles was driven each day into town to visit his barber, except for the not infrequent occasions when he was confined to his quarters. Then the barber's boy would visit him.

No. 82 became famous for its excellent dinners and all-night card parties. When at liberty, Charles would dine at Budan's, the most famous restaurant in town, where he had a private room. His favourite dish was cold partridge on canapé accompanied by several bottles of Alicante. He also had a passion for a Mont Blanc – a rich confection of grated sweet chestnut surrounded by whipped cream. He once confided to a friend: 'You see, my dear friend, after a good dinner there's nothing like a good cigar; and to go home in a pleasant low-slung little carriage so that one does not have to make the effort of raising one's foot very high in order to get into it.'[3] He bribed the head doctor at Saumur to give him a certificate that the state of his health precluded him from early rising.

The future General d'Urbal, a classmate, remembered the lifestyle:

Those who have not seen Foucauld in his room in white flannel pyjamas with brandenburgs, comfortably settled on his couch or in an excellent armchair, sampling a tasty *pâté de fois gras,* washed down with excellent champagne while reading Aristophanes in a handsome elegantly bound edition, cannot truly imagine a man happy to be alive.[4]

On 11 October 1879, Charles graduated from Saumur and was gazetted sub-lieutenant with the 4th Hussars at Pont-à-Mousson. He had achieved the position of eighty-seventh out of a class of eighty-seven. The Inspector General reported: 'He has a certain distinction and has been well brought up. But he is empty-headed and thinks of nothing but amusing himself. Deprived of leave because of his conduct and numerous punishments.'[5] These totalled twenty-one days of simple arrest and forty-five days' confinement to quarters.

Charles had inherited his large fortune on his twentieth birthday, 15 September 1878, and had no intention of allowing the 4th Hussars to interfere with his lifestyle. Certainly he refrained from attempting the traditional feat of the cavalry officer to get through thirty kilometres, three women and three bottles of champagne in three hours. His pleasures were more relaxed. He dined well and chose his women from among the many who were available to someone of his wealth and breeding. He made one odd decision, choosing to establish as his mistress one Marie C. (her full name has not survived, in spite of the effect she had on his career), daughter of an honest Lorrain workman. He moved her into an apartment at Pont-à-Mousson. His friends and family were uneasy but did not interfere, as Marie had the personality to ruin his career or, even worse, to marry him. They were much relieved when the 4th Hussars were posted to Algiers. A separation would surely end the affair.

But Charles did not surrender his comforts easily. He decided to send Marie ahead to set up a comfortable nest for them both, and gave her a ticket to Sétif in the name of his wife. With the help of letters of introduction from him and her own considerable and practised charm, she soon became a local celebrity, particularly among the officials, as the 'vicomtesse'. She was exposed by the arrival of an indignant contingent of officers' wives. They insisted that their husbands complain to the Colonel, who ordered Charles to ship Marie immediately back home and apologise to his fellow officers.

Charles was exaggeratedly polite. He assured the Colonel of his great respect for the honour of the regiment, but went on to doubt whether that honour was in any way touched by the conduct of an independent young lady who, being a civilian, was free to travel or stay where she pleased. The Colonel, unused to rebellion from influential junior officers, sent a report to the Minister of War and, on 20 March 1881, Sub-lieutenant de Foucauld was retired, by ministerial decision, from his post and placed on the non-active list. Charles responded by giving a sumptuous farewell dinner at the Hôtel de France, presided over by himself and Marie, before sailing home to settle with her at Evian on Lake Geneva.

Perhaps incessant proximity eroded the charm of the relationship. When Charles heard that his regiment was leaving for active duty the following May, he asked for permission to join them. This was refused. He insisted, and said that if he were not given his status as an officer he would enlist as a private soldier. To have had a viscount in the ranks would have proved an embarrassment, and he was allowed to join the 4th Chasseurs d'Afrique at Mascara.

A classmate at St-Cyr who also became a sub-lieutenant in the 4th Regiment of the Chasseurs d'Afrique, Laperrine, wrote of the change he saw in Charles when he returned to Africa in June 1881 and joined his regiment:

> In the midst of the dangers and the deprivations of the expeditionary columns this well-read playboy revealed himself to be a soldier and a leader, bearing the worst trials gaily, giving of himself constantly, taking devoted care of his men, he was admired even by the old Mexicans [veterans of the Mexican campaign under Napoleon III] of the Regiment, who were no fools.
>
> Nothing was left of the Foucauld of Saumur and Pont-a-Mousson except a tiny edition of Aristophanes and a very small remnant of snobbery which made him stop smoking when it was no longer possible for him to obtain his favourite brand of cigars.[6]

During the months of military campaign, Charles underwent two quite separate experiences which were to change his life. He had his first taste of the satisfaction of physically extending himself and he came into close contact with a people with a living faith. 'Islam has disturbed me deeply,' he was to say later on. 'The sight of this faith, of these souls living in the continuous presence of God has made me aware of something greater and more true than worldly preoccupations.'[7]

The 1880s was a period of European expansion in Africa. The

British were colonising their trading settlements; the Germans were seeking to move out of European politics to a *Weltpolitik*, and France, still smarting from the loss of Alsace-Lorraine, sought revenge by restricting German expansionism in Africa. Rivalry between the two was particularly bitter over Morocco, where both had economic ambitions. Charles, who had lost the city of his birth to the Germans, decided that he could play a part in opening Morocco to French influence by exploring the interior. He asked for leave from the Army, which was refused, so he resigned and went to Algiers to study Arabic and prepare himself for the journey.

His preparations were exhaustive. Each day he went on board a French naval vessel which happened to be under the command of a relative, to learn the use of the compass, sextant and other navigational aids; each evening he spent two hours with the President of the Geographical Society of Algiers learning geography and mathematics; he studied Arab history with a specialist at the Ecole Normale Supérieure and he ordered from France 25,000 francs worth of scientific instruments.

Since it was obvious that a defenceless Frenchman would not last long in the desert, Charles had to adopt a disguise. There were, he noted, only two religions in Morocco and he had to adopt one of them. Should he be Muslim or Jew? Other explorers had disguised themselves as Muslims, hoping to blend in with the majority population, but the disadvantage was that they were then bound to follow all the practices and ceremonies of that faith, which could be tedious and time-consuming but, worse, they were always likely to slip up in some small observance and give themselves away. To be a Jew meant to be an outsider, despised and ignored. Nobody would care who he was, where he came from or where he was going. Charles decided to be a Jew, and set himself to the study of Hebrew. He also found a guide and travelling companion in Mordecai abi Serour, a rabbi from Morocco who had long experience as a guide in the interior deserts and was happy to take on a leisurely journey at a monthly salary.

The full story of Charles's journey is told in his book *Reconnaissance au Maroc* and it reveals that the pampered, self-indulgent young man of Saumur and Pont-à-Mousson had developed into a hardened, self-reliant and resourceful explorer. The whole process of information-gathering was hazardous:

My whole itinerary was surveyed with the help of a compass and a barometer. While we were on the road I always had a notebook five centimetres square hidden in the palm of my left hand; with a pencil less than two centimetres long which was at all times in my other hand, I jotted down whatever noteworthy features the trail presented . . . I took the precaution of walking either in front or behind my companions so that, with the help of my ample garments, they might not perceive the slightest movement of my hands; the contempt in which the Jew is held contributed to my isolation . . .

What tales did we not invent to explain the sextant! Sometimes it served the purpose of reading the future in the sky, sometimes to give news of persons who were far away. In Taza it was a preventative against the plague, in the Tadla, it revealed the sins of the Jews; elsewhere it told me the time of day, predicted the weather, warned me of danger on the journey, anything at all.[8]

The report on Charles's exploration of Morocco so impressed the Geographical Society in Paris that he was awarded their Gold Medal. The citation reads:

In eleven months, from 20 June 1883 to 23 May 1884, one man by himself, M. Foucauld, has at least doubled the length of itineraries in Morocco which have been surveyed carefully . . . As far as astronomical geography is concerned, he has established 45 longitudes and 40 latitudes and where we had only a few dozen altitudes he has brought us 3,000. You will understand that a new era in the geographical knowledge of Morocco is indeed beginning, owing to M. de Foucauld.[9]

Charles settled back in Paris and enjoyed his celebrity. He took an apartment close to his Aunt Inés, who treated him as a son. She kept a distinguished salon, open each Sunday to ministers of state and savants, where Charles was agreeably entertained and admired as a writer and explorer. He also met there two people who were to act as channels for that grace which brought about his sudden conversion to Christianity.

The first was the Abbé Henri Huvelin, graduate of the Ecole Normal Supérieure, who had refused the position of Professor of History at the Institut Catholique to be an ordinary parish priest at the rather unprepossessing church of St-Augustin. His reputation as an intellectual and a confessor had made him widely popular and he lived a life under siege from penitents as well as being close friends with such disparate individuals as the mystical theologian Baron von Hügel and the rationalist philosopher Emile

Littré. Huvelin was not an aggressive missionary; he preferred to let each soul work out its own salvation. He once said: 'If you meet someone who is searching, don't preach a sermon at him; just show him that you love him'.

This was the attitude of Marie, daughter of Aunt Inés and the second person Charles met regularly at the salon who was to be responsible for his conversion. It was the renewal of a close relationship. They had been so intimate during Charles's adolescence that some biographers have suggested he was plunged into despair and atheism by her marriage, in 1874, to the Vicomte Olivier de Bondy. Certainly, Marie de Bondy loved him unwaveringly, and he came to recognise that the religion which inspired her life could not be totally absurd.

His experiences in Morocco had made him admire the Muslims, and he also felt a kinship with the Greek and Latin Stoics. The ancient virtues of self-reliance, asceticism, strict morality; the capacity to elevate himself by his own efforts – he had demonstrated all these and was attracted by the philosophy that extolled them. He read, he said, Christian books only to extract from them the pagan virtues which they taught.

Christianity seemed childish and irrational. It was the religion of the losers. In Paris, however, he met a number of otherwise normal people who seemed distinguished, intelligent and successful and yet were Christian. He later wrote to his friend Henri de Castries:

> When I was in Paris, having my journey to Morocco printed, I found myself with people who were very intelligent, virtuous and Christian. I told myself that perhaps this religion is not so absurd after all. At the same time I felt a very strong interior grace. I started to go into church even though I didn't believe. Only there did I feel at ease. I spent long hours repeating that strange prayer: 'God, if you do exist, make me know you'.

One day, towards the end of October 1886, he made the decision to consult Father Huvelin about his religious promptings. He went to the church of St-Augustin and found that the abbé was in the confessional. So he entered and asked for instruction in the faith. Huvelin simply told him to kneel down and make his confession. Charles objected that he did not believe, that he had not come to confess before a God whose existence he denied, but that he sought the first stages of instruction. Huvelin simply repeated that he should kneel and make his confession. So he did. Afterwards, the Abbé asked if he was fasting and, being told that he had not eaten that morning, sent him straight to communion.

From that time, he accepted Huvelin as his spiritual guide for life. He went to confession regularly and tried to take communion every day. He had not been moderate in his pleasures before conversion and was not lukewarm about his faith afterwards. He went on a pilgrimage to the Holy Land, arriving in Jerusalem on Christmas Day, where he followed the Via Dolorosa. Then he went to Calvary, to Bethany and to Nazareth, which made the greatest impression on him. He remembered the words Huvelin was fond of repeating: 'Our Lord has taken the lowest place in such a way that no one can take it from him'. Charles decided that the lowest place was the life Jesus led in Nazareth, the hidden life, and decided to spend the rest of his own life bearing him company there.

He began to search for a monastic order which would allow him to live in imitation of the hidden life of Jesus, and asked his publisher to send him three books which would help him decide. He read Montalembert's *Les Moines d'Occident*, an apologia for the monastic life in the secular West, and Abbé Fouard's *Vie de Jésus*, which is filled with geographical and historical detail about the Holy Land. But the book which most inspired him was Arnauld d'Indilly's translation of *Lives of the Desert Fathers*. In this he read of the humility, the asceticism, the total self-surrender which he sought. He wrote to his cousin Marie that his ambition was 'to follow the example of the hermits who pierced caves into the mountain on which Our Lord fasted, in order to fast all their lives at his feet'.[10]

He made a series of retreats with different Orders: to the Benedictines at Solemnes, to the Trappists at Soligny and Notre-Dame des Neiges and to the Jesuits at Clamart. He wrote to his sister in December 1889: 'I have been thinking about it for a long time. I have been in four monasteries, and in all four retreats I was told that God is calling me and that He was calling me to be a Trappist. My soul draws me to the same place; my director is of the same opinion. It is all resolved now.'[11]

The Trappists were the people with whom Charles felt it most likely that he could approach the conditions of deprivation and humility that he sought in imitation of the hidden life of Jesus. It was not only their Rule, which was of the strictest, but their location, which, unlike that of many of the monastic orders in France, was wholly without architectural elegance. The monastery at

Notre-Dame des Neiges is on the high plateau of Vivarais, in the Ardèche, far from urban civilisation, and is one of the less well endowed of monastic foundations. A further attraction for Charles was the existence of a daughter house in Syria which would take him back to the atmosphere of the Holy Land.

Charles arrived at Notre-Dame des Neiges on 16 January 1890. In accordance with the Rule, the Abbot asked him what he could do. 'Not a lot,' replied Charles. 'Can you read?' 'A bit.' So he was given the job of sweeping the floors.[12] He did this very badly but he was well content: he had achieved the lowest place.

After six months he went on to Notre-Dame du Sacré-Cœur, near to the village of Akbes, in Syria, poorest of the Trappist houses. It had been founded in 1882, when the Trappists in France feared expulsion by the increasingly powerful anti-clerical movement, and it consisted of a few little wooden houses with clay and wattle walls and thatched roofs in a desolate valley.

Charles wrote to his sister:

We are about twenty Trappists, including the novices. As you can see from the photographs, we live in rather large barracks. There are animals: oxen, goats, horses and donkeys, all we need for farming on a large scale . . . our great task is to work in the fields; sawing wood in the winter, labouring the vineyards in the spring and gathering hay and harvesting the crop in the summer . . . this work, which is harder than one thinks if one has never done it, gives such compassion for the poor, such charity for the workers, the labourers. One realises the value of a piece of bread so well when one sees for oneself how much toil it took to produce it. One has so much pity for all those who work when one shares their labour.[13]

He began woodcutting, but his hands were too soft and he seemed likely to injure himself or his companions so he was made librarian, then bell-ringer and then put to mending the clothes for orphans. He learned to knit and to sew. He was happy in the seclusion and asceticism of the monastery, and it remained only to disembarrass himself of his worldly goods outside. On 3 January 1891 he wrote to his sister:

Today I write to you particularly to make you a gift of all my flat in Paris contains; henceforth it is yours, to do what you please with it, sell, give, order what you like, it is just yours . . . The greatest joy that my little possessions have given me will be to get rid of them and to have them no longer.[14]

On the Feast of Candlemas, 2 February 1892, Charles made his solemn profession: 'About seven a.m. I pronounced my vows; about eleven a few locks were cut from my hair in church, then my head was shaved, leaving only the crown. And now I do not belong to myself any more in any way at all. My vows were of poverty, chastity and obedience to the Order of the Reformed Cistercians, the Trappist Order.' He took the name Brother Alberic, after one of the founders of the Order.

The most widely known characteristic of the Trappists is their vow of silence, which, for those of us outside the Order, seems to be part of their penitential way of life, since we think of silence between members of a community as a deprivation. But the penance, for some, is in the communal life itself: eating, working, sleeping, praying together. Silence gives some relief from this unremitting togetherness and is a safeguard for that solitude which is essential to a contemplative life.

Charles found the penitential life to his taste. He sought constantly to occupy the lowest place, to imitate what he saw as the life that Jesus had lived at Nazareth. But, more, he looked for opportunities for self-abasement, for abjection. This was not a part of the life at Nazareth, and it can easily be seen as a sign of psychological disorder. But many of the saints have displayed this need for abjection, for mortification, which stems from their meditations on the Passion of Christ. The mystery remains as to why Jesus chose to be subjected to humiliation, insults and torture on the cross. In submitting himself to this total abjection, he displayed his love for mankind, and those who choose to imitate him have often pursued the imitation into areas of mortification which helped them to identify with him. As the Prior-General of the Little Brothers of Jesus, an order inspired by Charles, expressed it: 'If we really love Jesus, can we help trying to prove our love for Him in the manner He Himself chose to prove His love to us?'[15] The conduct of Charles from his time with the Trappists onward can only be understood in the light of these words.

In April 1893 he was alarmed because the Holy Father authorised Trappists to use oil and butter as seasonings for their vegetarian diet. He opposed any relaxation of the rigour which had first drawn him to the Trappists and wrote to Marie de Bondy:

> For some weeks past we no longer have our dear cooking with salt and water, they put some sort of greasy stuff in our food . . . You understand how much I regret it . . . A little less mortification is a little less given to God; a little more expence is a little less given to

the poor . . . and then where will it stop? Down what slope are we sliding. May God preserve us.[16]

His disillusionment with the more relaxed approach to the monastic life increased during the summer of 1893 and he began to conceive a new Order:

> Seeing that it was not possible to live as a Trappist the life of poverty, humility and I would even say of recollection as lived by Our Lord at Nazareth, I asked myself if Our Lord had give me these desires solely in order that I might sacrifice them or if, since no congregation in the Church gives the opportunity today to live with him the life of this world, it were not possible to seek a few with whom one might form the beginning of a little congregation of this sort; the object would be to live as exactly as possible the life of Our Lord, living only from the work of one's hands, accepting no gifts either spontaneous or solicited and following all his counsels, possessing nothing, giving to everyone who asks, requiring nothing, depriving oneself of the most that is possible, first in order to be as like Our Lord as possible then and almost as urgently to give him as much as possible in the person of the poor . . . To form only little groups, little dovecotes like Carmels (big monasteries almost necessarily acquire a material importance that is inimical to abjection and to humility) to spread everywhere, particularly in the countries of the infidels which are so abandoned and where it would be so sweet to increase the love and the servants of Our Lord Jesus Christ.[17]

He told his confessor, Dom Polycarp, of his scheme and asked if these desires were from God or the promptings of the Devil. He received the traditional reply: 'It doesn't matter which. If they are from God he will see that they come to something. If they are from the Devil they will come to nothing,' and was told to await God's pleasure. He wrote to Father Huvelin, who was not encouraging. The programme which he felt right for Charles was:

> To continue your theological studies at least as far as the diaconate; to apply yourself to the inner virtues and particularly to self-denial; ask for the external virtues, to practise them by perfecting your obedience to the Rule and to our Superiors . . . for the rest, we shall see later. Moreover you are *not at all made* to be a leader of others.[18]

Charles obediently went back to his theological studies, which, he claimed, he enjoyed, though with the rider: 'It is admirable. But did St Joseph know much about it?'[19] And, although he lived contentedly enough, labouring ineptly in the fields, or more comfortably in the library, for eight hours a day and studying for two, the desire for a solitary life did not leave him and, at the end of 1895, Dom Polycarpe wrote to his confidante, Mother Clémence:

> Well, the good Father Alberic has got it into his head that he will leave us and become a hermit and live alone in the desert. We have tried to tell him that the Church no longer accepts this sort of life; that those who have had the same idea have ended up by apostatising or going mad. Nothing works. You absolutely must find a way of curing the good Father.[20]

But the intervention of the good Mother was not necessary. Huvelin opposed any change and Charles remained obedient. But he did not cease to dream. In 1896 he drew up the draft regulations for his 'dovecotes' who were to be called the Congregation of the Little Brothers of Jesus. They were to be established in small towns and suburbs 'where the poorest live'; they would rent small lodgings; there would be three rooms for each community: a chapel, a guest room and a room for the brothers. No chairs or beds, just stone benches round the walls. Round each house a small garden producing fruit and vegetables. A space would be set aside for the burial of deceased brothers.

The Order was to be strictly enclosed. No woman would be allowed to enter. Brothers would only go out when absolutely necessary, and then two by two. Inside the Order, there would be perpetual silence, except for matters concerning duty or work, and prayer. This would take up the whole day. Recreation time was specified as fifteen minutes in the morning and another fifteen minutes in the evening.

The clothing should be that of the local poor. There would be two meals a day: one gruel cooked with salt and water and the other half a pound of bread. On Sundays, a little milk, honey and fruits. The brothers would go barefoot and would sleep fully dressed on stone benches without mattress or pillow.[21]

This incredible passion for destitution did not go down well with Father Huvelin, to whom Charles sent a copy of his Rule. Huvelin replied:

> Your Rule is absolutely impracticable. The Pope hesitated to give his approval to the Franciscan Rule; he considered it too severe, but this Rule! To tell you the truth, it terrified me. Live at the gate of the community in the abjection for which you wish, but do not draw up a Rule, I beg of you![22]

The reference to living at the gate was to a subsidiary ambition of Charles, which was to occupy the traditional place of the fool for Christ. There was historical precedent for a situation in which a monastery would permit a hermit to live at its gate, outside the community, in total poverty, receiving a minimum of food and being permitted, from time to time, to receive communion. Since the Church refused him the status of desert hermit, Charles sought the position of fool for Christ at the gate of his monastery. The head of the Trappists in Algeria, Dom Louis de Gonzague, called him for an interview and, having heard his plea to be a hermit at the gate, ordered him to Rome for two years to study theology at the Gregorian University.

In October 1896 Charles left Africa for Rome, where he was delighted to be in the presence of so many ruins which were physical survivals of the early Church and moved by his studies of the Fathers, but frustrated in his most basic desires. He had, through demonstrating his obedience, been forced to give up the poverty and asceticism to which he was so strongly drawn. What could be further from the simple life of Jesus in Nazareth than to spend the days pondering the words of theologians in the company of scholars gathered in one of the world's most grandiose cities? Charles felt misplaced and anguished by the approach of 2 February 1897 – the date by which he had to either make his perpetual vows to the Trappists or leave the Order. He spent December in retreat and the week from 15–23 January, which he later said was the most important of his whole life, wrestling with the problem of finding his true vocation. He wrote to his superior, Dom Wyatt, setting out his spiritual condition and waited for a reply, which he was prepared to follow implicitly. On 23 January 1897 he received a letter saying that he was dispensed from his vows, that Dom Wyatt recognised his vocation to be a particular one, and that he should once more place himself totally under the spiritual supervision of Father Huvelin.[23]

On 11 February 1897, Dom Louis de Gonzague wrote a letter to his brother Dom Martin informing him that Charles was leaving the Order of Trappists:

To tell the truth, though he sincerely loved various people in our Order . . . he didn't really love the Order itself; he is a perfect specimen of our XIXth-century nobility: brave, generous with its blood and its money, on occasions saintly, but incapable of sustained obedience and discipline under a leader; he could become a saint; I hope it for him; but in his own way, not through obedience.

On 24 February 1897 Charles landed at Jaffa. He had given up the garb of a Trappist and was wearing a white cap which tried to imitate a turban, a long overgarment with a hood of blue and white striped material, blue cotton trousers and sandals. These were the garments of the poor of Palestine. Charles was only distinguished from Oriental beggars by the large rosary hanging from his belt. He had changed his name. No longer Vicomte de Foucauld or Brother Alberic; he was simply Frère Charles de Jésus. He belonged to no order; he was alone. He had taken private vows of perpetual chastity and poverty, which he defined as an undertaking never to possess more than a poor workman.

Seeking to imitate the hidden life of Christ, he went to Nazareth and asked for a job with the convent of Poor Clares. They offered him the gardener's house, but he thought it too grand and settled for a shed in the garden which he called a 'hermitage' and dedicated to Our Lady of Perpetual Help. He began to live there on 10 March 1897. As he insisted on working for his keep he was given some simple carpentry, which he did rather badly. Then he dug over the garden and tried his hand at dry stone-walling. As a gardener he turned out to be lethal: he watered the young plants in full sunlight so they scorched, and put fresh dung on them which burned them. A nun later remembered him with affection: 'He couldn't even plant a lettuce'.[24] Charles described himself as 'the servant, the domestic, the valet of a poor religious community'.

He was very contented with his life of deprivation and poverty, living on two meals of dry bread a day. The year was 1897, the year that André Gide published *Les Nourritures Terrestres*, which extolled the uninhibited satisfaction of the appetites. Charles wrote a meditation on the Book of Genesis in which he noted that God becomes present to humans in situations of solitude, poverty and extremity:

> It is at the moment when Jacob is on the road, poor and alone, when he sleeps on the bare ground in the desert to take his rest after a long journey on foot, it is at the moment when he is in the painful situation of the isolated traveller in the middle of a long journey in a strange and wild country with nowhere to sleep; it is at that moment when he finds himself in so sad a condition that God overwhelms him with incomparable favours.[25]

At this time Charles thought of himself as a hermit, living in a hermitage a life of solitude, prayer, asceticism and contemplation in accordance with a tradition which had been kept alive more vigorously in the Eastern than the Western Church. His inspiration was from the Desert Fathers, his mode of life far closer to the Russian skete than the monasteries of his own Church. But he had constant support from his Spiritual Father, who wrote to him on 15 October 1898, approving his situation 'with its opportunities for peace, silence and solitude which you still have need of'. Huvelin was only opposed to the repeated schemes which Charles put to him for a new Order to live out the way of Christian poverty he had discovered. On 8 February 1899, Huvelin wrote: 'Wait . . . The tree must grow a little before it can give any shade under which others may come to rest.'

Charles was ready to obey and wait, but not to abandon his project. In June 1899 he completed a revision of the Rule he had previously sent to Huvelin, this time calling it the Rule of the Hermits of the Sacred Heart. The manuscript runs to more than two hundred pages, the first two sections in Latin and French, following closely the Rule of St Augustine, the final section specifying in minute detail the way of life of the Hermits. They should live in small communities, each with a solitary cell, meeting regularly for communal meals and for Mass. Having completed his Rule, Charles waited for a sign that it was God's will he should seek to establish it.

Such a sign seemed to come when he heard that the Mount of the Beatitudes was for sale. He would buy it and install himself there as a hermit to await the arrival of others who would join his order and grow into a small community, living the simple life of Nazareth and witnessing for Christ. He wrote to Huvelin explaining his plan, and to his family asking for the necessary 13,000 francs. Huvelin replied that, if he could buy the mountain he should do so, hand it over to the Franciscans, and stay there with them: 'I do not believe that this idea of being a hermit-priest is from God. However, if you feel an irresistible urging, take your Rule, go to the Patriarch of Jerusalem, throw yourself at his feet and ask for enlightenment.'[26]

Charles did so. On 11 June 1900, he set out for Jerusalem and presented himself, with his Rule, at the door of the Patriarch. He was dressed in his old blue blouse with a tattered turban on his head and, his sandals having worn out, with pieces of wood held by straps to his feet. He hid the holes in his trousers by tying pieces of paper around the knees with string. As he had caught the sun on the way there, his face was swollen and flushed like a drunkard's. He had to wait for hours before being admitted to an affronted Patriarch, who heard him briefly and sent him away to wait.

Charles was overjoyed that he had secured an audience and was content to leave the decision on his Rule in higher hands. He had to make a more personal one for himself, which was whether or not to become a priest. The Reverend Mother of the Poor Clares had been urging him to do so, but Charles saw clearly that the change in his status would interfere with his life of solitude and abjection. He felt a strong vocation to the contemplative life and still clung to his desire to occupy the place which Jesus had in Nazareth. On the other hand, his power to influence others and to act as a channel of grace would be enriched by the sacrament of the priesthood.

Charles was also torn between his desire to live the life of a hermit and that of a poor worker. The two are not compatible, since a worker cannot earn his keep in the desert. He wrote in a meditation that Christ had lived three lives: that of Nazareth, the solitude of the desert and the public ministry: 'of these three lives, it is that of Nazareth that You lived the longest, ten times longer than Your public life, two hundred and seventy times longer than Your hermit life'. But he went on to say that all three ways of life were perfect and divine, so we must each follow according to our calling. And, of the desert life, he wrote: 'Forty days or forty years, it does not matter! One person can only bear witness after years of life as a hermit, another, after only a few months of solitude, will be called to speak. It is in the desert that this happy transformation is brought about from the silk worm to the butterfly.'[27]

He had thought of discussing the matter with Huvelin in person and had written to him in May 1900 indicating that he might travel to France, but adding: 'I think, as a general rule, that hermits should stay in the desert – or at Nazareth, which gives me the calm of the desert – and that they are not at home with steamships and roads . . . it seems best to me not to leave the hermitage and to look for you where I always find you and where I hope to be united with you for ages on ages – in Jesus'. But when Huvelin wrote supporting the Reverend Mother, Charles set sail for France.

He returned to the Trappist Monastery of Notre-Dame des

Neiges and in December was made sub-deacon, in March deacon, and on 9 June 1901 he was ordained as a priest. That year he was forty-two years old and thought of himself as an old man.

> My retreats for the diaconate and the priesthood had shown me that I must live this life of Nazareth which seemed to be my vocation, not in the beloved Holy Land but among the sickest souls, the most abandoned of the sheep. The divine Banquet of which I was becoming minister must be offered not to the relatives and to the rich neighbours but to the lame, the blind and the poor, that is to say to souls lacking priests. In my youth I had travelled all over Algeria and Morocco. In Morocco, big as France, with ten million inhabitants, not a single priest in the interior; in the Sahara, seven or eight times as big as France and much more inhabited than was thought in the past, a dozen missionaries! No people seemed to be more abandoned than these.[28]

He wrote to Dom Martin: 'I've just been ordained priest and I'm getting ready to go to the Sahara to continue "the hidden life of Jesus of Nazareth", not to preach but to live in solitude the poverty and the humble work of Jesus, whilst trying to do good to souls, not by the word but by prayer, by offering Holy Mass, by penance and by the practice of charity.'

He still had his dream of founding an Order and now he located it. The project for purchasing the Mount of Beatitudes had fallen through when the agent with whom Charles was dealing pocketed the money and disappeared. It turned out that he was a fraud and the land had never been for sale. In a letter dated 23 June 1901 to his friend Henri de Castries, Charles wrote:

> We would like to found, on the Moroccan border, not a Trappist house, not a large and wealthy monastery, not a farm but a kind of small humble hermitage where a few poor monks could live on some fruit and a little barley harvested by their own hands in a strict enclosure, for penance and the adoration of the Blessed Sacrament, not leaving their cloister, not preaching but giving hospitality to all comers, good or bad, friend or enemy, Muslim or Christian . . .[29]

He wanted to found what was called in Morocco, a 'zaouia'. He had seen these little centres of hospitality, run by Muslim brothers, and wanted to imitate them in the service of his faith by giving shelter and welcome to all irrespective of race or religion. It was a project which might well have been thought deserving of general support, but the times were not favourable. In metropolitan France there was a strong anti-clerical movement which led to the law against congregations of 2 July 1901 and the secularisation of schools by the Combes Government. In Algeria, the Government was hostile to any religious penetration by the Catholic clergy which might antagonise the Muslims. The White Fathers and Sisters, founded thirty years earlier, had to limit their activities to the running of orphanages and dispensaries, confining their apostolate to the European community. They operated from a large monastery, the Maison Carré, about ten miles from Algiers.

Here Charles arrived in September 1901 and enjoyed, for a time, the magnificent gardens, superb food and fine wines of the Fathers, whose aim it was to raise the Arabs to a higher level of civilisation. But Charles, who preferred to sink to theirs, was uneasy and sought the permission of the Director of the Bureau of Native Affairs to move into the desert and set up his hermitage. Fortunately, the Director happened to be Commandant Lacroix, an old classmate from St-Cyr, and permission was given. He was allowed to settle at the oasis of Beni Abbes, largest oasis of the interior Saoura region, where there was a detachment of French troops and about twelve or fifteen hundred farmers, mainly of Negro or Berber origin, in three villages close to a lake.

Charles arrived there on 28 October 1901 and, after an official welcome from the garrison commander, Captain Regnault, decided that he would live apart from the settled area, on the *hamada*, the hot, rocky plateau. Here, he bought a small hollow for 1,000 francs, sent to him by his sister Marie. With the help of Captain Regnault's soldiers, he cleaned out the wells, dug a vegetable patch and built a small hut, to be his hermitage, 500 yards from the nearest house, of clay bricks. About thirteen feet high, its ceiling was of big beams of palm trees held up by vertical palm trunks, plastered inside with dark grey mortar. In every way it resembled the Arab huts in the area and was distinguished only by the cross outside. Charles wrote to his friend, the Trappist Father Jérôme:

> One must pass though the desert and spend some time there in order to receive the grace of God; it is there than one empties oneself, that one drives away from oneself everything which is not God and that one empties completely the house of one's soul in order to leave all of it to God alone. . . . The Israelites went through the desert; Moses lived in it before receiving his mission; St Paul, St John Chrysostom also prepared themselves in the Desert . . . It is a time of grace, a period though which every soul wanting to bear fruit must

necessarily pass. It needs this silence, this withdrawal, this oblivion of all created things amidst which God established his reign and moulds the interior spirit in it . . . Go further . . . look at St John the Baptist, look at Our Lord. Our Lord did not need it but he wanted to set the example for us . . . Later, the soul bears fruit in the exact measure by which the inner self has been formed.[30]

Although he sought the seclusion and separation of the hermit, he found, in practice, that his isolation from the European community made him available to passers-by. He became known to the local Muslims as a marabout – a holy man noted for his asceticism. Charles lived a life of prayer and abnegation which they found astonishing in a race they had observed to be without religion.

He allowed himself two meals a day, consisting of unseasoned porridge made of boiled barley and crushed dates, or a kind of unleavened maize bread dipped in an infusion of a Sahara weed which was called 'desert tea'. So miserable was his diet that the two Negroes he engaged to help with the vegetable garden on terms including bed and board preferred to stay with their own people.

He slept curled up on the floor of the chapel 'like a dog at his master's feet' as he put it. But then he moved into the tiny sacristy. An officer questioned this: 'I thought you said you were comfortable in the chapel?' 'That's why I moved.' He could no longer stretch out as he lay down to sleep, and pointed out that this too was in imitation of Christ, who could not stretch out on the Cross.

He sent a schedule of his daily life to Father Huvelin:

4 a.m.	Get up and recite offices of Prime and Tierce followed by Mass.
6 a.m.	Eat a few dates followed by an hour of adoration of the Blessed Sacrament. From then until 11 work – both manual and intellectual.
11.30 a.m.	Dinner (as described).
12.30–2 p.m.	Stations of the Cross, reading extracts from the Old and New Testaments. Other saintly books and meditation and theological study.
2–3 p.m.	Teaching the catechism to Arab children or to any Frenchmen at the garrison who ask for instruction.
3–5.50 p.m.	Adoration of the Blessed Sacrament.
6 p.m.	Supper (same as dinner).
7–8.30 p.m.	Religious discussion with any soldiers who call. Prayers, benediction, then to sleep on the mud floor.
Midnight	Chanting the *Veni Creator* and reciting the offices of Matins and Lauds.
1 a.m.	Back to sleep.

In an official report, Captain Regnault wrote:

The Reverend Father de Foucauld, anxious to resume his cloistered life, has traced on the ground near his building, boundaries beyond which he never goes. With the help of a few natives whose work he has remunerated with his own resources, he has sown barley in the ravine situated to the west of his abode. He has dug a few wells which allow him to water his corn. He lives on dates and bread which he receives from the administration, The money he owns is used by him to buy flour, barley and dates which he distributes to the poor.

In spite of the repeated entreaties of the officers in the garrison, he has never been willing to vary his diet; the vegetables which are sent to him from the mess are generally given to the poor or to passing guests who are given shelter in the guest room . . . The natives of the Saoura have a profound veneration for the Reverend Father de Foucauld. His generosity, his self-denial are the object of their astonishment and their admiration.[31]

He had two guest rooms built where he received officers and common soldiers; Frenchmen, Arabs, and Berbers; Muslims Christians and unbelievers, even black slaves and beggars. When the Moroccan nomads passed by they were welcomed and entertained. Charles decided to do more than simply give them food and shelter: he would provide service:

To wash the laundry of the poor and to clean their rooms *myself* as much as possible. To do all the lowest chores of the house as much as possible *myself* and not to leave them to anybody else; to keep the premises occupied by the natives in a state of cleanliness; to take upon myself everything which is *service* and to resemble Jesus, who was known among the Apostles as 'the one who serves' . . . To cook for the poor, when I will be able to do so, to bring them drink, food, not leave this service to others.[32]

He wrote at this time to a Protestant friend: 'I am sure that God will welcome into heaven those people who are good and honest. They do not need to be Roman Catholic. You are a Protestant, others are unbelievers, the Tuaregs are Muslims. I am sure that God will welcome us all if we merit it.'

He was enthused by his work and repeatedly wrote to Dom Martin at Notre-Dame des Neiges asking for helpers to settle with him at Beni Abbes. For example, in a letter dated 24 April 1902, 'the following three conditions must be fulfilled: (1) They must be good, religious and above all obedient (or disposed to be so); (2)

They must be prepared joyfully to die of hunger and lack every-thing for Jesus; (3) They must be prepared joyfully to have their heads cut off for Jesus.' Between May and September, unsurpris-ingly, such entreaties produced no volunteers. Dom Martin's response may be gathered from his reply to Monsignor Guérin of the White Fathers, who wrote about this time to ask whether a few Trappists could not be found to join Charles:

> You exhort me to send him an assistant, a companion . . . Monsignor, my esteem for Father Alberic's virtues is profound and deeply rooted in my twelve-year knowledge of him. The only thing about him that surprises me is that he works no miracles . . . but I must confess that I doubt a little his prudence, his discretion. The austerities which he practises and which he thinks of exacting from his companions are such that I tend to believe the neophyte would die of them quite quickly. The intense application of mind which he imposes on himself and which he wishes to impose on his disciples seems to me so superhuman that I fear he might drive his companions mad by such intense application before causing their death by the excess of his austerities.[33]

The fierceness of these austerities may well have been in some way a recompense for the laxities of his former life. 'When one wants to write on a blackboard', he once said, 'one must begin by rubbing out what has been written there. I am always busy rubbing out'[34] But he became more and more conscious of the conflict between his desire for the isolation of the hermit's life and his need to serve others. His Rule of the Little Brothers had visualised a life of silence and peace so as to create an atmosphere suitable for adoration and prayer, but he had located himself in what had become a public place where every kind of human misery revealed itself. The people Jesus had asked him to love were pressing around him with demands he could not meet. He wrote to Marie de Bondy on 29 August 1902:

> I should like for myself, and also for you because it seems to me a good thing, a little solitude and silence. On the one hand I am very solitary here because I have here not a single person who has the slightest atttachment to me . . . But, on the other hand, from 4.30 in the morning till 8.30 in the evening I never stop seeing and speaking to people: slaves, the poor, the sick, soldiers, travellers, the curious . . .[35]

It was in response to this ambivalence that he conceived a plan to journey alone south into Morocco. He saw himself as the spear-head of a civilising mission of apostolic clergy who could, united in the service of France, eldest daughter of the Church, bring Morocco out of barbarism to civilisation and Christianity. He drew up in his diary in January 1903 an outline 'Project for Morocco' which he submitted to Monsignor Guérin at Easter: 'What I think it best to do for the conversion of Morocco is to organise a small legion of religious, vowed to contemplation and charitable deeds, living very poorly from manual work, whose Rule would be summarised in three phrases: "Perpetual Adoration of the Blessed Sacrament"; "Imitation of the hidden life of Jesus of Nazareth"; and "Life in the Mission land". This small mission would be an advance guard ready to throw itself on the field of Morocco.' His symbolism was military, though he had written, on 30 March, to Marie de Bondy: 'My vocation is to be a silent and contemplative monk' and, later the same year, to Monsignor Guérin: 'If only you knew how much like a fish out of water I am when I leave my enclosure'.[36]

On 19 August 1903, Monsignor Guérin agreed that Charles could leave Beni Abbes and set out to settle in the desert in a place where he would be 'totally isolated', without the solace of a priest, deprived of the ability to say Mass, which required a server. After several delays caused by civil disturbances and local skirmishes, Charles set out on 13 January 1904. He had overcome the disability to say Mass by recruiting a Negro altar boy, Paul Embarek, who accompanied him, together with two donkeys carrying few provisions and a portable chapel. They headed right into the very heart of the Sahara, the land of the Tuareg.

When the world was a ball of fire, according to Tuareg legend, God amused himself by throwing rocks at it. Where they fell, they created mountains. When he grew tired of the game, he threw what was left in his hand at the centre of the Sahara desert. That created the Hoggar, a group of volcanic mountains that rise to peaks between 6,000 and 10,000 feet above the stone plateau. It is a wild region, crossed by nomad trails, where Charles hoped to combine a life of solitude and service. He wrote of his intention:

To settle among the Tuaregs as deeply in the heart of the country as possible; I shall pray, study language and translate the Holy Gospel. I shall establish relations with the Tuaregs. I shall live without enclosure. Every year I shall return to the north to go to confession.

On the way, I shall administer the Sacraments in all the army posts and, as I pass by, I shall speak of God with the natives.[37]

He also wrote that he wanted to situate himself 'a little apart to have at the same time the silence of retreat and the proximity of men'.

For the final part of his journey to the interior, Charles travelled with a Captain Dinaux, who was heading a military and commercial mission to the Hoggar. Dinaux wrote of him:

> He walked rapidly and almost bent double, pulling by the bridle one of his baggage camels. Behind him his catachumen Paul followed with the other camel. Brother Charles's emaciated face partially covered by a bristly beard which he trimmed roughly with a pair of scissors was lit up by his burning piercing eyes and his broad smile gave one a feeling of affection and understanding and good will to all . . .
>
> His baggage was reduced to the barest minimum. A small tent under which to celebrate Mass a folding table used as an altar, a flask of communion wine which was eked out drop by drop and the other things essential for holding a religious service.
>
> For his personal needs, he carried a small reserve of dried dates and grilled barley, two water skins and two blankets. He also had a small portable writing desk in which the ink was made of a mixture of charcoal and camel urine.[38]

But 1904 was to be a year of travel and not of settling down. Charles went on a long tour with his friend Laperrine, almost as far as Timbuktu, journeying a total of 3,250 miles before returning to make a retreat with Monsignor Guérin and the White Fathers. He returned to Beni Abbes in January 1905 but, when permission came from the Tuareg leader, Moussa, for him to build a hermitage in the Hoggar, he packed his things and left, with Paul, for a settlement he had selected on the high central plateau.

It was in a dry lake bed 333 to 667 feet wide, in the centre of a rock-strewn plateau about two miles across, at an altitude of 5,000 feet and ringed by distant mountains. There were no trees and no shade. A few wells had been dug by the local Harratin people, who had built low huts in a cluster of about twenty, sufficient to be given a settlement name. The place was called Tamanrasset.

When the Tuareg called at this place they would pitch their low tents of red leather near the wells and barter with the Harratin for the little barley and few vegetables planted between the rocks. Charles hoped to come into contact with them and built a low house nearby, of stones and dry mud with thick walls and a flat roof. There were no windows, just vents in the walls twenty inches wide to let in the cooling breezes of early morning and evening, with wooden shutters to keep out the heat of the day and the occasional violent storms.

There was only a single room inside, with a curtained corridor that served as a chapel. It could accommodate six people, which was ample since Tamanrasset had no Christians. Charles set about his task of producing some with tact: he concentrated on getting to know the Tuareg and winning their confidence, following the example of St Paul: 'To the Jews I became as a Jew that I might gain the Jews . . . to the Gentiles a Gentile that I might gain the Gentiles . . . so I become all things to all men that I may gain some of them at any cost' (1 Cor. 9:20–22).

He began a Tuareg–French and French–Tuareg dictionary. The language is actually called Tamashek, a dialect of the Berber language. He wanted to encourage it partly because the alternative language, Arabic, was associated with Islam: 'The Tuareg should not be taught Arabic, which brings them closer to the Koran; on the contrary they should be weaned away from it. They must be taught Tamashek, an excellent, very easy language.'

He rarely left the hermitage. He had planned his life again to resemble that of Jesus at Nazareth. He wrote in his diary for 22 July 1905:

> Make, whether alone or with a few brothers, the life of Nazareth your objective in everything and for everything, in its simplicity and its breadth. . . . no special clothing – like Jesus in Nazareth; no enclosure – like Jesus in Nazareth; a house not far from an inhabited place, but close to a village – like Jesus in Nazareth; not less than eight hours' work a day (manual or other – as much as possible manual) – like Jesus in Nazareth . . . the unmost poverty in everything: Jesus in Nazareth.[39]

In abandoning Beni Abbes for Tamanrasset he was also giving up the idea of forming a community in favour of solitude. He realised that a community is always set apart from local people; a monastery is part of a local landscape but its monks are never part of a local community, however much they may wish to belong. But the solitary from another place can be in the closest possible contact with the natives. He wrote: 'Residing alone is good, even if one doesn't do much; one becomes *du pays* [of the place]'. He had the balance which he sought: he was a hermit, not a missionary, but an available hermit. 'When my poor neighbours wish to see me they find me; the rest of the time I am alone with the best company, the good God and one does not weary of a *tête-à-tête* with Him.'[40]

On 17 May 1906, Paul Embarek finally gave up his attempt to share the asceticism of his mentor and left. His departure affected Charles deeply because he was canonically unable to say Mass without a server. The only recompense was that his solitude became more intense, and he wrote to Marie de Bondy on 15 July:

> I find this desert life profoundly, deeply sweet. It is so pleasant and so healthy to set oneself down in solitude, face to face with the eternal things; one feels oneself penetrated by the truth. Also I find it hard to leave this silence and this solitude and to travel; but the will of the Beloved, whatever it may be, must not only be preferred but adored, cherished and blessed.[41]

One trip he did make was to the White Fathers, where he made a retreat, explained his plans to Monsignor Guérin and left exulting in having secured at last a helper to share his mission, one Brother Michael. Unfortunately, Brother Michael's constitution proved unequal to the rigours of the journey and he turned back before they reached Tamanrasset, where Charles arrived alone on 6 July 1907.

He carried on with the research into language and traditions. Laperrine recorded:

> It is a windfall for Father de Foucauld when he can get hold of a few old ladies of the Tuareg nobility because they know the most about the traditions, legends, genealogies and poems. Nothing is more amusing than to see him enthroned, pencil in hand, in the midst of an Areopagus of old dowagers sitting on the ground and talking while they sip their tea and smoke their pipes.[42]

This attention to the locals was also motivated by a genuine affection and concern for them. This was reciprocated. Lapperine also records:

> A noble woman of the Hoggar who felt great gratitude for Father de Foucauld ever since he had saved her 5 small children from the famine of 1907 said to me one day: 'How terrible it is to think that such a good man will go to hell when he dies because he is not a Muslim'. And she confessed that she and many of her companions prayed to Allah every day that the Marabout might become a Muslim.[43]

December 1907 brought the saddest Christmas for many years.

His diary entry records: 'This night, no Mass for the first time in twenty-one years.' He wrote to Marie de Bondy: "Right up to the last moment I hoped that somebody would come. But nobody came, not a Christian traveller, not a soldier, not the permission to celebrate Mass alone. I have had no letters for three months – for more than three months . . . may the will of the Well-Beloved be blessed in all things."[44] The permission he sought was obtained from Pope Pius X by Father Burtin of the White Fathers, who travelled to Rome and sought an audience to request special dispensation so that Charles could celebrate Mass alone. The dispensation was granted and arrived at Tamanrasset on 31 January 1908.

That year Charles reached the age of fifty and seemed to have arrived at an accommodation between the demands of his calling and of his situation. He wrote:

> By vocation, I ought to be living a hidden life in solitude, not talking and travelling. On the other hand, some travelling is required of me by the need of the souls in these lands where I am alone . . . I am trying to reconcile these two things. I have two hermitages a thousand miles apart. Every year I spend three months in the northern one, six months in the southern one and three months coming and going. When I am in one of the hermitages, I live there as an enclosed monk, trying to build for myself a life of work and prayer – the work of Nazareth. On my journeys I think of the flight into Egypt and of the annual journey of the holy family to Jerusalem. Both at my hermitages and when travelling, I try to make contact as much as possible with the native peoples.[45]

His contact with the Tuareg was from a position of sympathy rather than superiority. Whereas the attitude of the Catholic missions overseas had frequently been to attract native peoples through demonstrating a superiority in education, medicine or technology, Charles had the resources only to love them. 'My apostolate', he wrote, 'must be of kindness. In seeing me, people must say to themselves: "Since this is a good man, his religion must be good". And if I am asked why I am gentle and good, I must say: "Because I am the servant of someone far more good than I. If only you knew how good is my master, Jesus." ' When Dr Hérisson, in charge of a medical mission to the Tuareg, met Charles in 1909 and asked how he should set about winning their confidence, Charles replied:

> Don't be the assistant-surgeon or even the doctor with them; don't take offence at their familiarities or their easy manners; be human

and charitable *and always gay*. You must always laugh, even when saying the simplest things. I, as you see, am always laughing, showing very ugly teeth. Laughing puts the person who is talking to you in a good humour; it draws men closer together, allows them to understand one another better; it sometimes brightens up a gloomy character; it is always a charity. With the Tuareg you must always laugh.[46]

On his fifty-first birthday, 15 September 1909, Charles made a trip to a remote and beautiful mountain plain four days' journey south from Tamanrasset, where there was a heart-stopping view over the peaks that made him feel close to God. His yearning for total solitude was reawakened and he decided to build a hermitage there. The place is called Asekroum. It is at an altitude of 9,500 feet, which is 1,600 feet higher than the nearest place for water, and far from all routes of communication. There is no soil there – only black, green and red stone. It can be reached only by scaling a great cliff 330 feet high, and all the materials for the hermitage had to be hauled up there on men's backs. The simple stone hut measured 26 feet by 13 feet and was 6 feet 6 inches high. Charles moved in on 1 July 1911:

> I am completely alone on top of a mountain which towers over almost all the others and which is the orographic centre of the region: the view is marvellous, the eye encompasses the mountains of the Ahaggar which slope off to the north and south as far as the immense desert plains. In the foreground there is the most amazing tangle of peaks, rocky needles and piles of rocks in fantastic shapes. It is a beautiful and lonely spot which I love very much; close by there are a great number of ravines which, as soon as it rains, are covered with scented herbs and where the Tuareg immediately pitch their tents to drink the good mountain milk![47]

He explained to his superiors that he had retreated to the interior because the Tuareg were not often seen at Tamanrasset – to follow the nomads and be closer to them. Still he sought solitude whilst at the same time being available to the locals. On 6 December 1911, he wrote:

> One or two meals taken together, a day or half a day spent together put us on far better terms with one another than a great number of visits of half an hour or an hour, as at Tamanrasset. Some of these families are comparatively good, as good as they can be without Christianity. These souls are directed by natural lights; although Mussulmans by faith, they are very ignorant of Islam and have not been spoiled by it. In this direction, the work I am doing is very

good. Lastly, my presence is an opportunity for the officers to come into the very heart of the country.[48]

One of those officers, Captain Neiger, who visited the outpost frequently, noticed that Charles was less enthusiastic in his welcome for his fellow countrymen than he was for the Tuareg:

Foucauld only willingly let his solitude be violated in favour of the Tuareg, that is to say his apostolate . . . To relinquish his cherished isolation required an effort of renunciation and self-denial from him. I cannot forget that, one evening, pointing to the surroundings of his poor hut, he said: 'I have a horror of the world and its hypocrisy'. He was quite obviously speaking about our world.[49]

He was involved in that world more than he would have wished by the turn of international events and by his own deep patriotism. On 30 March 1912, Morocco became a French protectorate and Charles did not hide his hope that this might be a step towards annexation:

Algeria–Tunisia–Morocco–Sudan–Sahara! What a fine Empire! So long as we civilize it, gallicise it, and don't settle for just maintaining and exploiting it. If we try to civilise, to raise to our level, these peoples who are thirty million now and who will be, thanks to the peace, sixty million in fifty years' time, this African Empire will be, in half a century, a glorious extension of France . . .[50]

To 'gallicise' meant, ultimately, to Christianise according to the mission of the 'eldest daughter of the Church', but Charles was sensitive and realistic about the inadvisability of proselytising among the Tuareg. He wrote:

They are Muslim by faith but without any religious instruction and with very few practices; it is an Islam of the surface only. I have some excellent friends among them. There are not as yet any Christians among them. I do not want there to be any for some years to come. Before speaking to them about religion, we have to win their confidence and friendship; we should demonstrate our religion by practising its virtues in front of them rather than by words.[51]

Because of his close contacts with the Tuareg and long experience of life in their country, Charles was frequently consulted by visiting French missions on the development of policy in the country. He so distinguished himself that the French government wanted to award him the Légion d'Honneur, but he refused it with the explanation:

When the Tuareg see this decoration on the tunics of our officers they know that France has honoured their valour or some other meritorious act. As it concerns myself, I prefer to remain as insignificant as possible, like the divine carpenter of Nazareth. I am a monk, made for silence, not for speech or publicity, trying only to prepare the way for those who will follow me.[52]

The early years of the First World War had little effect on Charles in his isolation. He spent his time between hermitages, working on various projects to help the study of the Tuareg language: the Tuareg–French dictionary, a Tuareg grammar, a collection of Tuareg poems and proverbs with a French translation and a collection of Tuareg prose texts. It seemed, for a time, unlikely that hostilities would affect him. Turkey had entered the struggle on the German side, and a collection of tribes closely linked with the Turks of Tripoli, the Senussi, started to range the desert in raiding parties. They were staunch Muslims and represented a threat, though a distant one, to a lonely French Catholic. Charles saw the war through the eyes of a nineteenth-century French patriot. 'I never really understood the crusades,' he wrote, on 9 January 1916, 'but now I understand them. God will again save the world through the eldest daughter of his Church.'[53]

There was a drought that year which reduced the food supplies and made the little settlement at Tamanrasset a possible target for raiding parties. In June 1916 a small fort was built there where the locals could take cover if the Senussi attacked. Charles designed this and supervised the work. It was a massive square construction of unbaked bricks about 50 feet long, its walls 6 feet 8 inches wide at the base rose to 26 feet 8 inches high ending in a watchtower and battlements. There was only one entrance: a little bridge leading to a low door protected by a parapet. The lintel was nearly three feet high and the door so low that entry could only be gained by stooping. The door opened on to a low brick corridor leading to another door. Both were secured by stout locks.

Charles wrote to a friend:

The corner of the Sahara from which I write to you is still calm. However, we are on the qui vive on account of the increasing agitation of the Senussi in Tripoli; our Tuareg here are faithful but we might be attacked by the Tripolitans. I have transformed my hermitage into a little fort; there is nothing new under the sun; when I see my embrasures I think of the fortified convents and churches of the 10th century. How old things come back and how what we thought had disappeared is forever reappearing![54]

Charles had built the fort for the protection of the local farmers rather than himself. He could easily have escaped to a French garrison if danger threatened, and at the fort there was no military force to protect him. He carried on life there much as in the hermitage: daily Mass with his server Paul, who had returned, work on his collection of Tuareg language books. A letter to René Bazin dated 16 July 1916 shows his aims and ambitions at the time – and his sense of prophecy:

> Let us hope that when we have won the war our colonies will make fresh progress. What a beautiful mission for our younger sons of France, to go and colonise the African territories of the mother-country, not to get rich but to make France beloved, to make souls French and above all to obtain eternal salvation for them.
>
> I think that if the Mussulmans of our colonial empire of North Africa are not converted gradually and gently, a national movement like that of Turkey will come about: an intellectual elite will be formed in the large towns, educated *à la française* but having neither the French mind nor heart, an élite which will have lost all the faith of Islam but will keep the label in order to be able to use it to influence the masses . . . National or barbarian feeling will therefore become worked up in the educated élite . . . it will make use of Islam as a lever to rouse the ignorant mass and seek to create an independent Mussulman African Empire.[55]

On the evening of 1 December 1916, Charles was alone in the fort, Paul having returned to the village. He was securely locked in and had nothing to fear. He heard a knocking at the door and when he asked who was there the reply came in a voice which he recognised – that of El Madani, a local farmer – calling out that he had brought the post. He opened the door and was seized. There were about thirty Tuareg, all of them Senussi. They bound him in a kneeling position, his hands tied to his ankles behind his back, and threw him on to the embankment near the wall of the fortress. A fifteen-year-old boy, Sermi Ag Tohra, was given a rifle and told to stand guard over him.

For half an hour the Senussi carried out of the fort the things they wanted to steal. They were arguing about what should be done with the marabout when two camel drivers from the village appeared to collect their post. Charles tried to stand up and shout a warning to them but they were both shot dead and the boy, panicking, shot Charles through the right ear. The bullet emerged from the left eye and embedded itself in the wall of the tower to the left of the entrance to the fort. For a few seconds the body of Charles remained half erect, then it slid slowly down and curled on the ground.

His life seemed to have produced nothing. The civilisation and Christianising of North Africa, of which he dreamed, did not take place. His chapel at Beni Abbes became a school for teaching the Koran, and the fort where he died a barrack room for French soldiers. He had made only one convert in his life: an elderly Negro woman, and he had been deserted by the Tuareg he served. He had not succeeded in persuading any fellow priests to join him in the desert, and the Orders of Little Brothers and Sisters which he worked so hard to bring into being existed only as a Rule on paper. The grain of wheat planted by his death, to use an image he was fond of quoting, was a long time germinating. But it bore fruit in an order of men and women who experience and witness the long-forgotten reality that sanctity is possible in everyday life. And this witness is based on Charles de Foucauld's experience and teaching.

When he first experienced conversion he wanted to leave the world and dedicate himself completely to God. The Church has institutions which enable and encourage this complete severance from society. The basic context in which monastic life is lived is that of enclosure, and monasteries were built to be self-contained, so that their monks need never journey outside their walls. The promise of 'stability' made by each monk on entering the monastery means that he is prepared to spend the rest of his days behind its walls. When Charles became a Trappist it was with the expectation of cutting himself off physically from society for the rest of his life. And when he left the Trappists and first drew up his regulations for the Little Brothers of Jesus, he proposed that their enclosure should be 'very severe'. In his 1899 Rule, he proposed that the small house occupied by the Little Brothers should be 'entirely closed by solid walls in general 4 or 5 metres high'.[56]

Although he never succeeded in erecting such a barrier around his own hermitages, he did outline their boundaries and for a long time confined himself strictly within them. But his desire to shut out the world was confused by his wish to witness – if not to go forth and teach, at least to allow what Christ had worked in him to be seen. And this he did by welcoming and serving the Tuareg. So a gradual change took place in his attitude to his status as a desert hermit. From being a secluded abstracted role which needed the protection of barriers against the intrusions of the world, it became a commitment to break down barriers and create understanding.

The calling for solitude, which he never denied to the end of his life, developed into a need for separation from his own culture. He always resented the intrusion into his hermitages of civilised Westerners, but rarely that of the Tuareg. Indeed, he saw that a degree of apartness from his own culture was necessary to make him acceptable to the people he sought to serve, the poorest of the poor. And this insight has been built into the way of life of the Little Brothers and Sisters, who recognise that the clergy in our own society have a certain social rank which places them above and to a degree out of touch with the poor. However well-intentioned the priest, once he puts on priest's clothes and lives in the priest's house he is classified as belonging to the middle classes. He may wish it were not so and that priests were classless, but the social reality is that they are not.

This is why the Little Brothers and Sisters deliberately live among the poor, without distinctive clothes or special houses, to demonstrate that a truly Christian life can be lived in the conditions in which others are forced to live. The peace and seclusion of the great monastic houses create an atmosphere of tranquillity in which it is easy to imagine that God is at hand. When we visit them we sense a commitment to prayer and a consciousness of spiritual realities which we may, for a time, share so long as we stay within the walls. It soon evaporates in the world outside. We may be tempted to feel that it is relatively easy to lead a Christian life when cut off in a contemplative monastic order from the pressures and temptations of the world. But Christ himself did not lead a monastic existence. And the Little Brothers and Sisters of Christ, in imitation of his life, try to preserve and live according to their faith while fully engaged in the world. This is the inspiration of Charles de Foucauld. It is a kind of solitude in society.

CHAPTER SEVEN

The Waters of Contradiction:
Thomas Merton

The contradictions in the character of Thomas Merton and the situations which he faced for most of his adult life forced him to examine and justify the solitary calling to himself and to others. Merton loved people and yet needed solitude. He was for twenty-seven years a member of a strictly enclosed order of Christian monks, and yet was described, by *Time* magazine, as 'the most publicly visible Christian contemplative since Simon Stylites'.

During the years that followed his vow of silence he published over 300 articles and thirty-seven books, including an auto-biography that became a bestseller. In America it was called *The Seven Storey Mountain*; in Britain, edited by Evelyn Waugh, it appeared as *Elected Silence*. Merton was the hermit celebrity of his time; he sought solitude but had no particular commitment to obscurity. The story of his search throws light on every aspect of the hermit's life – emotional, practical, psychological and spiritual – because when Thomas Merton became committed to a cause, that commitment was fired by his unusual energy and intellectual power. His long pursuit of solitude was opposed by those he had a duty to obey, and so he set out to win them over by a mass of historical witness that ranged from Lao-Tse to Charles de Foucauld. There has never been so powerful, so well informed and so persuasive an apologist for the solitary life.

Merton's early years might well have encouraged independence of character. He had few national or family ties. He was born on the last day of January 1915 in the Eastern Pyrenees and so was technically of French nationality. He would often call himself a Catalan. But his father was from New Zealand and his mother was American. Both were artists without firm ties to their home countries. When Merton was one year old they moved to America, but by the time he was six his mother had died and he lived a nomadic existence, spending time with his father in Bermuda, Massachusetts and in France as well as staying with his grandparents in New York.

At the age of thirteen, he moved to England to attend preparatory school in Ealing, from where he went a year later to Oakham, a public school, in Rutland. There he won prizes in English, was a fair hand at boxing, and began to smoke Craven A cigarettes. He changed to a pipe when he became a prefect and kept his lips tight shut during morning prayers. He won an exhibition to Clare College, Cambridge, and went up in October 1933.

At Cambridge things went wrong for him. He ordered a set of tails, drank a great deal, 'ran with a pack of hearties' (his own phrase), and argued with his landlady about the girls he took back to his rooms. He fathered an illegitimate child, and his work was so disappointing that, when he visited his godfather in New York in 1935, he was persuaded to stay in America.

There he enrolled in Columbia University and became a part of the undergraduate literary scene, dressed in a three-piece suit with gold watch chain, topped by a soft felt hat. He became art editor of the Columbia *Jester*, whose editor, Robert Lax, was to become a lifelong friend, and he edited the Columbia Yearbook for 1937. He had found a congenial place where spontaneity was encouraged and wit applauded. Because of his later fame, his Augustinian confessions and the hagiographic strivings of later admirers, it is difficult to recapture the Thomas Merton of 1938, as he stood, unknown to himself, on the edge of conversion; but the evidence points to an energetic young man with a retentive memory and zest for life, a wider experience of the world than most of his contemporaries, but distinguished by no particular achievement, calling or commitment to hard work. If the hints of future greatness were there, they were no more than the normal transient but exhilarating convictions of omnipotence that visit all the top dogs of undergraduate society.

Of his conversion to Christianity much has been written. The simple Christian explanation is that he was touched by the grace of God. But grace tends to operate in situations which allow for it to be discounted. The secular or psychological analysis focuses on the admission into his life of the authority of mystery. When the intellect has been fine-tuned to become the key instrument for acquiring personal success, social status and the respect of friends, every experience or precept is validated by being checked against it. Intuition is intellectually sloppy; mysticism a cop-out. Mysteries are there to be solved, and their solution is only a matter of time and effort.

Merton had long admired the writings of Aldous Huxley, rationalist, novelist, intellectual and grandson of the man who coined the word 'agnostic', and when Huxley began to preach a sort of eclectic mysticism, finding realities in the teachings of Eastern religions, Merton was able to take those realities seriously. Huxley was, in Merton's words, 'too sharp and intelligent' to be taken in by the phony. A sign of his changing priorities was the decision to abandon his idea of doing post-graduate research into the eighteenth-century writer Richard Graves, the satirist of religious enthusiasts, and take up the study of William Blake, most enthusiastic of religious poets. He was committing himself to taking seriously those human experiences that lie beyond rational analysis.

He took the decision to become a Catholic one evening in late October 1938. He was sitting at home, reading a biography of Gerard Manley Hopkins. He had come to the point where Hopkins, a student at Oxford, is thinking of becoming a Catholic and writes to Newman for advice. The experience, the most crucial in his life, is best told in Merton's own words:

> All of a sudden, something began to stir within me, something began to push me, to prompt me. It was a movement that spoke like a voice.
>
> 'What are you waiting for?' it said. 'Why are you sitting here? Why do you still hesitate? You know what you ought to do, why don't you do it?'
>
> I stirred in the chair. I lit a cigarette, looked out the window at the rain, tried to shut the voice up. 'Don't act on impulses', I thought. 'This is crazy. This is not rational. Read your book.'
>
> Hopkins was writing to Newman, at Birmingham, about his indecision.
>
> 'What are you waiting for?' said the voice within me again. 'Why are you sitting there? It is useless to hesitate any longer. Why don't you get up and go?'
>
> I got up and walked restlessly around the room. 'It's absurd', I thought. 'Anyway, Father Ford would not be there at this time of day. I would only be wasting time.'
>
> Hopkins had written to Newman, and Newman had replied to him, telling him to come and see him at Birmingham.
>
> Suddenly, I could bear it no longer. I put down the book, and got into my raincoat and started down the stairs. I went out into the

street. I crossed over and walked along by the grey wooden fence towards Broadway, in the light rain.

And then everything inside me began to sing – to sing with peace, to sing with strength, and to sing with conviction.[1]

It is a characteristic of conversion experiences that they remain unconvincing to the non-believer. Merton's is no exception. An insistent inner voice urging a specific course of action leading to faith is not granted to most of us. Our inner promptings tend to be vague and often connected with anxieties about our situation or the satisfaction of our appetites. Most agnostics would say that they would happily listen to the voice of God if he would only speak to them and they take his silence to indicate either that he isn't interested or that he doesn't exist. The unanswered cry for a sign is as old as religion itself. But the voice that speaks unambiguously and with authority takes away free will and is rarely heard. Merton recognised authority in the prompting but doesn't tell us why.

Having become a Catholic, Merton toyed with the idea of becoming a priest – in fact the idea had come to mind even before his baptism. Instead, he returned for a time to his old way of life, only turning his attention to Christianity at Mass on Sunday mornings. Yet he was curious about the men and women who had made a more total commitment to the Truth he had accepted, and the idea of becoming a monk pressed in on him. He began to study the different Orders and found the Benedictines too likely to turn him into a schoolmaster and the Jesuits too disciplined. He was attracted to the scholarship of the Dominicans, but decided against them when he read a French book which described their sleeping together in dormitories. The Franciscans seemed to have an agreeable lack of order and external hierarchy in their simple attachment to poverty, and Merton went for a time to a Franciscan house in New York and became a member of the Franciscan Third Order, wearing two pieces of brown cloth under his clothes. But he decided that this was not the right path for him and turned elsewhere.

He records in *The Seven Storey Mountain* that he had learned about the Trappists from the Catholic Encyclopedia and that he was even more attracted by the hermitages of the Camaldolese:

What I saw in those pages pierced me to the heart like a knife. What wonderful happiness there was, then, in the world! There were still men on this miserable, noisy, cruel earth who tasted the marvelous joy of silence and solitude, who dwelt in forgotten mountain cells, in secluded monasteries, where the news and desires and appetites and conflicts of the world no longer reached them.

They were free of the burden of the flesh's tyranny, and their clear vision, clean of the world's smoke and its bitter sting, were raised to heaven and penetrated into the depths of heaven's infinite and healing light.

They were poor, they had nothing and therefore were free and possessed everything, and everything they touched struck off something of the fire of divinity. And they worked with their hands, silently ploughing and harrowing the earth, and sowing seed in obscurity and reaping their small harvests to feed themselves and the other poor. They built their own houses and made, with their own hands, their own furniture and their own coarse clothing, and everything around them was simple and primitive and poor because they were the least and the last of men, they had made themselves outcasts seeking outside the walls of the world, Christ, most poor and rejected of men.[2]

The article in the 1912 edition of the Catholic Encyclopedia which Merton consulted is more sober in tone and describes the Trappist life in detail, from the monks' diet to their underwear. Merton's reaction to it deserves comment, as it is characteristic of most of his writing for most of his life. He could be suddenly fired with enthusiasm by the essence of an idea which he would then celebrate in rhapsodic prose. There are writers so intoxicated by the power of words that they set down far more than they feel; but Merton was not one of them. He wrote more passionately than most because he felt more intensely.[3] He had the intellectual power to grasp the essentials of an idea and the emotional depth to be totally enthused by it. The article ends with an encomium: 'Too much credit cannot be given to these noble bands of monks, who by their lives demonstrated to a corrupt world that man could have a higher ambition than the gratification of the mere natural instincts of this ephemeral life'. Merton was inspired by this and made a retreat, in Holy Week of 1941, to the Trappist monastery at Gethsemani, in Kentucky, where he felt his faith nourished by the experience. But then came the appeal of good works, without which, as St James tells us, faith is dead.

He heard a talk by Catherine de Hueck, who was running an establishment called Friendship House, in Harlem, for Catholic Action. She spoke vigorously against the contemplatives who buried themselves in the study of dead subjects and did not notice the suffering around them. When somebody asked about the need for a life of prayer without ceasing, she replied: 'Baloney'. Merton was impressed and decided to help at Friendship House, where he moved in August 1941. He spent some weeks handing out clothes, mopping floors and visiting the sick, and he wrote in his journal of the need for the Catholic Church to be more aware of social injustice. But he was torn between the contradictions of his need to write, his wish to help the underprivileged and the strong pull of the contemplative life.

Towards the end of 1941, he planned another retreat at Gethsemani to consider his various options, but a letter from the Draft Board which arrived on 1 December firmed his purpose. He had previously been rejected for military service on medical grounds, but the letter stated that the requirements had been lowered and that he was likely to be drafted. The choice was starkly there: to join the Army or become a monk. He sent most of his clothes to Friendship House, gave away most of his books, and, carrying a small suitcase, set off for the Trappist monastery to seek admission as a postulant.

On 13 December 1941 Merton was accepted as a postulant to the choir at Gethsemani, and on 21 February 1942 he became Brother M. Louis Merton of the Cistercian Order of the Strict Observance. At this stage his commitment was to a secluded contemplative life in community with fellow monks. He wrote that 'By this time God had given me enough sense to realize at least obscurely that this is one of the most important aspects of the religious vocation: the first and most elementary test of one's call to the religious life – whether as a Jesuit, Franciscan, Cistercian or Carthusian – is the willingness to accept life in a community in which everybody is more or less imperfect'.[4] That willingness was to be put severely to the test.

The monastery at Gethsemani, like all Christian monasteries, lived according to the sixth-century Rule of St Benedict, This had been strictly interpreted by the Cistercians in the eleventh century and, still more strictly, by the seventeenth-century Abbé Armand-Jean de Rancé, Abbot of La Trappe, in France, who had founded the order of Trappists. Gethsemani tried to follow the French pattern of life. The monks there ate no meat, fish or eggs; they fasted rigorously during Lent and Advent. They wore long robes, scapular and cowl, made of thick woollen material in the winter, durable denim in summer. The vow of stability which they took confined them to the monastery for life. They lived, died and were buried within its enclosure. When Merton entered the walls of Gethsemani there was no reason to suppose he would ever again see the world outside.

The daily programme of activities at Gethsemani was:

2.00 a.m.	Rise, go to choir and recite Matins and Lauds.
2.30 a.m.	Meditation.
3.00 a.m.	Night Office.
4.00 a.m.	Priests say private masses or go to communion.
5.30 a.m.	Prime, followed by Chapter. (Small breakfast permitted to those who do not wish to fast until dinner.)
6.30 a.m.	Reading, study or private prayer.

After this time, the winter and summer programmes diverged.

Winter:

7.45 a.m.	(Tierce, High Mass and Sext)
11.07 a.m.	(None),
4.30 p.m.	(Vespers),
6.10 p.m.	(Compline), *Salve Regina*, followed by examination of conscience and bed at 7.00 p.m.

Summer:

9.30 a.m.	(Tierce, High Mass, Sext)
1.07 p.m.	(None),
5.15 p.m.	(Vespers),
7.10 p.m.	(Compline) *Salve Regina*, examination of conscience and bed at 8.00 p.m.

The intervening hours were spent in work, reading or private prayer. Meals were: Dinner at 11.30 a.m. (winter) or 11 a.m. (summer); Collation at 5.30 p.m. (winter) or Supper at 6.00 p.m. (summer). In the summer there was a 'Meridienne', or siesta, between 12 noon and 1 p.m.[5]

There was no privacy. The monks ate, worked, studied and slept together. In the dormitory each had a tiny curtained area containing a wooden bed with a straw-filled pallet and bolster which formed a rudimentary cell. Merton wrote later that 'two hundred and seventy lovers of solitude are packed into a building that was meant for seventy'. As for writing, the monks were permitted to send only four half-page letters a year.

But Merton was allowed, by special permission of the Abbot, to write poetry, and his first published book, *Thirty Poems*, appeared in November 1944. Two years later he was given permission to begin work on an autobiographical work, 'Something, as I see it now', he wrote to a friend, 'like a cross between Dante's *Purgatory* and Kafka and a medieval miracle play called "The Seven Storey Mountain". . .'[6] The book was published in 1948 and became an immediate success. Merton, and Gethsemani, became nationally, and shortly afterwards internationally, famous.

It was in the same year that he wrote to his friend Robert Lax about his need for solitude. He was wryly pragmatic about it at the time, pointing out that it would be difficult for him to live as a hermit since he could not cook and was not able to live on roots. But he was finding the perpetual togetherness of the Trappists more and more trying. He had professed his solemn vows on 19 March 1947, feeling at the time that God was asking him 'to give up all my aspirations for solitude and for a contemplative life'. He found some reassurance in the frustration, being convinced for a time that a sure sign that a course of action was approved by God was that it went against his own aspirations. But he was becoming too aware of the pitfalls of the spiritual life to hold firmly to such a conviction and discussed with the Abbot the possibility of joining the Carthusians, who lived in separate cells.

The Abbot was reluctant to release him. Not only were the royalties from *The Seven Storey Mountain* helping to repair the monastery, there had been an increase in applications from new postulants since the appearance of the book, and the Trappist way of life had found a wide and approving audience. It would be unfortunate if Merton, who had become a public figure, should be publicly seen to find that way of life unsatisfactory. The Abbot was discouraging and, indeed, refused to allow Merton to be ordained as sub-deacon until he promised not to leave and join the Carthusians. Merton made the promise and was ordained in the spring of 1949.

His health was not good, and from the autumn of 1949 to the end of 1950 he was frequently ill and in hospital. At this time he read Thoreau and mentioned in his journal the importance to him of the ideas in *Walden*. The ideal of the solitary life was still with him, but so was the notion that his ambitions might well be different from God's design. He was writing at the time *The Sign of Jonas*, so called because, as he explains in the Prologue: 'Like the prophet Jonas, whom God ordered to go to Nineveh, I found myself with an almost uncontrollable desire to go in the opposite direction. God pointed in one way and all my "ideals" pointed in the other. It was when Jonas was travelling as fast as he could away from Nineveh towards Tharsis that he was thrown overboard and swallowed by a whale who took him where God wanted him to go'.[7]

He was beginning to accommodate his ideas of solitude to the situation in the monastery. He writes in the same book: 'Solitude is not found so much by looking outside the boundaries of your dwelling, as by staying within. Solitude is not something you must hope for in the future. Rather, it is a deepening of the present and unless you look for it in the present you will never find it.'[8]

He asked the Abbot at this time for permission to spend several hours a day alone in the forest. The Abbot was not unsympathetic but needed a precedent and looked for one in the history of the Cistercians. He discovered that in medieval times there was indeed an official, under the cellarer, who was called the 'forester', and he made application to the General Chapter of the Order to revive the office at Gethsemani. Approval was given and Merton was appointed. This gave him the chance to be alone with the trees and, inspired by Thoreau, he began to learn their names. It was a release from the constant pressures of life in the community, but it was not enough, and Merton pursued his applications to transfer to another Order. At this time he had decided on the Camaldolese, who live in a collection of separate hermitages, and he wrote to them in 1952.

But he was still confused about how far he should follow his own inclinations, and in his journal for 10 October 1952 he wrote:

> What am I certain of? If it were merely a question of satisfying my own desires and aspirations I would leave for Camaldoli in ten minutes. Yet it is *not* merely a question of satisfying my own desires. On the contrary: there is one thing holding me at Gethsemani. And that is the cross. Some mystery of the wisdom of God has taught me that perhaps after all Gethsemani is where I belong because I do *not* fit in and because here my ideals are practically all frustrated.[9]

Merton felt keenly the pressure of his own desires and aspirations, particularly those which drove him to seek solitude. But he was always aware of the need to check those desires against some higher authority to avoid a backsliding into self-indulgence.

On October 22 he wrote:

> . . . a man cannot go on to be a hermit until he has proved himself as a cenobite. I have in no way proved myself as a cenobite. I have been beating the air. I am not really a monk – never have been

except in my own imagination. But it is a relief to know that. What exhausts me is the entertainment of all my illusions . . . I can make reparation for my impiety – not necessarily by imitating Abbot de Rance (everything in me says that he is not supposed to be my model) but by living as perfectly as I can the Rule and Spirit of St Benedict – obedience, humility, work, prayer, simplicity, the love of Christ.[10]

At Gethsemani he was taking a few steps closer to becoming a solitary. His earnings for the monastery had funded a building pro-gramme, and the workers had left behind a disused toolshed. It was hauled by Traxcavator to the woods beyond the horse pasture out of sight, and Merton was given permission to go there for med-itation. He could only use it for certain hours of the day and it was not exclusively his, but he loved it and called it 'St Anne's'. In his journal for 28 January 1953 he writes: 'Fine ideas in Picard's "World of Silence", a train of the old times sings in my present silence at St Anne's where the watch without a crystal ticks on the little desk'. Picard was a Christian existentialist who wrote about the need for silence and solitude in order to allow a person to develop an inviolable personal integrity. That essential and unique personhood is the place where one meets God – and other people – but it can only be reached through solitude. Merton was to expe-rience this and be transformed by it.

But he was held back by his commitment to the Trappist Order. At this time he read an article in the October 1952 issue of the jour-nal *La Vie Spirituelle* which seemed to further his cause. It was written by a Dominican writer and called 'L'Erémitisme dans la vie spirituelle et dans la vie religieuse'. Merton said it had the effect on him that Dale Carnegie might have on a despondent salesman. The article developed the argument for allowing monks to become her-mits in their own Orders without having to transfer to other Orders and marshalled historical evidence in support of this. Merton called it 'a modern spiritual classic on eremitism' and it prompted him to his own researches, which were published in an article 'Dans le désert de Dieu'. This was to appear only in French and Italian; he wrote that he could never get it past the American censors.

In the spring of 1955, the Abbot Visitor from Rome, during the annual visitation, reproved what he called the 'eremitical mental-ity' he had observed at Gethsemani, and Merton, having read of Charles de Foucauld, who had left the Cistercians for solitude in the desert, decided that the time had come for him to follow that example and quit. He applied to Rome for permission to join the Camaldolese.

It was while waiting for a reply that the post of Master of Novices at Gethsemani became vacant and Merton was appointed – a task he accepted in the spirit of obedience and service. He found himself again in the role of Jonas when the reply came from the Sacred Congregation for Religious denying his request.

In July 1956 Merton had a traumatic meeting with a distinguished psychiatrist. He was planning to write a paper on 'Neurosis in the Monastic Life' and thought some comments from a professional in the field might be helpful. Gregory Zilboorg was a recent convert to Catholicism and had built up an international reputation as an analyst, having treated Hemingway and a number of famous writers and artists. He had read Merton's books and was keen to meet him, so the Abbot agreed that Merton should attend a two-week workshop given by Zilboorg in New York on psychiatry and the religious life. Zilboorg had already formed an assessment of Merton's character from his writing, and this was confirmed when they met. It was not a charitable one. Merton records in his journal after a private interview that Zilboorg pronounced him neurotic and in bad shape: 'You like to be famous, you want to be a big shot, you keep pushing your way out – into publicity – megalomania and narcissism are your big trends'.

On Merton's desire for solitude, the judgment was: 'Your hermit trend is pathological'. Worse was to come. Although Zilboorg had told him not to tell anyone about his pronouncements, he arranged a meeting with the Abbot at which Merton was present where he went over it all again and finally turned to Merton and announced: 'You want a hermitage in Times Square with a large sign over it saying "HERMIT" '.[11]

All this ignored the fact that Merton, having joined the monastery of Gethsemani, had spent seven years without setting foot outside its walls; that he had scrupulously followed the directions of his superiors who denied his requests for solitude and insisted that he play his part in the communal monastic life; and that, far from being convinced of the need to get his own way, he was constantly aware of the possibility that, Jonas-like, his own plans and ambitions were quite likely to be heading in the wrong direction. It is a sign of Merton's true humility that, on hearing these words, he did not shake his head with disbelief but silently wept.

He continued with his duties as Master of Novices but kept alive the desire to be a hermit. He studied the Desert Fathers and published a book of extracts from the apophthegmata in which he demonstrated that the hermit life was part of Christian monastic tradition as well as urging its contemporary relevance:

> The Coptic hermits who left the world as though escaping from a wreck did not merely intend to save themselves. They knew that they were helpless to do any good for others so long as they floundered about in the wreckage. But once they got a foothold on solid ground, things were different. Then they had not only the power but even the obligation to pull the world to safety after them.
>
> This is their paradoxical lesson for our time. It would perhaps be too much to say that the world needs another movement such as that which drew these men into the deserts of Egypt and Palestine. Ours is certainly a time for solitaries and for hermits. But merely to reproduce the simplicity, austerity and prayer of these primitive souls is not a complete or satisfactory answer. We must transcend them, and all those who, since their time, have gone beyond the limits which they set. We must liberate ourselves, in our own way, from involvement in a world that is plunging to disaster. But our world is different from theirs. Our involvement in it is more complete. Our danger is far more desperate. Our time, perhaps, is shorter than we think.[12]

It was from the Desert Fathers that he found confirmation of his view that the search for solitude is a journey to discover the inner self. The monks fled to the desert to become ordinary. If they had gone there to be extraordinary this would have meant taking the world with them as a standard of comparison. They lived among the rocks because they wanted to be themselves and to flee a world that divided them from themselves. 'There can be no other valid reason for seeking solitude or for leaving the world'.

At this time Merton wrote to several bishops asking if there was a possibility of his living as a hermit in some remote part of their diocese. He was offered positions in the British West Indies, in Nevada and on an island off the coast of Nicaragua. He took advice and decided that he would be best suited to a hermitage attached to the monastery of Our Lady of the Resurrection at Cuernavaca, whose Prior had visited Gethsemani and asked for Merton's help. He wrote to Rome for permission and, on 17 December 1959, the rejection arrived. On that day he wrote in his journal: 'Actually, what it comes to is that I shall certainly have solitude but only by a miracle and not at all at my own contriving. Where? Here or there makes no difference. Somewhere, nowhere, beyond all "where." Solitude outside geography or in it. No matter.'[13]

Fifteen years had passed since he joined the Trappists and launched himself out on the contemplative life, but he was no nearer to the solitude he sought. An accident helped him on the way. In March 1960 there was a fire at the monastery which resulted in a rebuilding programme out of which he was given a new room – a 'special cell built over the new stairs by the infirmary . . . I think it ought to make a nice hermitage'.[14] Here he began to taste solitude and its effects on his study, which he recorded in his journal for 8 May:

> Reading in here is a totally different experience from anywhere else, as if the silence and the four walls enriched everything with a great significance. One is alone, not on guard, utterly relaxed and receptive, having four walls and silence all around enables you to listen, so to speak, with all the pores of your skin and to absorb truth through every part of your being. I doubt if I would be any better off in Mexico.[15]

There was another project. As part of the rebuilding work, the Abbot had accepted a plan for a retreat house on a small hill called Mount Olivet, outside the monastery walls. The plans were much discussed, amended and reduced by committees of visiting architects and the resident monks, including Merton, whose influence we can see in the final outcome, which he describes as 'no longer a shiny, smart little pavilion, but just a plain cottage with two rooms and a porch. Clearly it is a hermitage rather than a place for conferences.'[16] And so it became. He was given permission to spend a few hours every day there alone, and on 26 December 1960 his journal celebrates the end of a long quest: 'Lit candles in the dusk. *Haec regina mea in saeculum saeculi* – the sense of a journey ended, of wandering at an end. *The first time in my life* I really felt that I had come home and that my roaming and looking were ended.'[17]

It was in the initially short periods of isolation in the hermitage that he began to develop his thoughts on solitude. He wrote that most people try to avoid being alone and are able to evade situations of solitude 'by those occupations and recreations so mercifully provided by society which enable a man to avoid his own company for twenty-four hours a day'.[18]

The first problem of solitude is that it forces us to accept our own absurdity:

The anguish of realising that underneath the apparently logical pattern of a more or less 'well organised' and rational life there lies an abyss of irrationality, confusion, pointlessness, and indeed of apparent chaos. This is what immediately impresses itself upon the man who has renounced diversion. It cannot be otherwise: for in renouncing diversion he renounces the seemingly harmless pleasure of building a tight, self-contained illusion about himself and about his little world.[19]

But the first insight that impresses itself on those who choose solitude is that they are not cutting themselves off from, but discovering their unity with, the rest of humanity:

. . . one who is called to solitude is not called merely to imagine himself solitary, to live as if he were solitary, to cultivate the illusion that he is different, withdrawn and elevated. He is called to emptiness. And, in this emptiness he does not find points upon which to base a contrast between himself and others. On the contrary, he realises, although perhaps confusedly, that he has entered into a *solitude that is really shared by everyone*. It is not that he is solitary while everyone else is social: but that everyone is solitary, in a solitude masked by that symbolism which they use to cheat and counteract their solitariness . . .[20]

*

The solitary is one who is aware of solitude in himself as a basic and inevitable human reality, not just as something which affects him as an isolated individual. Hence his solitude is the foundation of a deep, pure and gentle sympathy with all other men whether or not they are capable of realising the tragedy of their plight. More – it is the doorway by which he enters into the mystery of God and brings others into that mystery by the power of his love and his humility.[21]

*

Every man is a solitary, held firmly by the inexorable limitations of his own aloneness. Death makes this very clear, for when a man dies, he dies alone.[22]

This question of bringing people to God, of fulfilling his duties as a Christian and a monk when cut off from society and his Church, was one with which his superiors had often taxed him. And he had a ready answer:

. . . a Christian hermit can, by being alone, paradoxically live even closer to the heart of the Church than one who is in the midst of her apostolic activities. The life and unity of the Church are and must be visible. But that does not mean that the invisible and spiritual activities of men of prayer are not supremely important. On the contrary, the invisible and more mysterious life of prayer is *essential* to the Church. Solitaries, too, are essential to her![23]

The morality of withdrawal from social and political activism, had much concerned Merton, who had made the decision to move from activist to contemplative:

Withdrawal from other men can be a special form of love for them. It should never be a rejection of man or of his society. But it may well be a quiet and humble refusal to accept the myths and fictions with which the social life cannot help but be full – especially today. To despair of the illusions and facades which man builds around himself is certainly not to despair of man. On the contrary, it may be a sign of love and of hope. For when we love someone we refuse to tolerate what destroys and maims his personality. If we love mankind, can we blind ourselves to man's predicament? You will say: we must do something about his predicament. But there are some whose vocation it is to realise that they, at least, cannot help in any overt social way. Their contribution is a mute witness, a secret and even invisible expression of love which takes the form of their own option for solitude in preference to the acceptance of social fictions. For is not our involvement in fiction, particularly in political and demagogic fiction, an implicit confession that we despair of man, and even of God?[24]

And as to the need to proclaim the Gospel rather than retreat to a hermitage:

The message of God's mercy to man must be preached. The word of truth must be proclaimed. No one can deny this. But there are not a few who are beginning to feel the futility of adding more words to the constant flood of language that pours meaninglessly over everybody everywhere from morning till night. For language to have meaning, there must be intervals of silence somewhere to divide word from word, utterance from utterance. He who retires into silence does not necessarily reject that language. Perhaps it is love and respect for language that impose silence on him. For the mercy of God is not heard in words unless it is heard, both before and after the words are spoken, in silence.[25]

*

The hermit has a very real place in a world like ours that has degraded the human person and lost all respect for that awesome loneliness in which each single spirit must confront the living God.[26]

*

We must remember that Robinson Crusoe was one of the great myths of the middle class, commercial civilisation of the 18th and 19th centuries:[27] the myth not of eremitical solitude but of pragmatic individualism. Crusoe is a symbolical figure in an era when every man's house was his castle in the trees, but only because every man was a very prudent and resourceful citizen who knew how to make the best out of the least and could drive a hard bargain with any competitor, even life itself. Carefree Crusoe was happy because he had an answer to everything. The real hermit is not so sure he has an answer.[28]

And finally, on the need for a measure of solitude in everyone's life, he wrote:

Without solitude of some sort there is and can be no maturity. Unless one becomes empty and alone, he cannot give himself in love because he does not possess the deep self which is the only gift worth of love. And this deep self, we immediately add, cannot be *possessed*. My deep self is not a 'something' which I acquire, or to which I 'attain' after a long struggle. It is not mine and cannot become mine. It is no 'thing' – no object. It is 'I'. The shallow 'I' of individualism can be possessed, developed, cultivated, pandered to, satisfied: it is the centre of all our strivings for gain and for satisfaction, whether material or spiritual. But the deep 'I' of the spirit, of solitude and of love cannot be 'had', possessed, developed, perfected. It can only *be* and *act* according to deep inner laws which are not of man's contriving but which come from God . . . It is only this inmost and solitary 'I' that truly loves with the love and the spirit of Christ. This 'I' is Christ Himself living in us: and we, in Him, living in the Father.[29]

As the years went by, Father Louis was gradually allowed to spend more time in the hermitage. But this allowance was a pittance. As one monk put it, his time there was doled out in bits and pieces. Occasionally he would be allowed a full day there, and in 1963 he had six full days. By 1964 he had bookshelves, a table, a few chairs and a bed there. He hung on the wall the nameplate that had hung over his cell in the dormitory with his monastic name 'N. Maria Ludovicus'. He installed an oil lamp, which tended to smoke but extended his reading hours. In that year he wrote:

What a thing it is to sit absolutely alone in the forest at night, cherished by this wonderful, unintelligible, perfectly innocent speech, the most comforting speech in the world, the talk that rain makes by itself all over the ridges . . . As long as it talks I am going to listen. But I am also going to sleep, because here in this wilderness

I have learned to sleep again.[30]

His journal records that his private thoughts were in line with his public utterances:

September 22 . . . There is no question, once again, that I am only fully normal and human when I have plenty of solitude. Not that I think a great deal when I am alone, but I live according to a different and more real tempo. I live with the tempo of the sun and of the day, in complete harmony with what is around me.

It would be infidelity to deny or evade the obvious truth that, for me, such a life is completely and fully right. I cannot doubt it was the life I was meant for. Most of my troubles come from my tendencies to half believe those who doubt it. But I have got to the point when I can no longer take them seriously.

Having won a measure of solitude for himself, Merton was keen to spread the benefit to his fellow monks. It was in October 1964 that the second American Meeting of Cistercian Abbots took place at Gethsemani, and he prepared a paper setting out a detailed proposal for setting up a hermitage at the monastery. His basic thesis, which he emphasised by typing it in capital letters, is 'that there is a real need to construct a hermitage at some distance from the monastery, with a facility for both relative and complete solitude, to provide for temporary and permanent vocations to solitude, without severing the bonds of the monk with the community of his vocation and of his Profession'.

He received a sympathetic response. The attitude of the Abbot was softening and, in the same month, he gave permission for an extension of Merton's quest into solitude by allowing him to sleep at the hermitage once in a while without special restriction or further permission. He did so for the first time on the night of 12 October 1964. A few days later he wrote:

October 20. . . . my heart tells me that in this question of the solitary life there is for me a special truth to be embraced. A truth which is not capable of logical explanation. A truth which is not rooted in my own nature or in my own biography, but is something deeper and something that may also cut clean through the whole network of my own recent works, ideas, writing, experiences and so forth – even those that in some way concern the solitary life and monastic renewal.

*

December 16 Yesterday for the first time I was able to live a complete day's schedule as it ought to be, at least in this transitional period at the hermitage . . .

Everything the Fathers of the Church say about the solitary life is exactly true. The temptations and the joys, above all the tears and the ineffable peace and *happiness*. The happiness that is so pure because it is simply not one's own making but sheer mercy and gift. Happiness in the sense of having arrived at last in the place destined for me by God: of fulfilling a purpose for which I was brought here twenty-three years ago.

The following year, 1965, was to be one of his most productive. It began well:

January 31 I can imagine no greater cause for gratitude on my fiftieth birthday than that, on it, I woke up in a hermitage.

The early months saw domestic improvements there which increased his comfort but troubled his conscience. If the Desert Fathers had found wisdom in the austerity of caves and the utter simplicity of a life in a barren place, to what extent was it possible that making himself more comfortable might be a check on his spiritual progress? He already had a hermitage which was more solidly constructed and spacious than many of the farms in the area. Was there a danger that further modernisation might turn his hermitage into a chalet?

February 16 At last the electric light is coming. All day they were working on holes, digging and blasting the rock with small charges. Young men in yellow helmets, good, eager, hard-working guys with machines. I was glad of them and of American technology, pitching in to bring light as they would for any farmer in the district. And it was good to feel part of this, which is not to be despised but admirable, which does not mean that I hold any brief for the excess of useless developments in technology.'

He was brought a 'big glossy' fridge and commented on 24 February: 'in many ways I wish I did not have it, but in summer it will be necessary . . . I might as well forget about feeling guilty, the thing is too splendid. But local people have such and they have TV too.'

The arrival of his fridge prompted him to ruminate on the past ascetic practices of the Church:

Now we have come to be openly doubtful of the intrinsic value of such practices. The sincerity was there and it obviously meant a great deal to them, but depth psychology and so forth have made these things forever questionable. They belong to another age and to another kind of consciousness. They presuppose a certain unawareness of the unconscious. But it is in the unconscious that the true purification and repentance have to reach down and happen. Artificially austere practices have a tendency to prevent this deeper change. They can be a substitute for change in depth, although it is not necessarily true that they can *never* be associated with deep change. But can they in our time?[31]

Although the issue of whether or not a hermit with a fridge can properly be considered ascetic may seem trivial, it leads to one of Merton's most important insights into the solitary life. This is that it can be judged only by the inner experience and not by the external surroundings. A person may live alone in a desert cave and not be a true solitary; equally, the inner life can be discovered by those with many social contacts. In fact, there is a danger in surrounding oneself with the props of the eremitical life:

. . . In any event the Christian solitary should avoid all trappings and decor of a theatrical eremitism – the hood, the costume, the retinue of devoted birds and squirrels (though they will be around anyway), the diet of bread and water, the stone pillow, the rosary of knotted string, the bed of twigs. These things are affectations, and we might as well recognize that even the classification of 'hermit' has its dangers.[32]

*

At the same time it is not altogether easy to be perfectly honest with oneself, and solitude brings this fact out. The wood may well foment new madnesses that one did not suspect before, But it would seem that solitude is not a satisfactory setting for concerted, thoroughgoing madness. To be really mad, you need other people. When you are by yourself you soon get tired of your craziness. It is too exhausting.[33]

In the hermitage, Merton continued to reflect in his journal on the dangers and the fruits of solitude:

February 26 I see more and more that solitude is not something to play with. It is deadly serious, and much as I have wanted it, I have not been serious enough about it. It is not enough just to 'like solitude' or love it even. Even if you like it, solitude can wreck you, I believe, if you desire it only for your own sake . . .

Solitude is a stern mother who brooks no nonsense. And the

question arises – am I so full of nonsense that she will cast me out? I pray that she will not, and I suppose that is going to take much prayer.

*

February 27 The solitary life makes sense only when it is centred entirely on the love of God. Without this, everything is triviality. Love of God in Himself, for Himself, sought only in His will in total surrender. Anything but this in solitude is nausea and absurdity.

*

June 8 The great joy of the solitary life is not found simply in quiet in the beauty and peace of nature or in the song of birds or even in the peace of one's own heart. It resides in the awakening and the attuning of the inmost heart to the voice of God – to the inexplicable, quiet, definite inner certitude of one's call to obey Him, to hear Him, to worship Him here, now, today, in silence and alone. It is the realization that this is the whole reason for one's existence.

*

July 5 Unfortunately, even in solitude, though I try not to and sometimes claim not to, I still depend too much emotionally on the idea of being accepted and approved and of having a place in society. But obviously there is no such thing as an absolute solitude. Even my solitude is my place in society.

He wrote on 9 August to Naomi Burton, his agent and close friend:

At the end of the month I am out of my office job and permanently in the hermitage. I am of course very glad and also I see that it will not be any joke either. The more I get into it the more I see that the business of being solitary admits of no nonsense at all, and when I see how full of nonsense I am, I see that I could wreck myself at it. Yet I really think God asks me to take this risk, and I want do do this . . . I am almost getting a humble and a chastened attitude towards the whole thing. Wouldn't it be amazing if after all this I really went at it in a spirit of humility and faith, instead of just making noises and demanding it all as a right?[34]

Three days later she replied, with the insight of an intimate who was aware of the contradictions in Merton's character between his desire for solitude and his need for people: 'Perhaps the worst thing that could happen to you, in one sense, would be your own realisation that it wasn't the right thing for you. That would be a terribly hard admission and take a lot of guts to accept.'

Merton was to come close to but never fully to accept that solitude was not right for him.

> August 10 The solitary life, now that I really confront it, is awesome, wonderful, and I see I have no strength of my own for it . . .
>
> It seems to me that solitude rips off all the masks and all the disguises. It tolerates no lies. Everything but straight affirmation or silence is mocked and judged by the silence of the forest. 'Let your speech be yea, yea'.

On 17 August the private council of the monastery met and approved his request for retirement to the hermitage. It had taken the man pronounced by a noted psychiatrist as a megalomaniac who wanted to be a big shot and kept pushing his way out almost twenty-four years to gain the privilege of living alone.

On 20 August he took up full-time residence in the hermitage.

> August 25, *Feast of St Louis*. The five days I have had in real solitude have been a revelation, and whatever questions I may have had about it before are now answered. Over and over again I see that this life is what I have always hoped it would be and have always sought. It is a life of peace, silence, purpose and meaning.

It was also a productive life. In the spring of 1965 he completed *The Way of Chuang Tzu* and *Gandhi on Non-Violence*, as well as three collections of essays. In an article 'Rain and the Rhinoceros', published in *Holiday Magazine* in May 1965, he refers to Ionesco's play *Rhinoceros* and uses its imagery to link the life of the hermit with contemporary existential thought. In the play, people turn themselves into rhinos through conforming to social pressures, while the hero tries to hang on to his essential humanity by remaining alone. Merton sees the play as a work very close to Zen Buddhism and to Christian eremitism, seeing modern man as 'the man in a rush, the man who has no time', the man afflicted with 'Rhinoceritis' – the sickness that lies in wait for those who have lost the sense and the taste for solitude.

Alone in the woods, Merton is free to understand the message of the rain:

> The rain I am in is not like the rain of cities. It fills the woods with an immense and confused sound. It covers the flat roof of the cabin

and its porch with insistent and controlled rhythms. And I listen, because it reminds me again and again that the whole world is run by rhythms that I have not yet learned to recognize, rhythms that are not those of the engineer.[35]

But even in the solitude of the hermitage, where the quail whistle in the wet bushes, the sounds of the outer world impinge: 'Over at Fort Knox the Rhinoceros is having fun'.

His translations of the poems of Chuang-Tzu were published in 1965, and that summer Merton, in his enthusiasm for the Tao philosopher, wrote two introductions to the work. Chuang Tzu, the fourth-century-BC follower of Lao-Tse, was a witness to the notion that the desire for solitude is as old as humanity and Merton noted that there have always been, in all cultures, men who have claimed to find something superior to society in solitude. The monastic outlook, in fact, is as old as humanity.

But Merton was writing in the 1960s, when ideals of retreat from the world into self-realisation were highly fashionable, and he entered a caution that personal freedom is not to be found in simply throwing off inhibitions and social obligations to live alone in self-absorption. Such a course, he wrote, 'results in the complete decay of the true self and of its capacity for freedom'.

He was later to reserve the right 'to forget about being myself, since in any case there is very little chance of my being anybody else. Rather, it seems to me that when one is too intent on "being himself" he runs the risk of impersonating a shadow'.[36]

In a letter to Robert Lax at the end of 1965 he wrote: 'Yes it is true I sleep in the woods, I eat in the woods, I come down to the monastery only to say an occasional fie upon the commandant and to subvert the troops . . . In my house in the woods I resist war. I resist everything. That is why the hermit life is called the "pièce de resistance".'[37]

By the beginning of 1966, his hours at the hermitage were being shaped into a structure. He wrote to the Sufi scholar, Aziz Ch. Abdul in January 1966, and gave a detailed account of his schedule:

I go to bed about 7.30 at night and rise about 2.30 in the morning. On rising, I say part of the canonical office, consisting of psalms, lessons, etc. Then I take an hour or an hour and a quarter for meditation. I follow this with Bible reading, and then make some tea or coffee . . . with perhaps a piece of fruit or some honey. With breakfast I begin reading and continue reading and studying until about sunrise. Now the sun rises very late, in summer it rises earlier, so this period of study varies, but it is on the average about two hours.

At sunrise I say another office of psalms etc., then begin my manual work, which includes sweeping, cleaning, cutting wood, and other necessary jobs. This finishes at about nine o'clock when I say another office of psalms. If I have time, I may write a few letters, usually short (today is Sunday and I have more time). After this I go down to the monastery to say Mass as I am not yet permitted to offer Mass in the hermitage. Saying Mass requires an altar, an acolyte who serves the Mass, special vestments, candles and so on. It is in a way better to have all this at the monastery. It would be hard to care for so many things and keep them clean at the hermitage. After Mass I take one cooked meal at the monastery. Then I return immediately to the hermitage, usually without seeing or speaking to anyone except the ones I happen to meet as I go from place to place (these I do not ordinarily speak to as we have a rule of strict silence). (When I speak it is to the Abbot, whom I see once a week, or to someone in a position of authority about necessary business.)

On returning to the hermitage, I do some light reading and then say another office, about one o'clock. This is followed by another hour or more of meditation. On feast days I can take an hour and a half or two hours for this afternoon meditation. Then I work at my writing. Usually I do not have more than an hour and a half or two hours at most for this, each day. Following that, it being now late afternoon, (about four), I say another office of psalms, and prepare myself a light supper. I keep down to a minimum of cooking, usually only tea or soup, and make a sandwich of some sort. Thus I have only a minimum of dishes to wash. After supper I have another hour or more of meditation, after which I go to bed.[38]

It was a schedule from which he frequently diverged. His health was poor and he often had to leave the hermitage for treatment. Then there were the letters. As his fame increased so did his correspondence and he was a focus of interest for contemplatives from different traditions around the world – students of Celtic solitaries, Zen mystics, Buddhist writers and spiritual masters of Islam. All seemed to think of him as a solitary within their own tradition. And there were the uninvited visitors. Although the monks tried to protect him by turning people away at the gate house, he had told his friends of a back way to the hermitage and they had of course told their friends. So his peace was liable to be interrupted at any hour of any day. He had to admit that he was not always displeased by this. He could offer a glass of wine and occasionally tea and toast, not on the menu of the monastery. He had a record-player.

He was not only sociable but concerned that in solitude he should not lose touch with the issues that were concerning people in the world outside. He did not want to lose contact with that world by drifting off into rarefied spiritual contemplation. He wrote to a Catholic theologian, who had become a regular correspondent:

> My hermit life is expressly a *lay* life. I never wear the habit except when at the monastery and I try to be as much on my own as I can and like the people living around in the country. Also I try to keep up valid and living contacts with my friends who are in the thick of things and everybody knows where my real 'community' is. I honestly believe that is the right place for me (woods, not Gethsemani) in so far as it is the right battleground . . . I am not by any means turning my back on other people, I am as open as the situation (of overcontrol) permits and want to make this more open as time goes on. Lots of people would like me to get out and join them in this or that, but I just don't see that I could do it without getting into some absurd role and having to act a dumb part or justify some nonsense or other that I don't really believe in . . . I can't say where and when my life is eschatological, because as far as I can see I am a tramp and not much else. But this kind of tramp is what I am supposed to be. This kind of place is where I am finally reduced to my nothingness and have to depend on God. Outside, I would be much more able to depend on talk.[39]

By retreating into his hermitage, Merton was not cutting himself off from contemporary problems, but hoping to be able to consider them more deeply and to speak on them with authority. He wrote: 'A contemplative will, then, concern himself with the same problems as other people, but he will try to get at the spiritual and metaphysical roots of these problems – not by analysis but by simplicity.'[40] The hermits of the past had been similarly involved:

> In all the great religious traditions men and women have dedicated themselves to contemplative lives in which, under special conditions of silence, austerity, meditation and worship, it has been possible for them to deepen and broaden their spiritual consciousness. In so doing, they have have become able to explore realms of experience which, though unusual, have profound implications for the ordinary lives of their fellow men. Whether from the point of view

of psychology, ethics, art, religion, or simply in the development of man's deepest capacities, the contemplative experience is in touch with what is the most basic in human existence.[41]

But the place of the hermit in the society of his time had changed fundamentally since the days of the Desert Fathers. Merton had experienced the one and studied the other:

Whereas in the fourth century monks were determined to prove their solitude charismatic by showing it to be beyond the human, the situation today is quite the reverse . . . The hermit exists today to realize and experience in himself the ordinary values of a life lived with the minimum of artificiality. Such a life will from the beginning seem itself artificial because it is so completely unlike the lives of other people.[42]

*

Today more than ever we need to recognize that the gift of solitude is not ordered to the acquisition of strange contemplative powers, but first of all to the recovery of one's deep self and to the renewal of an authenticity which is twisted out of shape by the pretentious routines of a disordered togetherness.[43]

Merton had moved on from the position he publicised to such acclaim in *The Seven Storey Mountain*. He had discovered, in solitude, that the contemplative is not necessarily an ascetic who scorns the world and seeks God through heroic acts of self-denial which aspire to self-annihilation but a person who seeks his true self, a self known to God, the self he was created in order to become. And that the true value of solitude is that it withdraws a person from the distorting influences of society and allows him to rediscover his own nature.

Contemplation is not and cannot be a function of this external self. There is an irreducible opposition between the deep transcendent self that awakens only in contemplation, and the superficial, external self which we commonly identify with the first person singular. We must remember that this superficial 'I' is not our real self. It is our 'individuality' and our 'empirical self' but it is not truly the hidden and mysterious person in whom we subsist before the eyes of God. The 'I' that works in the world, thinks about itself, observes its own reactions and talks about itself is not the true 'I' that has been united to God in Christ. It is at best the vesture, the mask, the disguise of that mysterious and unknown 'self' whom most of us never discover until we are dead.[44]

On the solitary life he wrote:

Some men have perhaps become hermits with the thought that sanctity could only be attained by escape from other men. But the only justification for a life of deliberate solitude is the conviction that it will help you to love not only God but also other men. If you go into the desert merely to escape from people you dislike, you will find neither peace nor solitude; you will only isolate yourself with a tribe of devils.[45]

*

What is the 'world' that Christ would not pray for, and of which He said that His disciples were in it but not of it? The world is the unquiet city of those who live for themselves and are therefore divided against one another in a struggle that cannot end, for it will go on eternally in hell. It is the city of those who are fighting for possession of limited things and for the monopoly of goods and pleasures that cannot be shared by all.

But if you try to escape from this world merely by leaving the city and hiding yourself in solitude, you will only take the city with you into solitude . . . For the flight from the world is nothing else but the flight from self-concern. And the man who locks himself up in private with his own selfishness has put himself into a position where the evil within him will either possess him like a devil or drive him out of his head.

That is why it is dangerous to go into solitude merely because you like to be alone.[46]

According to one of his biographers, he expressed in one sentence the essence of his thinking on this over a lifetime: 'The only true joy is to escape from the prison of our own selfhood . . . and enter by love into union with the Life who dwells and sings within the essence of every creature and within the core of our minds'.[47] And perhaps this is one of his most valuable insights: that people and all living entities are more like God the more they are simply and naturally themselves.

A tree gives glory to God first of all by being a tree . . . The more a tree is like itself, the more it is like Him . . . No two created beings are exactly alike. And their individuality is no imperfection. On the contrary, the perfection of each created thing is not merely in its conformity to an abstract type but in its own individual identity with itself. This particular tree will give glory to God by spreading out its roots and raising its branches into the air and light in a way that no other tree before or after it ever did or will do.[48]

It's harder for people. We have a choice. 'We can be ourselves or not as we please. But the problem is this: since God alone possesses the secret of my identity, He alone can make me who I am, or rather, He alone can make me who I will be when I at last fully begin to be.'

The fallen world and condition of man make it hard to know who we really are:

All sin starts from the assumption that my false self, the self that exists only in my own egocentric desires, is the fundamental reality of life to which everything else in the universe is ordered. Thus I use up my life trying to accumulate pleasures and experiences and power and honor and knowledge and love, to clothe this false self and construct its nothingness into something objectively real.[49]

In a study of Merton, Dom John Eudes Bamberger, the monastery's psychiatrist and a close friend, pointed out that at no time in his life did he ever become a true hermit. He had friends all over the world – Vietmanese Buddhists, Hindu monks, Japanese Zen masters, Sufi mystics, professors of religion and mysticism from Jerusalem's university, French philosophers, artists and poets from Europe, South America and the United States, Arabic scholars, Mexican sociologists etc. These wrote regularly and turned up on his doorstep having travelled thousands of miles to see him. Furthermore, although the medieval hermits also had visitors, Merton had a need for human companionship. He had an intense longing for solitude and yet found that he sought out people – not always for conversation or human contact: just people with whom he could simply be present.[50]

Only Merton's sudden death, apparently by electrocution from a faulty electric fan in a Bangkok hotel in December 1969, brought an end to the contradictions in his life. A close friend, Dom Patrick Hart at Gethsemani, said of his desire to be a hermit: 'It was like a *leitmotif* that ran through the course of his life. No one can say which side would have won out in the controversy over the social side versus the solitary side of Merton. I think that both would have endured up to the end if he had survived Bangkok.'[51]

Merton's life had been vastly productive. He changed the way Catholics saw other faiths and revealed many of the spiritual riches of the Catholic tradition to a wide audience. His long search for solitude won reforms in the Church which were far-reaching. Jean

Leclercq, a Benedictine writer on solitude, wrote of him, after his death:

> By patience and obedience, yet always faithful to what he clearly recognised as a call from God, he won approval to live as a hermit himself, and it was easy to see that he became, not only more a monk, but also more human: close to men, to all men, more universal. Before he died he saw his former abbot become a hermit and his community elect as successor a novice whom Merton had trained and who was living, as he did, in a hermitage not far from the monastery. And now, from the North to the South Pacific, from Oregon to Santiago de Chile, and elsewhere throughout the world, I have encountered Trappists who are living as hermits to everyone's satisfaction.[52]

The contradictions in the life of Thomas Merton produced the tensions that enriched his creativity. To the end of his life he sought to keep in balance his need for solitude and companionship, and he never felt secure from the need to retreat yet further. On 19 July 1968, he noted in his journal:

> More than anything I want to find a really quiet, isolated place –
> – where no-one knows I am (I want to disappear)
> – where I can get down to the thing I really want to do and need to do
> – from which, if necessary, I can come out to help others . . .[53]

This last observation ties in Thomas Merton with the great hermits of the past. St Antony of Egypt had shut himself away for twenty years in a deserted fort only to return to the world and make himself available to an unending stream of visitors; St Gregory of Palamas spent most of his life in secluded hermitages for five days a week, returning at the weekends to celebrate the Eucharist and give counsel to his fellow monks. Finally he returned to the city and spent the last years of his life fighting social injustice as Archbishop of Thessaloniki. The whole tradition of solitaries across the cultures has been, as we have seen, a retreat to acquire insights which are then passed on. Merton gave copiously to the world of the insights he gained from his hard-won solitude. That he felt the need for human companionship does not exclude him from the great tradition of hermit contemplatives, but unites him with that tradition. His insights were into the nature of solitude, its risks and its benefits. And, from time to time, he had a glimpse into the reality of the world around him that could come only to a lone observer. On 6 September 1965, he saw three deer in a field – a stag and two red does.

> The thing that struck me most – when you look at them directly and in movement you see what the primitive cave painters saw. Something you never see in a photograph. It is most awe-inspiring The *muntu* or the 'spirit' is shown in the running of the deer. The 'deerness' that sums up everything and is sacred and marvelous.
>
> A contemplative intuition, yet this is perfectly ordinary, everyday seeing – what everybody ought to see all the time. The deer reveals to me something essential, not only in itself, but also in myself. Something beyond the trivialities of my everyday being, my individual existence. Something profound. The face of that which is in the deer and in myself.[54]

CHAPTER EIGHT

A Hermit for Our Time:
Robert Lax on Patmos

Today the hermitages of Patmos stand empty and abandoned to the casual intrusions of the curious. Their windows are securely shuttered, their churches locked and barred to seal away the icons and other saleable commodities that once inspired veneration and would now fetch a good price on the international antiques market. Their gardens are overgrown, and the only touches of colour to be seen among the tangled undergrowth, are from empty cigarette packets and jettisoned picnic wrappings. The Age of Communication is with us, and those who once occupied remote and peaceful places on this island in their search for silence have been driven away by the outboard engine and the hired motor bike.

But there is, here on Patmos today, a witness to a kind of solitude that may well be the way ahead. Each day, in the busy port of Scala, a lean figure with a broad-brimmed straw hat and the white spade-beard of a Pilgrim Father moves quietly among the crowds heading for the fishing boats. The American poet Robert Lax is collecting food for his cats. Or, as he would say, for the cats who choose to live alongside him.

Robert Lax was born in Olean, a provincial town in New York State, in 1915. At Columbia College he was among a group of students who became renowned as the precursors of the 'beat generation': Allen Ginsberg was an early admirer of Lax, and Thomas Merton a life-long close friend. He taught literature for two years and became an editor at the *New Yorker*; later he wrote film reviews for *Time* magazine and went to Hollywood as a scriptwriter. He had converted to Catholicism in 1943, and ten years later he was appointed 'roving editor' for the liberal Catholic magazine *Jubilee*, which position allowed him to travel in Europe. In 1960 he visited Greece for the first time, and two years later returned there to stay. For the last thirty years he has lived on the island of Patmos.

His poems have been published in Britain, America, Italy and Switzerland. He writes every day, and thinks that only about ten per cent of his writings have so far been published.

Robert Lax loves people. As he passes along the streets of Scala, the port of Patmos, his progress is slow because of the many local men and women who stop him to exchange a few words. He looks carefully at each one, focused completely on the person who speaks to him. And they all leave him smiling, buoyed up by the meeting.

Yet, although he claims that the people he knows are one of the reasons he's most glad to be alive, he lives alone, as he has lived for forty years. He did not, he says, choose to live alone. Life just worked out that way. In fact, he did live with a friend for some years in New York. They never spoke to each other in the house. They would pass each other in the rooms without exchanging a word and then, once a week, on Fridays, would have long telephone conversations, office to office, 'to catch up'. Neither thought of this as odd.

This kind of solitude is necessary to Robert Lax because he is a writer and can only work when free from distractions. Solitude is, for him, above all a working environment – the only one in which he can write. And his writing is, above all, a search for meaning. Insights come from time to time, and if he can work them into a language he can understand, he feels they may be of use or interest to others. Here are some of those insights:

From Journal C:

22 July 1969 (PATMOS)

one feels that all philosophies, zen and yoga are ways of approaching wisdom & 'enlightenment' – they are ways of approaching an 'enlightened' state in which one's behaviour is always or almost always 'spontaneously' right.

to be 'enlightened' is not to shine: nor to bring multitudes to the hill where one sits cross-legged, to listen.

it is rather to know what one is doing (& even, perhaps, to enjoy it).

21 August 1969 (after swimming in the sea)

sea calls to the blood, waking those members farthest removed from the heart to a new circulation: the blood within, the brine without, calling to each other as day to night, as night to day.

a feeling, experienced by all the old men who swim daily, of being reborn in the sea. and they are shaped, licked like bear-cubs by their mother, and they issue from a summer of sea remade.

the undersea vision may (in fact) be a foetal vision: full of dim light, full of a bright, if far off, hope.

25 November 1969 (PATMOS)

night seems lighter, less heavy here than in kalymnos, and considerably less heavy than in new york. the weight of people stirring around at night, the weight of their thoughts, the weight of their plans seem to create a physical pressure in the air above all the cities: creates, that is, a psychological pressure so strong that it seems tangible, physical, bears down like a weight on the shoulders.

it would be hard to imagine a similar weight bearing down on so small an island. being gathered even from the nocturnal fantasies (for much of it rises from fantasies) of so small a community. perhaps it could. but just as new york seems heavier than kalymnos and london perhaps even heavier than new york, the size itself of the city and the number of perambulant dreamers within it seem to affect the magnitude of the weight that hangs above it and presses down.

for perhaps the same reason, an incident taking place (& i still mean at night) in the city has not the same weight as one that takes place in a smaller town; an anecdote told at night in the city has not the same resonance as would have exactly the same anecdote told in an island village. there are paradoxes to be discerned here, because although life in a city seems to be constantly changing, each violent occurrence within it, each brutal fact seems to be permanent, seems to become part of its unchanging face, in an island village the opposite is true: the hills about it are permanent. the seasons come and go in a stable rhythm; houses are built to stand till they fall; children carry the names of their forebears, and, within this mostly cosmic framework, incidents in the life of man seem smaller, more ephemeral: parts, rather, of a cosmic pattern than isolated omens of good or ill.

as a result, a country man takes news philosophically, whereas a city man is likely to hear it with panic.

25 February 1970

three bad ways (bum circuits) of thought in the west bear the reasonably attractive names of chiliasm, angelism and quietism. the three, together and singly, are generally ill-thought-of by christian mystics and theologians.

if they exist as ways of thought at all in the east (& almost certainly the latter two do) they must have been given different names, and perhaps have had quite different careers.

chiliasm, (coming from greek χιλ-root meaning thousand) begins with the idea that the millenium (the golden age (?), the end of the world, the second coming, all at once) is about to dawn, and that, as a result, a number of restraints on human liberty, which had prevailed up to now, should be abandoned, if only as a gesture of welcome for the time to come. among the first restraints (usually) to be abandoned by ardent chiliasts are clothing and sobriety. sitting quietly is not a chiliast attitude; dancing is (mixed and naked): so are parades and demonstrations (naked and mixed).

chiliasts have often been billy-clubbed and even shot down (in various parts of the western world): angelists and quietists seldom run into trouble with the civilian law.

the fault of the angelist is to imagine himself more angel than man; to identify himself (perhaps) with his own guardian angel, and to imagine, not only that he must do no wrong, but that he can do none.

angelists usually live in monasteries and, right or wrong, have seldom gained the approval of their superiors here below.

the quietist does not believe that he is an angel, may not even believe that he has one. he waits instead for direct inspiration (of the Holy Spirit); waits and waits, doing as little as possible that might interfere with his state of holy receptivity.

quietists, too, are often monks, and, if they manage to fulfil their *monastic duties, are usually left to pray as they like. it is only when they are moved to write quietist tracts that they find themselves in trouble with the authorities. tracts then are usually written against them (even bulls and encyclicals(?), and their ideas declared, if not heretical, at least out of bounds.*

one feels that there is narrowness in the thought that condemns these attitudes (all three) and that narrowness, perhaps, has had its day (a long one) in the west, and could well be abandoned.

narrowness and neatness seem to go together in philosophic and religious thought, at least in the west; thought runs to systems: whatever doesn't fit into the system must be considered heretical, out of bounds.

in the west, all things that are things are looked upon as (man-made) things. example of man-made things: a box, a rabbit hutch.

a box, any box, is apparently the result, at least, of all four aristotelian causes: material, efficient, formal and final. it is made of wood, by a maker of wooden boxes, in the form of a box, to be used as a box.

on to tragedy made of words by a maker of verbal tragedies, in the form of and to be used as tragedy.

what is the use of a tragedy? to cleanse the viewer of pity and fear.

on to civilisation, the social structure, churches, the church, men, mankind, man.

on to music, the stars, the music of the stars.

whatever is a thing in the west is some kind of box.

naturally, including all natural things: trees, fish, cats, the sea.

these can all be understood through the four aristotelian causes. or, if they cannot be so understood, the fault is more likely in the thing than in the causes.

an anomalous thing: a mysterious thing.

things in the west are made-things, even if they grow, having been 'created'. they are made things.

even if they leap, like Athena, full blown from the mind of Zeus, they are from that moment on to be seen as boxes.

*in most western languages (would it be true in sanskrit too?) 'to do'
and 'to make' are one. (lat. facere, fr. faire) no making without
doing. of course. but no doing without making, either. to act is to
make. (all action – at least in the west – some kind of making.)*

*all this (it occurs to me) may be a phase: an early, even primitive
phase of thought: tectonic thinking.*

26 February 1970

*a tragedy, or any other literary work, in the west, will have a begin-
ning, a middle and an end. (indian stories go on and on.) western
musical works, whether symphony or opera, have beginnings and
middles. and they leave you in no doubt about when the end has
come: a crashing finale.*

*indian music starts as if from nowhere (as the casual tuning of a
sitar), rises to unpredictable heights (of anguish, joy, or meditation),
descends again, and trickles off to nowhere. (you know it all has
ended when the last note is sounded and nothing, nothing follows.)*

*it has solved no problems: it has given no lasting insights. it is not
likely, even, ever to be played again.*

*the instrument will be played again; the musician, too, may play
again (molecules in both of them having changed): something
abides; but not a frowning score.*

From Journal D

28 February 1973

*i have listened to all the desires of my heart. i have not bounded off
on every suggestion. (i have bounded off on some; perhaps on too
many.) but i have listened to all my heart has had to say; have
allowed it to speak its own language.*

when it speaks again, i will listen . . .

*i have given my mind a long romp, too. it has said whatever thing
came to mind, often. i have written down the form of these echoes
in the mind . . .*

*to watch and to listen; hardly to watch or to listen; not to act
unless called upon; a passive way of life. but one that leads often*

to great and real activity. what is given up is vain action, and what remains is true activity. participation in eternal life, which has been defined as pure act. (he who does not act at all, but does not sleep, approaches this state of true activity.) the best activities of mind, soul & body are those that proceed from this pure state. (they are empty acts, goal-less acts, acts that proceed without calculation or conscious effort.) like respiration or digestion they are acts that take place usually without being noticed, and yet they advance the life of the whole.

14 April 1973

creativity & order, creativity & rationality
seem (to romantics) to be at odds, but can
perhaps (must perhaps) be brought to a living
fusion. order, just by itself, is a plane
without fuel.

gasoline, just by itself, is only a fire waiting
to happen, or good fuel ready to evaporate.

From *Psalm*

if experience is a seed it must be a seed of wisdom –
not just moral wisdom that becomes a proverb.
not (exclusively) wisdom as celebration or expression of the high-
est form of love which becomes a psalm,
but wisdom as consciousness, wisdom which sharpens man's
awareness of the meaning & conditions of life, which remains as
instinct & contributes to his survival.
does the seed die? does any seed literally die, or simply become
transformed?
what was seed & had life now becomes a plant & lives & devel-
ops with that same life which was hidden & enclosed in the seed.
the seed's outer husk disintegrates, but the fire of its life con-
tinues to glow in the plant.
the outer trappings (the particular circumstances) of an experi-
ence must disintegrate or undergo metamorphosis, but its essence
lives on in consciousness, in wisdom, or in a fruit (& further
seed) of wisdom, as in a poem.

I first met Robert Lax on Patmos in 1989, casually, in the streets of Scala. And for four years after that I met him there from time to time when we were both shopping. We would stand under the shade of a tree holding our white plastic bags – mine full of groceries and his of fish for the cats – and exchange a few words. Then I would leave with a fresh idea, a new perspective on nature or eternity or Louis Armstrong. And I would be smiling and a touch more glad to be alive, like all the people who meet Robert Lax.

When, in 1993, I began research on the Merton chapter of this book, I discovered that Robert had been Merton's best friend for many years and asked if I might visit him to discuss my writing. He agreed and I began to call on him, climbing the steep narrow street to his little house perched over the harbour and talking for an hour or so once or twice a week. We ranged over Merton's personality and experiences, particularly his search for solitude, and this led us into discussing Robert's own situation, which is in some ways more solitary than that which Merton finally achieved.

He mentioned one day that our conversations were .helping him to sort out his thoughts, and I asked if I might use a tape recorder to preserve them for both of us. He agreed.

Conversation with Robert Lax – Patmos, summer 1995

PF   How did you come to settle in Greece?

RL   I had been living in New York quite a bit, and spending a lot of time with New Yorkers, and wherever I was I was hearing the same – the New York – answer to every question, and I realised that both the questions and the answers that I was hearing were New York-based. And I realised that neither the questions nor the answers were the ones I was asking myself but I was surrounded by this language that had the questions and the answers knitted into it. And the only way out was to leave the city. When I got to Greece I didn't want to get caught up again in a whole web of questions and answers that didn't interest me, and so for a while, as I couldn't speak the language, I escaped.

PF   You've lived alone here for thirty years, but, for you, living with someone isn't all that different from living alone.

RL   If it *is* very different, it doesn't happen. I do feel attached to this little thing I like to do – writing. It helps me keep in touch with myself, and myself is somebody I like keeping in touch with. I like being with myself. I enjoy being with myself.

Maybe other people enjoy being with themselves too. I did run into a sentence the other day, someone quoting a Frenchman as saying. 'People who can't stand being alone make the worst company'.

PF   But you're not misanthropic. Is it important for you to inter-act with people?

RL   I guess so.

PF   How often?

RL   I'm not so conscious of those time things. We could play this game about how long you could take it on a desert island. I think if there were living creatures on the desert island I'd have my eye out for the rescue ship, but not for the company it would bring. I've only recently, maybe because of our con-versations, been conscious of living alone. I haven't actually consciously looked for solitude. All I've looked for are decent working conditions. I think if I didn't like to write, to do something that works best without interruptions, I might not be so interested in being alone for most of the day . . .

PF   If you need the solitude for most of the time, did you ever think of becoming a hermit?

RL   That sounds to me like too much of a professional, too self-conscious a thing to do. I don't feel at all embarrassed about being or thinking of myself as a writer. I'm not using the word as an honorific term. I'm not a novelist or a writer of mystery stories. I'm just a writer who writes what's in his mind. I've always been a writer in this sense.

PF   Do you write to discover what you have in mind?

RL   More to keep it from getting away. I think that, from moment to moment, I usually know what I have in mind and I also seem to know that five minutes from now I won't be able to rediscover it unless I've written it down. It's close to that – that doesn't really sound to me like perfect accuracy, but it's about what I mean. And it does satisfy me. I look back through my notebooks and remember the different things that have happened and read what I said about it at the time, and you won't be surprised to hear that I usually agree with it.

PF   But you don't think of yourself as having a message for the world?

RL   No. When I was thirteen years old maybe I thought I did, and the image stayed a while and felt good. I also had a fantasy, a heroic fantasy, where all the children in the school are walking down a flight of stairs and the banister – we're on the fourth floor now – the banister is about to give way and they could fall, and I grab the banister and keep it steady and they don't fall. And I was pleased about this fantasy for a time.

PF   Is there an element of helping people, stopping them falling downstairs, in your poems?

RL   Well, yes. I think, first of all, I have this confidence that if I ever manage to clear things up for myself I'll be helping clear them up for some other people, and if I put it in language that I can really understand and find simple enough to communicate to myself in then some other people too will be able to pick up on it. And my feeling really is that if what I'm finding for myself is good medicine then I hope it gets passed around, and if it's bad medicine then I hope it gets tossed into some place where it won't hurt anybody.

PF   Can you spell out for me now any of the insights you've had that might be good medicine?

RL   Well, this is feeling like one: that what I feel there is enduringly in the universe is what we might call a creative stream and maybe along with it a process that may be going on in the universe that I've never read fully about – like what Bergson called creative evolution. Maybe this is synonymous with grace. So that a creative solution is a graceful solution, a happy solution. With insight that kind of solution comes through, and you couldn't have thought of it if you hadn't been an artist yourself at finding grace.

PF   Merton spoke of the need for solitude not only to gain insights but to escape from the artificial self that is created by responding to other people's expectations. Does this apply to you?

RL   I'm not so conscious of this. I've never been in a position that I can remember where I was in need of a false persona. I never had to check into an office and say jolly things every morning or anything like that.

PF   But you're not indifferent to other people. You're not the sort of person who doesn't give a damn about what anybody thinks.

RL   I do give a damn about what *everybody* thinks. Because I think we all should care about what all of us think. It's good to think of other people's feelings, and it's good to check on what they're thinking about you too. The gift of seeing ourselves as others see us *is* a gift.

PF   But doesn't this modify the way you are?

RL   Maybe so, but it doesn't give me a false persona. We're all part of one sea of consciousness, and I think that any tips we can get from each other on how we're moving along in it probably help us. We check with each other, and I suppose that if you really were too far from the sea of consciousness you might – anyone might – get pretty quirky and you might be glad if somebody reminded you to put your hat on when you should, or tie your shoe laces and things like that. If you're doing something offensive, you won't mind if somebody sets you right.

PF   So other people help you to an understanding of yourself?

RL   Here we go. I do think so. I think if there weren't any other people around, then the trees and the ants and the gazelles could help you. And if there weren't any living creatures around then you should listen to any angel voices you can hear at that point that could help you too. But people shouldn't hiss at you. If you find you're part of a community that starts to hiss at you it's time to leave.

PF   But you have never chosen to live far from other people.

RL   That's because I'm not all that self-sufficient. I don't mean in my personality but in my abilities, and if there wasn't somebody around to remind me how to boil an egg I could forget. I think it's like that. Besides, my picture of what you have to do if you're a hermit – a classical hermit – is to chop wood. I tried that once, without great success, and I don't think that it's the sort of challenge I'd want to respond to if I didn't have to.

PF   One of the strangest things I'm discovering about the solitaries is that people flocked to them for advice, not on how to be solitary, but on how to get on in society: they came with their problems of living together to people who had chosen to live alone. Can you explain this?

RL   The scientists work alone to cure a social disease. The scientist works alone because he has to be alone to do his work, even when it is for the benefit of society. I don't think that's the whole answer, but it's maybe part of the answer.

       I ran into this the other day and think it's some way related to where we're at: it's from St Augustine: 'Who can map out the various forces at play in one soul? Man is a great depth, O Lord. The hairs of his head are easier by far to count than his feelings, the movements of his heart.' And so he's aware of that, and any kind of ideal hermit should be aware of that just by his own experience in solitude; he's found out what a rich and full and complex thing there is inside one human being. If he's at all understanding about what goes on in the world, he understands that as many things as go on inside his own mind and soul are going on inside the minds and souls of other people. So, if they come to him with problems that they haven't had the time to solve or even look at, he may have some insights that might help them just by having had this luxury of some time to himself to think about them. Time without distractions.

PF   So the value of solitude for you is no more than that it keeps you away from distractions.

RL   I need to escape distractions in order to do something which is not, I think, antisocial. I don't think I'd be comfortable with it if it was. We all need each other far too much for somebody to take off and do nothing or do something destructive. So long as you do something creative – even if it's just blowing bubbles – then it's OK, even if it means staying alone. It's OK if you stay alone for fifty years and end up inventing the crossword puzzle. If you've found something creative that you can do in solitude when you're alone then that really is good news for the whole world. Because they may not be ready for it yet but they may be at another time.

PF   Is there any general advice you can pass on to people who are thinking of becoming solitaries?

RL   Well, I knew a man who was a very busy astro-physicist, one of the men involved in planning the space programme, and he told me he loved to go, from time to time – he lived near a lake – and stare at the water. And his wife would ask him, 'What are you doing staring at the water?' When he heard that I was living alone and could stare at the water all day he was pleased to find that other people did it. And it was reaffirming for him as it was good for me to know that people so much engaged still felt the need for solitude and silence. So I do think it's there in people. Maybe we could issue a booklet of general advice for would-be solitaries . . .

PF   One problem is that many people feel they need other people to recharge their batteries. Where does the energy come from when you're living alone?

RL   You know [pointing upwards]. All the energy comes from there.

PF   Do you mean through prayer?

RL   Well, that's a good way. If you've heard of it and it's one of your regular things to do, then that must be it, that's where it comes from.

PF   But if you don't pray?

RL   Well, if you're on your own and you're not up to something destructive, it will probably still come through something that any angel would define as prayer anyway, so long as what you're doing is one of these creative things. And that will recharge you. I think anything that's creative must count as prayer.

PF   And what should I watch out for? Are there any things you could warn me against if I'm a would-be solitary who comes to you for advice on living alone?

RL   Well, to answer that I'd need to know you personally.

PF   So our booklet isn't going to work?

RL   No. What we need is not a booklet but an institute!

PF   But surely there are some, maybe just a few, general principles for the would-be solitary?

RL   Well, yes, just a few. Get a house with a wooden floor, not a tiled floor. Tiled floors get cold in winter. Screen the windows so you don't have the dilemma of wondering whether or not to kill any mosquitoes and flies that come in. Then you need a source of fire that works and isn't dangerous. Just physical, common-sense things. Ask me another question.

PF   What about books?

RL   Take the five books you'd take to a desert island and keep re-reading them.

PF   A radio?

RL   Well, I didn't have one for a long time but then somebody gave me one and now I listen regularly to the BBC. And I'm glad of that. I think it helps me to know what's going on in the world.

PF   Do you have any problems with the news broadcasts? Do you have any sort of moral duty, I mean, to be informed of all the disasters you can do nothing about?

RL   I just don't think we're ever in a position of being able to do nothing. Because – take an analogy from science – if a man is working on the discovery of penicillin, I think he's right to keep on with his work even if all the cities in the world are falling. He should keep to that work. We'll need some penicillin. I don't think you can rush off with a gun on your shoulder every time there's an alarm. I think if there is destruction and turmoil in the world, people need penicillin. They need any good thing you can produce.

    I'm not sure it's a moral duty. My idea of morality, of right behaviour, is that whatever we can do as living beings to contribute to the whole unfolding or flow or progress or evolution of life on earth is a move in the right direction. Anything we do that can honestly be characterised as that, whether we know that's why we're doing it or not, is good.

PF   How do we know that, in solitude, we're on the right lines? What sort of good things should we be looking out for?

RL Well, the spirit of peace. Somebody said: 'He who acquires the spirit of peace will save thousands of souls around him'. That simply acquiring the spirit of peace is of benefit to everyone. So that is the criterion too: if you find that you're actually spending peaceful days, that you can feel your days are more peaceful with less anxiety and tension and panic, then that's a good sign that the thing is working.

PF What about meditation?

RL It's a nice elastic term, actually. I think if someone can be taught to meditate formally for half an hour in the morning or at night, then bravo, that's a good idea. But, if not, doing whatever you do as if it were a form of prayer or meditation then that's fine too. And what I mean – what I'm coming to believe I mean by that – is keeping your mind on what you're doing. It isn't how many '*Aves*' you say along with what you're doing. I've read – and even written – stuff about being 'present to the present moment', but I find that pretty abstract as an expression. If you're just stirring the soup and watching that you're stirring the soup then, so long as you're watching what you're doing, that's being present enough to the present moment as I understand it. The talk of concentrating on a candle flame and emptying your mind is maybe something I can get around to one day, but it's pretty difficult and I find that just concentrating, or focusing on what you're doing – which also helps you evaluate what you're doing – is as close as I can come to meditation.

PF If you come out of a life which has structure, should you, when alone, try to structure your life in some way: so much time for writing, meditation, prayer or whatever? Or should you just let things happen?

RL I think the classic answer is to structure it. I should say that first. But there's a psalm that says something like it's vain for you to set aside time for prayer and sleep, because the saints praised God upon their beds. And I think that if you keep in mind the main purpose of all your activities then whatever seems to feed into it in a good way for you is probably right. I tend to go to sleep and wake up at what seem to me to be the natural times. Whatever structure there may be in my life has just come about in that way.

PF   And do you have any sort of central purpose for your activities?

RL   I think I might say it's trying to discover something inside me that I might call the spirit of peace. It's not looking for peace first of all between nations but the spirit of peace that may be discoverable within. I think if I can maybe discover the spirit of peace within myself and then can point it out to you, then you can discover it within yourself too.

PF   But the most important insights I've had have always come through people. Are we in danger of cutting ourselves off from this source of revelation if we choose solitude?

RL   Yes, but if you have a genuine vocation for solitude I suppose you couldn't have that sort of vocation unless heaven was prepared to send an angel with you. You'd be called to it because you were ready for it. I do think that, whoever you are, if you've even heard of the word 'vocation' and the word means something to you then I think that trying to discover your vocation is the number one priority, and that if you can do this by asking yourself questions that's good. If you can do it by asking a spiritual director that's good too. I've had a lot of help from spiritual directors.

PF   How do you set about finding a good spiritual director?

RL   Use all the radar you've got. If you find someone that people speak of as a good one then go and see him and find out if he's talking your language or just everybody's. Listen around for people who've been recommended, and then see if you hit it off together. I really think if you're serious about things like this you should have one.

PF   Can we talk about the 'search for the self', which is what many people think solitude is all about? You once told me that your friend the Hindu monk Bramachari said: 'The Self is the knower and never the known'. Doesn't that mean there's no point in searching for it?

RL   I think it helps to distinguish, as typesetters do, between the 'self' with a small 's' and the 'Self' with a capital 'S'. The really deep Self is the divine part of us which is united to the divine Self. So if you go in search of that Self, you are looking for your true self, your deep self, all with a small 's', and you will happily encounter the divine Self with a capital 'S'.

PF   But does this mean you can have an encounter with the divine Self but never know it – since that is the Self which can never be known?

RL   Well, in my experience it's never an encounter with – it's rather tumbling into than encountering. Also, I think that by definition God is unknowable to us, except within the limits of our capacity to know him, so he can know us as we know ourselves, but we can never know him as he knows himself. What I understood Bramachari as meaning was that if the Self is the knower, then the very fact that it is the knower keeps it from being known: the knower keeps backing away from the known so it can see what it knows. The deeper it gets in, the more it sees, but it is itself engaged in the act of seeing: it can never see itself seeing itself.

There is no point outside the knower from which we can observe the knower. We are the knower, and the fact that we are the knower makes it logically impossible for us to know that knower.

PF   But is that knower the same for all of us?

RL   Yes, I believe it is. That true knower that none of us can know is God, and it's as much of God as is allotted to us to make use of in our knowing.

PF   But as there is a false self, is there a false Self? That quality which enables us to know is, for some intellectuals, the rational faculty, and this can lead us astray or not take us very far. Have they adopted a false knower?

RL   I think there can be a false knower. If we think we know with the intellect then we have it wrong, because essentially it's the heart that knows; and if the heart isn't the vocabulary you like it's the soul that knows. Or if you can't take that then it has to be the Self – the real one.

PF   Have you any ideas as to how people can tell if the self they're seeking, the knower they're finding, is not the false but the right one?

RL   It seems to me it takes an experience. Something happens and they can really say to themselves – sincerely and not for the brochures – 'This is the real me. At last I'm feeling like myself.' Maybe it happens on a vacation, maybe what happens isn't really very pleasant, but they can say to themselves: 'My reaction to this was – that was really me'. I think things like that do happen. That break down façades for people who've been doing a great job keeping them up – and sometimes there are other people around and they can say: 'Yes, that was the real him', and if he's at all perceptive he can see it too.

Other times it can happen in church. Maybe you go into a church you didn't intend to visit and perhaps sit there for a moment and you suddenly feel more like yourself than you have since you were a child. And that gives you a clue to your identity. If you're in a fairly falsely rigged society, a fairly falsely rigged town where you go through the streets and you have to go through these formulas that have nothing really to do with you, and you come to one of these moments then all that protective coloration drops away. All the protective coloration that you needed in this funny place drops away and you can say: 'This is the real me. I shouldn't be living in this town – I should get out into the country' or something like that. And by the time you're ready to go into the country, it's you and you alone who are going there – the real you.

I have to say 'true' self and 'false' self is not a language I like using. I think of it more as 'deep' self and 'shallow' self – keeping it all to the one self. Just variations of self at different levels. The protective coloration goes on at the surface, but all the time the deeper self is there to be discovered.

I think that here on Patmos the farmers and the fisherman have only a minimal difference between the two selves: they're pretty close to being who they are night and day and at all times. It's only in the artificial societies where, in order to hold down jobs – even to be admitted to the intellectualised schools that we have that – the surface gets all that coloration that warps the perceptions.

PF   Is it possible to get so much coloration on the surface that we can no longer see, or be aware of, the existence of our deeper self?

RL   I think that what happens to somebody who's so much into that sort of rat race that they never have much contact with their real self – what happens to them often, it seems to me, is that physically they destroy themselves. Perhaps the poor old deep self says: 'I can't stand living in this mad-house any longer – let's drink ourselves to death. At least I'll be up and out of it then'. The shallow one's habits get to be so much that biologically he can't stand it any more, but he may have the good fortune to collapse and be taken to the country or to a good hospital and come up with his real self.

PF So should the people who are looking for their inner self stop looking for an entity in there and simply concentrate on finding a different way of knowing – of seeing the outside?

RL I like that better. It would be a good test of whether they were getting anywhere if they were seeing the outside in a truer way. I think the idea that you can search for your true self as though it were a little doll that's living inside is just another trap. So if you're sitting staring at a candle flame in search of your true self, then keep on looking at the candle flame. But tell whoever told you to do that to tell you more about just why you're doing it. I think the people who started those traditions knew what the process was all about – knew that it had to do with actually getting in touch with the deeper self which is indestructible and is part of the divine Self – a *rayonnement* from the divine Self. So, if you're getting your idea of sitting there out of a book – go see the author.

In general, anyone who is serious about this should look for a spiritual director in whatever tradition he's able to feel at home with. You can get help from people who've had experience in the search. You need the solitude; but you also need direction about how you're using it, how you're living in it.

PF There seems to have been, since the sixties, a vogue for internal voyages of discovery of the self. Does this have something to do with the society we're living in?

RL The falser the culture a man lives in, the falser will be his shallow self – because it is a product of that civilisation and the producer of that civilisation. The two interact, and sometimes, if things get too bad, as they did in Babel and in Babylon, then – bam! – it goes.

PF   What is falsity in a culture?

RL   Falsity is inappropriateness to the nature of the world or the universe. If you build a nice little straw house in the middle of a stream it's going to float away down the stream or be knocked to pieces by it, because it has nothing to do with the stream. The falseness is that it could never work. And there have been all these false cultures that have come through history . . .

PF   Where are we now, in a period approaching truth or falsity?

RL   I think there are a lot of false things and a lot of things that have to be adjusted, but things don't seem to me particularly bad – there are many promising things in our culture.

PF   Can you name a few?

RL   Well, there's our friend Merton for one, and the Merton Society. That's one thing. And there are many others that make me feel that the cultures of the world are beginning to understand each other and, more importantly, beginning to understand what they were put together for to begin with, which had something to do with living on this planet and possibly even bringing it to blossom.

PF   Have things improved in your lifetime?

RL   I think so, When I was young I remember thinking that the fact that *some* people could understand what was good about jazz made it seem possible that *many* people could. The messages that are implied in that kind of music are communal messages and have to do with joy in life. Ideas that were once the property of monks and scholars are now available on any bookshelf or in paperback books. And anybody can find these ideas. There is always, of course, a down side as well as the up, but I seem to remember somebody telling me from the study of physics that the affirmative is the stronger force in the universe than the negative – that you can count on it to be the stronger of the two.

PF   As an ex-media person I may have a blighted view, but I've had to accept that anything worthwhile is commercially suicidal. The programmes, books, films that are most successful today are the sensational ones with least to say.

RL   I think this is just an appearance. I think that if I were to be given stock in a company that would bring some income, I would like to be given stock in something like the Everyman Library, the Modern Library – something that went on producing classics year after year and kept selling them – rather than have stock in some company that was specialising in violent films – not because of the moral repugnance I feel about companies that produce violent films, but just because I don't think they will last as long as Everyman. You'd make more money in the long run. Those other things are just not good investments. In the media, if you were given the choice of managing 'Words of Faith', a religious series on BBC radio, or a programme series that was very successful because it was more sensational, you might be in for a better steady job with 'Words of Faith'.

I really think that all through history most of the bad stuff quietly eliminates itself in its particular form from generation to generation. It may be replaced by other bad stuff, but the fashion disappears. Whereas the good stuff renews itself. Anything that was good in the writing of Sophocles some good director will discover again and will reproduce. But the bad stuff – when it's forgotten, it's gone for ever. I can't remember all that about Shakespeare and the Bear Pit but I think that at the time people were saying: 'Isn't it terrible, Mr Shakespeare is writing all these classics and people are rushing to the Bear Pit'.

References

Prologue: Dawn in China
1 See 'The Individual in Chinese Thought' by Y.P. Mei in *The Status of the Individual in East and West* ed. Charles A. Moore, Hawaii, 1968
2 *Analects* XII, 22
3 ibid XI, 11
4 It is no longer accepted that Lao-Tse wrote the *Tao te Ching* or that he even existed. But the tradition persists.
5 ibid p.41

Chapter I: The Emergence of the Individual
1 The myth is recalled in Plato's dialogue *Protagoras*.
2 ibid p.322
3 *The Iliad*, Bk 1
4 ibid Bk 6.
5 Plato, *Symposium*.
6 H.D.F. Kitto, *The Greeks*, Penguin Books, London 1951
7 Plato, *Hippias Minor*
8 Xenophon, Memorabilia of Socrates, in *Socratic Discourse, Plato and Xenophon*, Everyman's Library, London 1910, p.30
9 *ibid* p.32
10 the above quotations are from Plato's dialogue *Crito*.
11 Xenophon, *Symposium* iv, 34
12 For these assessments of Herakles and Cyrus, I am indebted to R. Hoistad, *Cynic Hero and Cynic King*, 1948. See also D.R. Dudley, *A History of Cynicism*, London 1937.
13 Herodotus, *Histories* 3:38
14 Cp. the instructions of Jesus to his disciples (Matt. 10:10, Mark 6:8, Luke 9:3). Before Odysseus lands in Ithaca, Athena disguises him as a beggar by dressing him in a deerskin cloak and giving him a staff and a wallet with a shoulder strap. (*Odyssey*, Bk 13, lines 434–8).
15 Bertrand Russell, *History of Western Philosophy*, p.255
16 Diogenes Laertius, *Lives of the Philosophers*, Diogenes.
17 There is information on this traffic obtained from ancient Indian

writings in E.J. Rapson, *Cambridge History of India,* 1922, Vol. I pp.212–3, and David M. Robinson, *Ancient Sinope,* p.137 ff.

18 *Histories* 3: 38–94–98 and 7: 65–8

19 *Florida* 15

20 Diogenes Laertius, *Lives of the Philosophers,* 9,35

21 Quoted in Robin Lane Fox, *Alexander the Great,* London 1986 p.349

22 Report by Strabo quoted in F. Sayre, *Diogenes of Sinope,* London 1938, p.42

23 Fragment 6

24 Dudley, op. cit. pp.47–8

25 See *Cynic Epistles: a study edition* by Abraham J. Malherbe, Scholars Press, Montana, 1977.

26 Another suggestion has been that he was suspected of parricide and handed over his patrimony to escape detection.

27 Quoted Dudley, op. cit. p.205

Chapter II: The Desert Fathers

1 Deuteronomy 32:10

2 The *Life of St Antony* by St Athanasius is in R.T. Meyer, *Ancient Christian Writers; the Fathers in translation,* London, 1950

3 Matthew 11:19

4 Gibbon, *Decline and Fall,* Ch. 37

5 Quoted Waddell *The Desert Fathers,* London 1936

6 That the hermit was also missing out on what Lecky felt were the essentials of good living is evidenced by his imaginative reconstruction of what went on in the hermit's 'delirious brain':
'The shady groves and soft, voluptuous gardens of his native city would arise and, kneeling alone upon the burning sand, he seemed to see around him the fair groups of dancing girls on whose warm, undulating limbs and wanton smiles his youthful eyes had too fondly dwelt . . . In the arms of Syrian or African brides, whose soft eyes answered love with love they might have sunk to rest; but in the lonely wilderness no peace could ever visit their souls.' (from his *History of European Morals,* quoted James O. Hannay, *The Spirit and Origin of Christian Monasticism,*1903, p.114)

7 Waddell op. cit. p.16

8 ibid p.29

9 The main sources I have used here are Migne, *Patrologia Graeca* and the excellent editions of the apophthegmata translated into French and published by Solesmes, see *Les Sentences des pères du désert,* Solesmes, 4 vols 1966–1981.

10 Philip Rousseau, *Ascetics, Authority and the Church,* London 1978, p.12

11 Cuthbert Butler, *The Lausiac History of Palladius,* Cambridge 1898

12 'God be merciful to me, a sinner' (Luke 18:13)

13 Soloviev, Vladimir, *The Justification of the Good*, London 1918
   p.58
14 Proverbs 30:8–9
15 Mark 105:25

Chapter III: Lying Low in the Dark Forest: The Russian Startsy
   1 The quotation is in a book by I. Smolitsh *Moines* p.18 and is quoted
      in John B. Dunlop, *Staretz Amvrosy: model for Dostoevsky's Staretz
      Zossima*, Belmont, Mass. 1972, p.53
   2 *The Orthodox Church* by Kallistos Ware, 1963, p.269
   3 G.P. Fedotov, *The Russian Religious Mind*, 2 vols, 1946 and 1966,
      vol II pp.195–6
   4 The image is that of my own spiritual father, Bishop Kallistos of
      Diokleia, to whose writings I am much indebted – in particular, for
      the chapter, 'The Spiritual Father in Orthodox Christianity' *Cross
      Currents*, Summer–Fall 1974, pp.296–313
   5 See *The Northern Thebaid* published by Saint Herman of Alaska
      Brotherhood, 1975
   6 Ware op. cit. p.128
   7 See the article '*Le Starets Léonide*' by Vladimir Lossky in *Contacts:
      Revue Française de l'Orthodoxie* No. 34, p.99–107, and the biogra-
      phy *Elder Leonid of Optina* by Father Clement Sederholm, St
      Herman of Alaska Brotherhood, 1994
   8 Quoted in John B. Dunlop, op. cit., p.34
   9 The story is recorded in Bolshakov, Sergius, *Russian Mystics*, 1977,
      pp.180–81
10 ibid p.182
11 ibid p.183
12 See the article 'Le Starets Macaire' by Vladimir Lossky in *Contacts:
      Revue Française de l'Orthodoxie* No. 37, p.9–19 and *Elder
      Macarius of Optina* by Father Leonid Kavelin, St Herman of Alaska
      Brotherhood, 1995
13 Kavelin, op. cit.
14 ibid p.100
15 ibid p.143–4
16 Quoted ibid p.299
17 See *Russian Letters of Direction* edited by Julia de Beausobre,
      St Vladimir's Seminary Press, 1975.
18 See *Starets Amvrosy; model for Dostoevsky's Staretz Zossima* by
      John B. Dunlop, Belmont, Mass. 1972 and the article 'Le Starets
      Ambroise' by Vladimir Lossky, *Contacts*, No 40, pp.219–236
19 Education in a seminary in Eastern Orthodox countries, unlike the
      West, does not necessarily point to a clerical career.
20 This was the position of novice or pupil of the *starets* which
      involved domestic chores and daily contact.
21 Spiritual father of St Augustine, whose knowledge of Greek helped

him introduce Eastern theological ideas to the West.

22 Dunlop, *op. cit.*, p.44
23 Quoted Dunlop, op.cit., p.48
24 ibid pp.49–50
25 ibid p.51
26 'Batiushka' means literally 'Little Father' but is used as a term of affectionate respect for a priest.
27 Quoted Dunlop, op. cit., p.54
28 ibid p.57
29 ibid p.134
30 ibid p.141
31 ibid p.142
32 ibid p.63
33 ibid p.65
34 ibid p.65
35 ibid p.65
36 ibid p.74
37 ibid pp.74–75
38 ibid pp.75–76
39 ibid p.60
40 ibid p.61
41 Quoted in Dunlop. *op. cit.*, p.59–60
42 *The Brothers Karamazov*, Penguin Classics edition, 1982, p.368

Ornamental Hermits: an Interlude
1 Diderot. *La Religieuse*, written 1760, publ 1796, vol iv p.627.
2 Quoted in *Follies and Grottoes* by Barbara Jones, 2nd edition, 1974, a rich and inspiring work to which I am indebted for information and much reading pleasure .
3 See *Notes and Queries* 7 February 1852,
4 Lady Croom in Tom Stoppard's *Arcadia,* act II, scene 7, 1993.
5 Quoted in Edith Sitwell, *English Eccentrics*, Penguin Books, 1971, p.42
6 *Notes and Queries* 9 August 1856
7 ibid 13 Nov 1852
8 Jones op. cit. p. 186

Chapter IV: By Walden Pond: Henry David Thoreau
1 In 1957 the American Literature Group of the Modern Language Association included Thoreau in its bibliographic survey *Eight American Authors.*
2 Quoted in Walter Harding, *A Thoreau Handbook*, N.Y. 1959
3 *Walden*, chapter 11, 'Higher Laws'.
4 Jonathan Katz, *Gay American History*, N.Y. 1976.
5 Article on Brook Farm in 11th edition of *Encyclopedia Britannica*.
6 See the elegant article on Emerson in the 11th edition of the

References

Encyclopedia Britannica by Professor Henry van Dyke of Princeton.
7 Frederick Copleston, *A History of Philosophy,* Vol 8 Part II, p.20
8 ibid p.20
9 Article on Emerson in 11th edition of *Encyclopedia Britannica*
10 Copleston op.cit. p.19
11 Thoreau,*Walden,* Signet Classics edition, p.66
12 Quoted George P. Whicher, *Walden Revisited,* Chicago 1945
13 *Walden* pp.34–75
14 ibid p.35
15 ibid p.38
16 ibid p.40
17 There is a colourful account of Thoreau at Walden in Walter Harding's, *The Days of Henry Thoreau* Princeton, 1982 to which I am indebted.
18 *Walden* p.50
19 In Greek mythology the son of Poseidon and Gaea (the earth). He compelled all strangers to wrestle with him and every time he was thrown received fresh strength from contact with his mother. Hercules defeated him by lifting him up and crushing him.
20 *Walden* p.109
21 The phrase was too good to waste and Thoreau uses it in *Walden,* 'Economy', p.17
22 Harding quotes the delightful assessment by Sam Staples of Emerson, the Sage of Concord: 'I suppose that there's a great many things than Mr Emerson knows that I couldn't understand: but I *know* there's a damned sight of things that I know that he doesn't know anything about.' op.cit. p.37
23 Journal 24 July 1846
24 *On the Duty of Civil Obedience,* Signet Classic edition, p228
25 ibid p.230
26 ibid p.231
27 ibid p.240
28 *Walden* p.11
29 ibid p.12
30 ibid p.55
31 ibid p.14
32 ibid p.29
33 ibid p.19
34 ibid p.20
35 quoted Whicher, op. cit. p.50
36 ibid pp.50-1
37 ibid p.49
38 *Walden* p.79
39 ibid p.91
40 ibid pp.93–4
41 ibid p.95

42 ibid p.96
43 ibid p95
44 ibid p.97
45 ibid p.97
46 ibid p.100
47 ibid p.77
48 Journal I, p.306
49 Journal V, p.207
50 Journal II p.413
51 Journal V, p.410
52 Quoted in *The Living Thoughts of Thoreau* by Theodore Dreiser, London 1939
53 *Walden* p.143
54 ibid p.145
55 ibid p.211
56 ibid p.10
57 ibid pp.17–18
58 ibid p.19
59 Journal II p.181
60 ibid p.337
61 ibid p.406
62 Journal IX p.38
63 ibid p.379
64 Journal XIV p.181.
65 Quoted Dreiser op.cit.
66 *Walden* p.69
67 ibid p.70
68 ibid p.215
69 ibid p.216
70 Journal XI, p.325
71 Journal XII, p.47
72 Journal V, p.210
73 See the next chapter. This belief is still at the heart of Eastern Orthodox Christianity.
74 Journal I p.409
75 See Chapter, I, p.15
76 Journal I p.409
77 Journal II p.4
78 There is an account of the enthusiasm of Emerson and Thoreau for the Hindu scriptures in *Vedanta for Modern Man* ed. Christopher Isherwood, London 1952.

Chapter V: Light from the East: Ramakrishna

1 From The Laws of Manu, Book VI quoted in 'Social, Ethical and Spiritual Values' by T.M.E. Mahadevan in Charles Moore, (ed.), *The Indian Mind,* Hawaii, 1967

2 A mythical figure to whom is credited a collection of laws in twelve books, the oldest extant legislation in India.
3 These quotations, from Book VI of The Laws of Manu are quoted in the article 'Asceticism' in Hastings, *Encyclopaedia of Religion and Ethics*
4 Quoted in Christopher Isherwood, *Vedanta for Modern Man*, London 1952, p 124
5 Max Müller, *Ramakrishna, his life and sayings*, London, 1898
6 See Max Müller, op. cit., Swami Sarananda, *Sri Ramakrishna: the Great Master*, Madras, 1952, Swami Nikhilananda, *Ramakrishna, prophet of New India*, London, 1951, Christopher Isherwood, *Ramakrishna and his disciples*, London, 1965, G.C. Banerji, *Keshab Chandra and Ramakrishna*, Madras, 1931
7 Quoted in Isherwood, op. cit.
8 Max Müller, *India; what it can teach us*, London, 1883, p.6
9 This and the following sayings are collected in Max Müller, op. cit.

Chapter VI: Hermit of the Sahara: Charles de Foucauld
1 Lives of Charles de Foucauld abound. The most helpful I read were Marguerite Castillon du Perron, *Charles de Foucauld*, Paris, 1982; M. Carrouges, *Charles de Foucauld, explorateur mystique*, Paris 1954, J.F. Six, *Itinéraire spirituel de Charles de Foucauld*, Paris 1958, and *Vie de Charles de Foucauld*, Paris 1962, René Bazin, *Charles de Foucauld . . . ermite du Sahara*, Paris 1921, R.V.C. Bodley, *The Warrior Saint*, London, 1954 and Ann Fremantle, *Desert Calling*, London 1950
2 Castillon du Perron op.cit. p.54
3 ibid p.67
4 Carrouges op.cit. p.4
5 Castillon du Perron op.cit. p.73
6 quoted in Fremantle op.cit. p.20
7 ibid p.21
8 ibid pp.43–4
9 ibid p.77
10 Castillon du Perron op.cit p.185
11 ibid p.188
12 ibid p.191
13 ibid p.209
14 Bazin op.cit. p.99
15 R. Voillaume, *Seeds of the Desert*, London, 1972, p33
16 Fremantle op.cit. p.111
17 ibid p.113
18 ibid p.115
19 Castillon du Perron, op.cit. p.222
20 ibid p.224
21 ibid pp.227–8

22 ibid p.229
23 ibid pp.236–7
24 ibid p.240
25 Fremantle op.cit. p.160
26 Castillon du Perron op.cit. p.283
27 ibid p.261
28 Fremantle op.cit. p.151
29 ibid p.153
30 ibid pp.162–3
31 ibid p.165
32 ibid p.168
33 Castillon du Perron op.cit. p.302
34 Fremantle op.cit. p.239
35 Castillon du Perron op.cit. p.308
36 ibid pp.309–10
37 Fremantle, op.cit. p.199
38 Bodley, op.cit. p.214
39 Fremantle op.cit. p.227
40 Quoted Philip Hillyer, *Charles de Foucauld*, Minnesota, 1990, p.126
41 ibid p.129
42 Fremantle, op.cit. p.245
43 ibid p.247
44 Castillon du Perron op.cit. p.397
45 Hillyer op.cit. p.131
46 Bazin op.cit. p.284
47 Fremantle op.cit. p.258
48 Bazin op.cit. p.298
49 Hillyer op.cit. p.136
50 Castillon du Perron op.cit. p.455
51 ibid p.456
52 Bodley op.cit. p.241
53 Castillon du Perron op.cit. p.476
54 Fremantle, op.cit. p.282
55 Bazin op.cit. p.333
56 R. Voillaume, *Au Cœur des Masses*, vol I p.184

Chapter VII: The Waters of Contradiction: Thomas Merton
1 *The Seven Storey Mountain*, p.212
2 ibid pp.309–310
3 I am indebted to Robert Lax for first pointing this out to me, and my ideas about Merton have been influenced by many conversations with him.
4 *The Seven Storey Mountain* p.374
5 From appendix to *The Waters of Siloe,* London, 1950
6 Quoted in *The Seven Mountains of Thomas Merton*, by Michael

References

Mott, Boston, 1984, p.226

7 Prologue to *The Sign of Jonas*, N.Y. 1948

8 Quoted in *Merton, a biography*, by Monica Furlong, London, 1980, p178

9 Quoted Mott, p.273

10 Quoted Mott, op. cit. p.299

11 Quoted Mott, op. cit., p.297

12 *The Wisdom of the Desert, Sayings from the Desert Fathers of the Fourth Century*, by Thomas Merton, New Directions, New York, 1960 p.23

13 Quoted Mott op. cit. p.333

14 Journal for March 31, quoted Mott op. cit. p.348

15 Quoted Mott, op. cit. p.351

16 ibid p.352

17 Quoted Mott p.337

18 'Notes for a Philosophy of Solitude' in *Disputed Questions* London 1961, p.178

19 ibid pp.179–180

20 ibid p.188

21 ibid pp.188–9

22 ibid pp.180–1

23 ibid p.192

24 ibid p.192–3

25 ibid p.194–5

26 ibid p.199

27 *Robinson Crusoe* was first published in 1719–20. Defoe wrote *Reflections on Robinson Crusoe* in 1720 claiming that it was an allegory of his own life .

28 *Notes for a Philosophy of Solitude*, pp.201–202

29 ibid p.203

30 *Raids on the Unspeakable*, New York, 1964, quoted Furlong op. cit. p.283

31 Journal on 24 February, the day the fridge arrived.

32 *Contemplation in a World of Action* pp.241–242

33 ibid p.245

34 Quoted Mott op. cit. p.429

35 Quoted Mott op. cit. 405–6

36 Quoted Mott, op. cit. p.465

37 Quoted Furlong op. cit. p.278

38 Quoted Mott op. cit. p.432

39 Quoted Furlong op. cit. p.301

40 Quoted Furlong op. cit. p.264 (from *Faith and Violence*, Notre Dame 1968)

41 *Contemplation in a World of Action*, London 1971 p.166

42 *ibid* p.241

43 ibid p.267–8

44 ibid p.7
45 ibid p.52
46 ibid p.79
47 Furlong op. cit. p.149
48 ibid pp.149–50
49 ibid p.150
50 Article in *Continuum* 7(2) Summer 1969 quoted Furlong op. cit. pp.286–7
51 'The Mystery of Thomas Merton: an interview with Patrick Hart' in *The Critic*, Winter 1988 p.104
52 *Contemplation in a World of Action* by Thomas Merton, introduction by Jean Leclercq, OSB, London, 1971 (from intro p.*x*)
53 quoted Mott p.529
54 In 'Vow of Conversation', unpublished journal 1964–5.

Bibliography

Anson, Peter, *Hermit of Cat Island*, London, 1961.

Anson, Peter, *The Call of the Desert*, London 1964

Athanasius, *Life of St Antony* in *Ancient Christian Writers: the Fathers in translation*, trans. R.T. Meyer, London, 1950

Aubrey, John, *Brief Lives* (various editions)

Auster, Paul, *The Invention of Solitude*, London, 1988

Banerji, G. C., *Keshab Chandra and Ramakrishna*, Madras, 1931

Bazin, R., (ed.), *Charles de Foucauld; hermit and explorer*, London, 1933

Bazin, R., (ed.), *Meditations of a Hermit*, London, 1930.

Beausobre, Julia de, (ed.), *Macarius: Russian Letters of Direction*, London, 1944

Bell, Rudolph, *Holy Anorexia*, Chicago, 1985

Bennet, Glin, *Beyond Endurance*, London, 1983

Berdyaev, N. A., *Solitude and Society*, London, 1938

Bodley, R. V. C., *The Warrior Saint*, London, 1954

Boissieu, P. de, *Le Père de Foucauld*, Paris, 1945

Bolshakov, S. *Russian Mystics*, London, 1977

Bolton, J. D. P., *Glory Jest and Riddle*, London, 1973

Bouyer, Louis, etc., *A History of Christian Spirituality*, 3 vols., New York, 1963-69

Bratton, Susan Power, *Christianity, Wilderness and Wildlife*, New York, 1933

Brown Peter, *The Body and Society: Men, Women and Sexual Renunciation in Early Christianity*, London, 1989

Budge, Wallis, *The Wit and Wisdom of the Christian Fathers*, London, 1934

Butler, Cuthbert, *The Lausiac History of Palladius*, 2 vols., Cambridge, 1898–1904

Carrouges, M., *Charles de Foucauld, explorateur mystique*, Paris,

1954 (Eng. trans. *Soldier of the Spirit*, London, 1956)

Cashen, R. A., *Solitude in the thought of Thomas Merton*, London, 1981

Castillon du Perron, Marguerite, *Charles de Foucauld*, Paris, 1984

Chadwick, Owen, *John Cassian: A Study in Primitive Monasticism*, Oxford, 1950

Chitty, Derwas J., *The Desert a City*, London, 1966

Clay, R. M., *The Hermits and Anchorites of England*, London, 1904

D'Anvers, N., *Lives etc. of the Hermits (4th–8th cent.)*, London, 1902

Darwin, Francis, *The English Medieval Recluse*, London, 1944

Davies, K. R. *Anabaptism and Asceticism: a study in intellectual origins*, London, 1974

Dodds, E. R., *The Greeks and the Irrational*, California, 1951

Dreiser, Theodore, *The Living Thoughts of Thoreau*, London, 1939

Dudley, D. R., *A History of Cynicism*, London, 1938

Dunlop, John B., *Staretz Amvrosy: Model for Dostoevsky's Staretz Zossima*, Belmont, Mass., 1972

Eliade, M., (ed.) *The Encyclopedia of Religion*, article on 'Eremitism'. New York, 1987

Evening, Margaret, *Who Walk Alone: a study of the solitary life*, London, 1974

Festugiere, A. J., *Personal Religion among the Greeks*, Berkeley, 1954

Fosbroke T. D., *British Monachism*, London, 1817

Fox, Robin Lane, *Alexander the Great*, Harmondsworth, London, 1986

Freemantle, Anne, *Desert Calling*, London, 1950

Furlong, Monica, *Merton: A Biography*, London, 1980

Gale, N. R., *Solitude*, London, 1913

Gautier, E. F., *Oasis Sahara*, London, 1905

Gougaud, L., *Ermites et Reclus*, Paris, 1928

Halmos, P., *Solitude and Privacy*, London, 1952

Hamilton, Elizabeth, *The Desert is my Dwelling; a study of Charles de Foucauld*, London, 1968

Hannah, Ian, *Christian Monasticism*, London, 1924

Hannay, James O., *The Spirit and Origin of Christian Monasticism*, London, 1903

Harding, Walter, *The Days of Henry Thoreau*, Princeton, 1982

Hardman, O., *The Ideals of Asceticism: An essay in the comparative study of religion*, London, 1924

Harper, R., *Seventh Solitude – Man's Isolation*, London, 1965

Hawes, John C., *Soliloquies of a Solitary*, London, 1952

Hérisson, R., *Avec le Père de Foucauld et le Général Laperrine*, Paris, 1937

Hillyer, Philip, *Charles de Foucauld*, Minnesota, 1990

Hoistad, R., *Cynic Hero and Cynic King*, Oxford, 1948

Huxley, Aldous, *Heaven and Hell*, London, 1956

Isherwood, Christopher, *Ramakrishna and his Disciples*, London, 1965

Isherwood, Christopher, (ed.), *Vedanta for Modern Man*, London, 1952

Jones, Barbara, *Follies and Grottoes*, London, 1953

Kirk, G. S. and Raven, J. E., *The Presocratic Philosophers*, Oxford, 1957

Lacarrière, Jacques, *The God-Possessed*, London, 1963

Les Sentences des pères du désert, Solesmes, 4 vols 1966–1981

Leyser, Henrietta, *Hermits and the new Monasticism*, London, 1984

Lialine, Clément, and Doyère, Pierre 'Eremitisme' in *Dictionnaire de Spiritualité*, Vol 4, Paris 1960

Lloyd, T., *Desert Call, the story of Charles de Foucauld*, London, 1948

Louth, Andrew, *The Wilderness of God*, London, 1991

Malherbe, Abraham J., *Cynic Epistles; a study edition*, Scholars Press, Montana, 1977

Merton, Thomas, *Conjectures of a Guilty Bystander*, New York, 1968

Merton, Thomas, *Contemplation in a World of Action*, London, 1971

Merton, Thomas, *New Seeds of Contemplation*, New York, 1962

Merton, Thomas, 'Notes for a Philosophy of Solitude' in *Disputed Questions*, London, 1961

Merton, Thomas, *Raids on the Unspeakable*, New York, 1964

Merton, Thomas, *The Monastic Journey*, London, 1978

Merton, Thomas, *The Seven Storey Mountain*, New York, 1948

Merton, Thomas, *The Sign of Jonas*, New York, 1953

Merton, Thomas, *The Way of Chuang Tzu*, New York, 1965

Merton, Thomas, *Thoughts in Solitude*, New York, 1958

Mott, Michael, *The Seven Mountains of Thomas Merton*, Boston, 1984

Müller, Max, *Ramakrishna: his life and sayings*, London, 1898

Neihardt, John G., *Black Elk Speaks . . . 1932*, repub: Nebraska, 1961

Nikhilananda, Swami, *Ramakrishna: Prophet of New India*, London, 1951

Oman, J. C., *The Mystics, Ascetics and Saints of India*, London, 1905

Picard, Max, *The World of Silence*, London, 1952

Plato, *The Symposium*, trans. W. Hamilton, Harmondsworth, 1951

Pourrat, P., *La Spiritualité Chrétienne*, 4 vols Paris, 1920–28

Powys, John Cowper, *A Philosophy of Solitude*, London, 1933

Preminger, Mation M., *The Sands of Tamanrasset*, London, 1963

Price, R. M., (trans.), *Lives of the Monks of Palestine, by Cyril of Scythopolis*, Cistercian Studies, 114

Quesnel, R., *Charles de Foucauld*, Paris, 1956

Rolland, Romain, *Prophets of the New India*, London, 1930

Rousseaux, Philip, *Ascetics, Authority and the Church*, London, 1978

Saradananda, Swami, *Sri Ramakrishna: The Great Master*, Madras, 1952

Saudreau, A., *La Pieté à travers les Ages*, Paris, 1927

Sayre, F., *The Greek Cynics*, London, 1948

Sayre, Robert F., *Thoreau and the American Indians*, Princeton, 1977

Seabrook, J. R., *Loneliness*, London, 1973

Six, J. F., *Itinéraire Spirituel de Charles de Foucauld*, Paris, 1958

Soloviev, Vladimir, *The Justification of the Good*, London, 1918

Storr, Anthony, *Solitude*, London, 1988

Suso, *The Life of Blessed Henry Suso by Himself*, trans. T. F. Knox, London, 1913

Theophan, Bishop, ed *Unseen Warfare*, trans. E. Kadloubovsky and G. E. H. Palmer, London, 1952

Thoreau, Henry David, *Walden* (1st publ. 1854), Signet Classics, 1960

Tournier, P., *Escape from Loneliness*, London, 1962

Turnbull, P., *Sahara Unveiled*, London, 1940

Bibliography

Voillaume, R., *Seeds of the Desert*, Paris, 1955

Waddell, Helen, *Beasts and Saints*, London, 1949

Waddell, Helen, *The Desert Fathers,*, London, 1936

Whicher, George P., *Walden Revisited*, Chicago, 1945

Winnicott, Donald, 'The Capacity to be Alone' in *The Maturational Processes and the Facilitating Environment*, London, 1965

Woodcock, George, *Thomas Merton: Monk and Poet*, Edinburgh, 1978

Workman, Herbert B., *The Evolution of the Monastic Ideal*, London, 1913

Yale, John, *A Yankee among the Swamis*, London, 1961

Zaehner, R. C., *Evolution in Religion: A study in Sri Aurobindo and Pierre Teilhard de Chardin*, Oxford, 1971

Zaehner, R. C., *Mysticism Sacred and Profane*, Oxford, 1957

Zimmerman, Johann George, *Solitude*, London, 1797

Index